STUDIES ON VOLTAIRE
AND THE EIGHTEENTH CENTURY

214

GENERAL EDITOR   HAYDN MASON
                 DEPARTMENT OF FRENCH
                 UNIVERSITY OF BRISTOL
                 BRISTOL BS8 1TE

SIMON DAVIES

Paris and the provinces in eighteenth-century prose fiction

THE VOLTAIRE FOUNDATION
AT THE TAYLOR INSTITUTION, OXFORD

1982

ISSN 0435-2866

ISBN 0 7294 0292 4

Typeset by Cheney & Sons Ltd, Banbury, Oxon OX16 8EY

Printed in England at The Alden Press, Oxford OX2 0EF

to Anne

to my mother

to the memory of my father

Contents

Acknowledgements

DEBTS one acquires can never be adequately acknowledged so what follows is merely a brief expression of gratitude to various people who have helped me over the years. To Jack Reynolds who first interested me in the French language and things French. To Robert Niklaus who introduced me to the pleasures and pains of eighteenth-century literature and has never failed to encourage me with his customary acumen and humanity. Vivienne Mylne offered me both invaluable bibliographical information in the early stages of my research and later some constructive criticism. Haydn Mason suggested I revise the thesis long after I had abandoned thoughts of seeing it in print and then kindly accepted it for publication. Gillian Johnson and Carina Rourke cheerfully showed a resilience characteristic of many eighteenth-century heroines in typing my manuscript. Finally my wife, Anne, read the proofs with admirable equanimity and forbearance.

Preface

THIS study is a revision of a doctoral thesis presented at the University of Exeter in 1972. The eighteenth-century novel had received considerable re-evaluation at that date and has since continued to attract much critical scrutiny as our bibliography amply testifies. The subject-matter of the study was selected on account of its importance in the social, political and literary history of France.

As will be seen, the relationship between Paris and the provinces is a theme of recurrent interest in eighteenth-century literature. It is found in all types of fiction, *mémoires*, *nouvelles*, *contes moraux*, epistolary novels, and is also portrayed in a variety of tones, comic, libertine, sentimental, didactic, etc. To quantify the presence of this theme in the fiction of the period is a tempting but perilous enterprise. Can one equate its treatment in a short story or intercalated tale with its presentation in a four volume novel expressly composed to illustrate it? Any statistical calculations have proved here to be of little value. Furthermore although over 250 titles were read in preparing this monograph, no claim could ever be made to exhaustive coverage. Yet what one can confidently assert is that Diderot, Rousseau, Voltaire, Restif de La Bretonne, Marmontel, Baculard d'Arnaud dealt with the subject to a greater or lesser extent in their creative writings. Moreover though the last two authors are nowadays read only by scholars, their tales were best-sellers in the eighteenth century, as numerous re-editions bear witness.[1]

A thorny problem in the discussion of Paris and the provinces is a definition of terms. In various works Paris may mean all or some of the following: the seat of political power, the centre of culture, the world of the *bonne compagnie*, the largest urban development in France, even the nation itself. The provinces are depicted as representing everything in France outside the capital, the location of small communities, the countryside in general or more specifically the site for agricultural pursuits. We have therefore used the terms Paris and the provinces in a comprehensive way for even if particular aspects are under consideration, they are frequently emblematic of a general observation.[2]

To pursue the theme we have delved into the fiction of almost the whole century, taking 1789 as a terminal date so as to avoid any repercussions from the Revolution. The multiplicity of unfamiliar works has obliged us to quote at length and often detail similar plots to illustrate our argument. Accumulating evidence in this manner necessarily entails a cursory treatment of some works at what may appear regrettably a breakneck pace. Our investigation underlined that fiction at that period could not have evolved untouched by its issues and ideas. It is therefore in both the literary and ideological climate of the eighteenth century that we have tried to bring out the relevance of our theme to the development of prose fiction.[3]

Introduction

In the course of the seventeenth century the monarch exercised an increasing influence over the French nation. Urban development in Paris enhanced the city's prestige and dominance over the rest of the kingdom. During his ministry Colbert envisaged the capital as a new Rome, as the centre of law, order and culture for France.[1] The centralising policies diminished the status of the provinces and deprived them of many forceful and ambitious noblemen. The officers who, having fought for their country, would once have returned to their domains, now increasingly stayed at court with a view to preferment.

Nevertheless the vast majority of the French population lived in rural areas and small communities. The advent of the eighteenth century saw little change, as C. B. A. Behrens claims that only 15% of Frenchmen resided in towns of over 2,000 inhabitants as late as 1789.[2] Further statistics reveal a gradual growth in population from 19 million in 1715 to 26 million in 1789. But what of the capital itself?

An accurate figure is impossible to compute. Some estimates have put the population as high as 1,000,000 but this would seem to be a gross exaggeration. The first reliable census was taken in 1801 and recorded a figure of some 547,000 inhabitants for the capital. It would appear probable therefore that in the preceding period the population was of the order of 500,000 to 600,000, with a gradual increase as the century unfolded.[3] Louis Chevalier believes that the demographic increase was due largely to a rising birth-rate rather than an influx of provincials.[4] Nonetheless there were many peasants who drifted to the capital in search of public assistance in the years of famine and unemployment, however alien this may have been to their conservative instincts.[5]

The expansion of Paris must be seen in relation to the stagnation of the provinces where time-honoured practices and customs held sway: 'La France demeure un assemblage de provinces rurales, aux mentalités traditionnelles, aux techniques archaïques, à la monnaie longtemps rare, aux liaisons difficiles, où la quête du pain quotidien demeure l'essentiel où chaque groupe humain tente de "vivre du sien", en "bon ménager"' (*L'Ancien Régime*, p.69). There were of course large towns outside the capital though none could be compared with it (p.191):

Nous savons déjà que le fait urbain était largement minoritaire. Paris n'atteignit le demi-million qu'au dix-huitième siècle, et ne groupa guère plus de 2% des Français; six villes entre soixante et cent mille âmes, une dizaine autour de trente ou quarante mille, moins de gros marchés et de petits centres administratifs: le total arrive difficilement à 3 millions de personnes, à peine 15% des Français.

Thus Paris in the eighteenth century was clearly demographically as well as politically dominant.

Though Louis XIV had moved to Versailles to the detriment of the capital, Paris gained revenge in the succeeding reign. When the Sun King died in 1715, his palace was abandoned for eight years. The young Louis was housed in the Tuileries while the Regent took up residence in the Palais Royal. Despite Louis xv's return to Versailles in 1723, the habits of town life had become so familiar to his courtiers that residence in the palace never regained its erstwhile attraction. Paris became therefore the cultural and social centre of the Age of Enlightenment. Louis Réau asserts: 'à notre avis un des caractères essentiels de l'art français au xviiie siècle [est] la substitution de Paris à Versailles, de la ville à la cour comme centre de production artistique et foyer de rayonnement'.[6] Royal patronage was no longer the sole source of success for artists since financiers paid handsomely too. Writers eventually achieved an enhanced status in the intoxicating society of the capital.

The 'art de société' in the salons of mme de Lambert, mme Du Deffand, mme Geoffrin, etc., replaced court etiquette as the zenith of gracious manners. In these gatherings writers mingled with the old nobility of birth as well as the new aristocracy of wealth. Conversation ranged over the wide gamut of human enquiry; the arts, literature, science, religion, morality. Foreigners flocked to the French capital to join these eloquent and stimulating assemblies. The Russian author, Karamzin, analyses his feelings as he approaches the city:

'There it is', I thought. 'There is the city which for so many centuries has been the model for all Europe, the fount of taste and fashion; the city whose name is pronounced with reverence by the learned and unlearned, by philosophers and fops, artists and fools, in Europe and Asia, in America and Africa, whose name became known to me almost together with my own; the city about which I have read so much in novels, have so often dreamed, so often thought! There it is! I see it and soon shall be in it!'[7]

Karamzin yearned to meet the literary luminaries of the late century, especially Florian and Mercier, but others sought less exalted company and journeyed principally to sample the capital's pleasures.

In his brochure on Paris La Peyre praises its attractions:

cette cité qui est la Déese de la terre, le berceau des Héros, attire dans son sein des gens de toutes les nations. Ils y sont conduits, les uns par la curiosité, le plaisir, et même par l'amour du désordre; les autres considérant que la Fortune répand dans ce séjour ses biens plus abondamment qu'ailleurs, y ont été attirés par l'espérance de jouir un jour de ses avantages.[8]

Paris beckons the nobility of neighbouring lands who relish their visits to such a centre of entertainment where they can indulge in the latest fads and fashions. Tilly underlines the capital's magnetism:

Paris, où affluait alors l'élite de la France et du reste de l'Europe, devint aussi pour moi, comme pour tant de jeunes gens et même d'hommes faits, un tourbillon de dissipation, de distraction, et de jouissance, si l'on peut appeler ainsi l'habitude des spectacles, la fréquentation du foyer des acteurs et des Phrynés du bon genre; de plus, les dîners et les soupers fins, les bals, les jeux, les concerts; toutes choses qui n'excluaient pas de voir ce qu'on appelait la bonne compagnie.[9]

The abbé Leblanc bemoans in fact the ambiguous nature of Parisian manners and their charm for strangers: 'Paris est à quelques égards en possession de la gloire dont Athènes et Rome ont joui successivement: les étrangers y abondent de toutes parts; [...] il serait à souhaiter et pour eux et pour nous que la sagesse de nos mœurs les y attirât autant que la politesse de nos manières!'[10] Be that as it may, there is no doubt that Paris was the favourite abode of many expatriates.

Could the abbé Galiani ever reconcile himself, in Naples, to the lost joys of his French sojourn, or Casanova remember without regret the scene of so many triumphs? Where else could the Teutonic Grimm and d'Holbach discover such agreeable and diverting company?

But what of the other social groups in the capital? The financiers profited from the continued disdain for commerce affected by the aristocracy. The bourgeoisie was in a position to exploit business opportunities unhindered, and, accordingly, played a significant role in the economy of the country. The richest strata of the middle-classes desired to imitate the life pattern of their superiors, that is to live idly and pleasurably. Having made their pile, they often forsook commerce to live solely on their means, buy non-productive land and 'vivre noblement'.

The lower echelons of the bourgeoisie, the lawyers, doctors, tradesmen, shopkeepers, frequently harboured a disapproving even contemptuous opinion of their betters. What were, after all, the upper-classes to them? Surely an ostentatious collection of individuals who were often in debt and whose only claim to a useful existence was a rare military victory or the occasionally fair administration of an ecclesiastical sinecure. They, on the other hand, had to work hard for their livelihood, yet were subject to taxes from which their masters were exempt.

Below them came the artisans, the craftsmen still clinging to their guilds with their lengthy apprenticeships and strict regulations. Many were engaged in luxury trades, the sole manufacturing concerns of any dimensions in Paris before the Industrial Revolution at the turn of the century. Indeed, luxury goods were known as 'articles de Paris' throughout Europe.

At the bottom of the social scale were the workmen, vendors, jacks-of-all-trade, frequently eking out pitiable existences in the sordid quarters of the capital. It is easy to form a picturesque image of the hubbub of the streets, the 'crieuses de vieux chapeaux', the 'ravaudeuses', the 'crocheteurs', but one only has to turn to the vivid pages of Mercier's *Tableau de Paris* (Amsterdam 1782-1788) to appreciate the squalid reality of a high percentage of the population. His moving descriptions of institutions such as the Enfants Trouvés, the Hôtel-Dieu, where insanity and putrefaction, senility and youth often lay literally side by side, give the lie to any facile idealisation of the happy lot of the poor.

Just as in the modern city Paris was noted for its noise and the speed and urgency of its life. The noise was often associated with the hustle and bustle of coaches. Not only were these vehicles irksome in terms of decibels but also dangerous on account of the narrow roadways. At the end of the seventeenth century out of 665 streets only about 30 were more than 5 yards wide, the others rarely exceeded 1 1/2 to 3 yards in width.[11] The rushing cabs and traffic jams endangered the lives and limbs of pedestrians; one remembers Rousseau's traumatic experience.

One method of escaping from the hazards of the streets and the whirligig of the social round was to seek refuge in the cafés. These had usurped the role of the cabarets and were to increase in number in the course of the century. At the beginning of the Regency there were merely 300 cafés in the capital, by 1723 roughly 80 more had been added, yet in 1788 1,800 have been counted.[12] The customer could sup his 'bavaroise' and listen to the chattering 'nouvellistes' or the writers in the Procope, Gradot, Parnasse, or perhaps study the chess players in the Régence like *Moi* in Diderot's *Le Neveu de Rameau*:

Si le temps est trop froid, ou trop pluvieux, je me réfugie au café de la Régence: là je m'amuse à voir jouer aux échecs. Paris est l'endroit du monde, et le café de la Régence est l'endroit de Paris où l'on joue le mieux à ce jeu. C'est chez Rey que font assaut Legal le profond, Philidor le subtil, le solide Mayot; qu'on voit les coups les plus surprenants, et qu'on entend les plus mauvais propos.[13]

Then there were the famous Café de Foy, Café du Caveau and others in the Palais Royal which was to be such a hot-bed of politics and debauchery during the Revolution. While for the poor Parisians in search of enjoyment or oblivion the cheap *guingettes* were the favourite ports of call.

We shall now leave the historical reality of Paris in the eighteenth century and turn to a consideration of the portrayal of Parisians and provincials in the literature of the preceding era. In the theatre of the seventeenth century the relationship or rather the contrast between the Parisian and the provincial is a theme of recurrent interest. The comedies of Molière and his contemporaries abound in satirical thrusts at the pretensions and antiquated opinions prevalent in the provinces. One area of attack is the desire to ape Parisian fads or at least what the provincial regards as a metropolitan fashion. This provokes the gibes of Molière in *Les Précieuses ridicules* (1659, scene 2):

MAGDELON   Il faudrait être l'antipode de la raison, pour ne pas confesser que Paris est le grand bureau des merveilles, le centre du bon goût, du bel esprit, et de la galanterie.
MASCARILLE   Pour moi, je tiens que hors de Paris, il n'y point de salut pour les honnêtes gens.
CATHOS   C'est une vérité incontestable.

If knowledge of Paris is so indispensable, it follows that he who has not even visited the capital is an incomplete person. In *La Comtesse d'Escarbagnas* (1671) the protagonist is exceedingly proud of her stay there and demands extra respect accordingly. She is mortified when she finds flattery is not forthcoming and her opinions are not accorded supremacy: 'le mal que j'y trouve, c'est qu'ils veulent en savoir autant que moi, qui ai été deux mois à Paris, et vu toute la cour' (act 1, sc.3). Contact with the metropolis should enhance one's prestige and grant one an almost superhuman aura.

Once in Paris, woe betide the stranger who fails to acquaint himself with the fashionable manners and does not conform. In Pierre Corneille's *Le Menteur* (1642), Dorante from Poitiers is aware of this danger and tells Cliton (act 1, sc.1):

> Ce qu'on admire ailleurs est ici hors de mode;
> La diverse façon de parler et d'agir
> Donne aux nouveaux venus souvent de quoi rougir.
> Chez les provinciaux on prend ce qu'on rencontre;
> Et là, faute de mieux, un sot passe à la montre.
> Mais il faut à Paris bien d'autres qualités;
> On ne s'éblouit point de ces fausses clartés;

> Et tant d'honnêtes gens que l'on y voit ensemble,
> Font qu'on est mal reçu, si l'on ne leur ressemble.

Many of his compeers are less astute and suffer at the hands of the wide-awake Parisians, M. de Pourceaugnac being a signal example. In Molière's play of 1669, the eponymous hero is the butt of derision when he arrives in the city (act 1, sc.3): 'Hé bien, quoi? qu'est-ce? qu'y a-t-il? Au diantre soit la sotte ville, et les sottes gens qui y sont! ne pouvoir faire un pas sans trouver des nigauds qui vous regardent et se mettent à rire.' The Baron de La Crasse receives a similar welcome when he pays a visit to the court and stands on his dignity:

> Un Baron, dit l'huissier, un Baron! place, place
> A Monsieur le Baron! Que l'on s'ouvre de grâce!
> L'on croyait à la cour les Barons trépassez;
> Mais pour la rareté du fait, dit-il, passez.[14]

The poor man is abused by the courtiers for whom the feudal title of baron had become exclusively associated with the 'hobereaux de province'.

In *Le Campagnard* (1657), Gillet de La Tessonerie's hero is duped continuously during his stay in Paris. His stupidity is further emphasised when he makes an idiotic proposal of marriage to the disdainful Philis (act 4, sc.4):

> Mais enfin je vous donne une âme toute en feu,
> Et puisque la nature est contente de peu,
> Je crois que trois chasteaux avec trois métairies,
> Huit cents arpens de terre, et quatre bergeries,
> Deux haras bien peuplés, et quatre ou cinq moulins,
> Trois granges en bon ordre et trois ailleurs tout pleins,
> Plus de trente coureurs dedans mes écuries,
> Quatre meutes de chiens, bassets, moyens et grands,
> Epagneux, lévriers, mâtins et chiens courants,
> Dix oiseaux excellents, une assez bonne table,
> Quelque rente foncière, et du bien raisonnable,
> Parmi deux cents voisins d'honneur et de vertu,
> Vous mettront à votre aise.

Needless to say such a vulgar declaration of property goes unrequited.

As will be manifest the country nobility was depicted as coarse, gullible, dim-witted. Cléandre describes his mistress's mother in the following terms:

> Elle est si disposée à se fier à moi
> Qu'elle croit mes discours comme articles de foi.
> Pour tout dire en un mot, elle est provinciale,
> C'est-à-dire, grossière, étourdie, inégale,
> Qui se laisse duper sans s'en apercevoir,
> Qui prend le vrai pour faux et le blanc pour le noir.[15]

Accompanying this obtuseness there was frequently an insufferable arrogance. An example of the latter defect is to be encountered in M. and Mme Sotenville in Molière's *George Dandin* (1668). They treat their rich son-in-law with contempt despite their own poverty simply because of his peasant status. In addition they seize every opportunity to show off the glories of their lineage. In an amusing scene with Clitandre, M. de Sotenville declaims the valorous deeds of his family (act 1, sc.5):

M. DE SOTENVILLE   Mon nom est connu à la cour, et j'eus l'honneur dans ma jeunesse de me signaler des premiers à l'arrière-ban de Nancy.

CLITANDRE   A la bonne heure.

M. DE SOTENVILLE   Monsieur, mon père Jean-Gilles de Sotenville eut la gloire d'assister en personne au grand siège de Montauban.

CLITANDRE   J'en suis ravi.

M. DE SOTENVILLE   Et j'ai un aïeul, Bertrand de Sotenville, qui fut si considéré en son temps, que d'avoir permission de vendre tout son bien pour le voyage d'outre-mer.

This hubristic attachment to the exploits of their ancestors incited mockery on the stage more especially as the provincial nobility's state was often portrayed unfavourably in relation to their paper glory.[16]

Let us close our cursory examination of the theatre by quoting analogous sentiments expressed in an early eighteenth-century play, Lesage's *Turcaret* (1709). When Mme Turcaret arrives from the country, she is the unwitting subject of the traditional barbs of derision. The marquis cajoles her and she retorts (act 5, sc.6):

Vous êtes trop poli, monsieur le marquis. Ces flatteries-là pourraient me convenir en province, où je brille assez, sans vanité. J'y suis toujours à l'affût des modes; on me les envoie toutes dès le moment qu'elles sont inventées, et je puis me vanter d'être la première qui ait porté des pretintailles dans la ville de Valognes.

And to his ironic eulogy of a 'petit Paris' she proudly adds:

Oh! je ne vis pas comme une dame de campagne, au moins. Je ne me tiens point enfermée dans un château; je suis trop faite pour la société. Je demeure en ville, j'ose dire que ma maison est une école de politesse et de galanterie pour les jeunes gens.

The provincial is not merely a figure of fun in the theatre but is also jeered at in fiction. The 'gentilhomme campagnard' is a ridiculous character in the satirical work of Agrippa d'Aubigné, *Les Avantures du baron de Faeneste* (1617). Here a baron sets off for Paris and the court, doomed to meet successive disasters. Recounting his adventures in his Gascon dialect, he proves to be the empty-headed braggart that his station invariably demanded:

Nous estions à la Comédie aux poids pilez, un Parisien bestu de biolet se leboit à tous coups et m'empêchoit la bue des youurs; ye lui crie rudement, 'Hola bioulet, biras bous d'aquiou.' Ce fat tournant la teste, me respond, 'Je n'en ferai rien.' Et moi resolut quant et quant, je redouvle: 'Demouras y donc.' Et par ce moyen il ne fit rien sans mon commandement.[17]

Scarron in his *Roman comique* (1651-1657) scoffs at the outmoded manners and etiquette of the provinces. He remarks on the clumsy attentions paid to actresses by the young bucks:

Les mains d'Angélique estoient quelquefois serrées et baisées, car les provinciaux sont fort endemenez et patineurs; mais un coup de pied dans le dos des jambes, un soufflet ou un coup de dent, selon qu'il estoit à propos, la délivroient bien tost de ces galans à toute outrance [...] Mademoiselle de l'Estoile estoit d'une humeur toute contraire; [...] Elle estoit tout habillée sur un lict, environée de quatre ou cinq des plus doucereux, estourdie de quantité d'équivoques qu'on appelle pointes dans les Provinces, et sousriant bien souvent à des choses qui ne lui plaisoient guères.[18]

This lack of refinement is also noted disparagingly by the abbé de Pure. Aricie relates an excrutiatingly boring interview with a provincial:

Il parloit éternellement, rompit en visière aux gens à tout bout de chant, n'escoutoit jamais autrui et n'avoit autre soin et d'autre tache que de débiter ce qu'il sçauroit à tort et à travers sans faire aucune réflexion sur soy-mesme, sur son peu de mérite et de condition, et sur la nécessité qu'un bon esprit a de se ménager avec un peu de conduite dans les conversations pour n'estre pas importun à ceux qui l'escoutent, et pour se faire escouter agréablement.[19]

This absence of polish renders conversation a most disagreeable exercise.

Seventeenth-century literature, therefore, viewed the provincial with an amused if not hostile eye. Ignorant and gullible as he was, he was better advised to remain in his antique 'gentilhommière' than risk the ridicule of sophisticated Parisians, such at least is the counsel of Jodelet in *Le Campagnard* (act 5, sc.7):

> Et vous, beaux campagnards, accordés ou maris,
> Gardez-vous d'amener vos femmes à Paris,
> Pour y voir le Pont-Neuf et la Samaritaine,
> Plus de mille cocus s'y font chaque semaine,
> Et les godelureaux y sont si fréquemment
> Qu'une femme de bien s'y trouve rarement.
> Prenez-y donc exemple, et devenant plus sages
> Faites-leur voir Paris au fond de vos villages,
> Parmi vos partisans faites les cupidons,
> Et demeurez toujours les rois de vos dindons.

Stay at home, the game is not worth the candle!

The delineation of the conventional attitude of the Parisian portrayed in these works towards his provincial brethren leads to an evaluation of that of his descendants in the following century. Did it develop, harden or change radically?

1. The ascendancy of Paris

THE prose fiction of the eighteenth century is greatly preoccupied by Paris and its position in the life of France. The attitudes of writers to this relationship vary, but they testify almost unanimously to the ascendancy of the capital over the provinces, be it for good or ill. In the following pages we shall sketch the changing climate of expression on this relationship before embarking on a detailed analysis of its literary development.

Charles-Pinot Duclos is one of the most perceptive writers of the first half of the century and may usefully be taken as a representative of its opinion. What does he write of Paris and the provinces? On the one hand he comments on the backwardness of the Provinces: 'quelle différence, quelle opposition même de mœurs ne remarque-t-on pas entre la capitale et les provinces? Il y en a autant que d'un peuple à un autre. Ceux qui vivent à cent lieues de la capitale, en sont à un siècle pour les façons de penser et d'agir.'[1] On the other, he asserts that the Parisian loses his fashionable characteristics when away from the capital: 'Qu'un homme, après avoir été longtemps absent de la capitale, y revienne, on le trouve ce qu'on appelle rouillé: peut-être n'en est-il que plus raisonnable: mais il est certainement différent de ce qu'il était' (p.13). In this work, first published in 1750, Duclos echoes the seventeenth-century attitude to the provinces; they are backwaters and any man of merit would reside in Paris.

Similarly, his *Les Confessions du Comte de **** (1742) carries the conventional mockery of the pretentious provincial. The hero is amused by the efforts of an 'intendante' to emphasise her social standing: 'elle n'oubliait rien et outrait tout pour me persuader de la dignité et de l'éminence de l'intendance, et pour me faire oublier qu'étant souveraine en province, elle n'était qu'une bourgeoise à Paris'.[2] Prestige in Paris is still employed as a yardstick by which to judge the importance of a provincial. The 'intendante' is aware of her insignificance in the eyes of the Comte and strives to conceal her feelings of inferiority by pressing the claims of her local empire. Duclos will later introduce her humiliation in Parisian society.

Most novelists publishing works prior to 1760 continue the derisory presentation of the Provinces. Thémidore, the rakish protagonist of Godard d'Aucour, finds little to whet his appetite during a trip to Picardy: 'Un de nos soupers d'hiver vaut une éternité de ces plaisirs champêtres. En vain voulais-je chercher quelque aventure amusante, les circonstances ne se présentent pas.'[3] Life outside the capital is monotonous and seems incapable of providing a suitable setting for a literary hero.

Just as in the comedies of the seventeenth century, the 'gentilhomme de campagne' is a target of abuse, as we see in Yon's description of a vainglorious squire:

Il s'était battu dans sa jeunesse, il avait reçu et rendu plusieurs coups d'épée; manie excusable dans les provinces, où l'on est brave par insolence, peu endurant parce qu'on est noble, et inutile à sa patrie par esprit d'indépendance. On n'y veut point servir, parce qu'il faut commencer par obéir, et que le commandement choquerait des gens qui, depuis trois siècles, n'ont d'autres maîtres que l'oisiveté, l'ignorance et l'inflexibilité héréditaire de leurs aïeux.[4]

Here is a traditional attack in the vein of La Bruyère.

If the provincial 'hobereau' is ridiculed, so is his female counterpart. Marivaux lampoons such an unprepossessing lady:

Otez à la campagnarde de qualité son masque qu'elle porte, quand, montée sur sa haquenée, elle traverse d'un château à l'autre; ôtez-lui sa vanité crue sur les antiquités de sa famille, son ton bruyant, son estomac redressé par intervalles de réflexions, l'embarras total de sa contenance, et sa marche à mouvement uniforme; car tout cela compose l'économie de sa figure; ôtez-lui son fils le marquis et le chevalier, petits enfants qu'elle dresse devant vous à la révérence villageoise, et qui, par fatalité, sont toujours morveux quand ils arrivent, afin d'être mouchés du mouchoir de la mère; passez-moi le portrait; ôtez-lui, dis-je, toutes ces choses, il ne vous reste rien de curieux chez elle, si ce n'est la langueur ou le ton emphatique des compliments qu'elle fait, quand elle est en ville.[5]

She is drawn for the amusement of his readers and for no other motive, his public would have expected nothing else.

Duclos too enjoys this sport in his *Histoire de Mme de Luz* (1741), where we are offered a cameo of a provincial nobleman. The Comte de Maran is an admirer of the heroine and is painted as follows:

Il était un homme d'une naissance assez ordinaire pour ne pas dire obscure. Il était venu du fond d'une province éloignée pour s'attacher à la cour; et, comme on y reçoit aussi souvent les hommes sur leurs prétentions que sur leurs droits, il s'y était donné pour un homme de qualité, et avait été reçu pour tel; ou plutôt on ne s'était guère embarrassé de lui disputer un titre qui n'intéressait personne, par le grand nombre de ceux qui le portent ou l'usurpent.[6]

The proliferation of petty noblemen witnesses the usual portrayal of ignorance and pretentiousness as a literary cliché.

We are presented with the Parisian's patronising treatment of the provincial by Bridard de La Garde. His heroine, Thérèse, recounts her first meeting with fashionable ladies: 'Les premiers compliments faits, ma tante me présenta à ces Dames, qui d'un ton ironique dirent qu'elles me trouvaient assez jolie pour une provinciale.'[7] This condescension is well conveyed since she is not even accorded the courtesy of being addressed as a 'demoiselle de province'.[8] There is, however, an implicit rebuke to the arrogance of the Parisian in this passage which can be encountered elsewhere in pre-1760 works.[9] Fanfiche upbraids the inhabitants of the capital for their overweening claim to be the sole arbiters of taste: 'Il y a une antipathie singulière en fait de goût entre Paris et la Province. L'imbécile Parisien, qui ne croit pas qu'il y ait de salut hors de sa ville, ne peut se figurer que l'on puisse avoir du goût ailleurs.'[10] Yet despite this jeering comment, one finds no wholesale attack on the superiority and importance of Paris in the novels of this period. In literature, the capital is generally accepted as the proper location for plots and delineation of character, the growing realism is social not critical. We use the term 'social realism' to mean that writers were concerned to present contemporary society as it was and not, as in 'critical realism', as a means to suggest how it should be.

This distinction can be best illustrated by comparing two texts. During her stay in the capital, Thérèse follows the custom of joining a party in the country. Writing to her correspondent she declares:

Rien n'annonce ici la nature plus que dans la ville d'où nous sommes sortis. Ni la table, ni les logements ni les actions ne se ressentent de la simplicité champêtre [...] Nos dames à la vérité ont, pour accroissements de plaisirs, trois ou quatre médiateurs de plus par jour, et les hommes la liberté de perdre trois ou quatre fois plus d'argent qu'on n'en perd ordinairement à Paris, et d'en varier un peu davantage les moyens. Voilà les seuls agréments dont l'on jouit dans cette retraite.[11]

Here is a satirical thrust at the falsehood of pretending to enjoy the countryside; such visits are merely a continuation of town life. Jean-Jacques Rousseau comments on the same travesty in a letter from Saint-Preux to Milord Edouard: 'Les gens de ville ne savent pas aimer la campagne; ils ne savent pas même y être; à peine, quand ils y sont, savent-ils ce qu'on y fait [...] Les habitants de Paris qui croient aller à la campagne n'y vont point; ils portent Paris avec eux.'[12] Town dwellers are so removed from country life that they find it impossible to comprehend and appreciate its essence. Rousseau is censuring a society which cannot understand the basics of its existence. Whereas the first extract makes a particular social point, the second passes a general critical observation. Bridard de La Garde mocks a particular self-deception but Rousseau bemoans a general impotence.

The increasing critical awareness in post-1760 fiction is due to diverse factors which will command close examination in a later chapter.[13] For the present, let us exemplify this critical trend in a few quotations. In the past, literature had generally reserved its barbs for the ignorant provincial, now it was the turn of the Parisian. The tone of Marmontel's *Le Connaisseur* is gentle and certainly not censorious, yet it attacks the predominance of Parisian taste. Célidor, regarded as a prodigy in his home town, is dispatched to the capital by his father to lodge with M. de Fintac who summarises the state of literature in France: 'en province [...], les lettres sont encore au berceau. Sans le goût, l'esprit et le génie ne produisent rien que d'informe, et il n'y a du goût qu'à Paris.'[14] The tale, published in 1761, ridicules de Fintac and his narrowminded attachment to the ideas of the capital. Paris is no longer portrayed as the unique fount of all worthwhile knowledge and expertise.

The balloon of Parisian arrogance is also pricked by Barthe in *La Jolie femme ou la femme du jour*. His marquise experiences revulsion at the prospect of leaving Paris for the provinces. In a manner reminiscent of society's reaction to Montesquieu's Persians, she exclaims: 'Comment peut-on vivre en province! ah, dieux! quelle triste atmosphère quand on a respiré l'air de la capitale!'[15] The comic effect through exaggeration is well conveyed and shows the art of a practising dramatist. The marquise is ridiculous and consequently undermines the ludicrous attachment to the life of the capital. This procedure is paralleled by Barbé-Marbois in *La Parisienne en province* where another marquise is presented on the point of a dreaded departure:

la marquise prête à quitter Paris, en regretta les délices: nous n'abandonnons jamais sans peine des lieux auxquels le plaisir nous a habitués [...] D'ailleurs Paris est si attrayant! la Marquise y a passé des jours délicieux! Ils pourraient renaître: et, pour satisfaire un vain mouvement de curiosité, elle s'exposait de périr d'ennui; car, comment peut-on vivre en province?[16]

Again one is confronted by a jibe at Paris, all the more effective through the powers of oblique suggestion.

The 'cri de cœur' of Barthe's marquise is assuaged by her friend, Mme de Lorevel, who answers:

Comment? on y vit fort bien, on ne se gêne point, on donne la loi, on se moque de ce peuple de sots; et c'est ainsi qu'on leur impose. Le provincial, idolâtre de tout ce qui vient de la capitale, n'a ni goût ni dessein, ni volonté; on nous écoutera, et nous donnerons absolument le ton. Plus il sera impertinent, plus sur ma parole, il sera trouvé admirable.[17]

The Marquise is relieved to hear this prediction but will later be rather chagrined when it fails to materialise. The provincials are not portrayed in fawning costumes in this novel and the visitors suffer by contrast.

The same attack through ridicule is evident in La Salle d'Offement's *Le Maladroit*. The Vicomtesse de X*** has travelled to Picardy with considerable apprehension. However, her fears were not justified, as she confesses to the Duc de Y***: 'savez-vous bien que j'ai trouvé des gens qui avaient l'air de raisonner supportablement, quoiqu'habitant à quarante lieues de la capitale'.[18] The presumption of the Vicomtesse is deftly insinuated while her correspondent serves as both a representative of Parisian prejudices and of an audience which needs re-education. The happy experiences of this lady show that Picardy has been rethought in literary terms since the days of Godard d'Aucour's *Thémidore*.

The critical attitude to the Parisian is not merely presented in humorous terms, but is often conveyed in the delineation of social stereotypes. A ubiquitous character in the eighteenth-century novel is the rake turned mentor who embodies, in this instance, the traditional disdain for the provincial. M. de Fauxfilter scolds the Comte de Joinville for interesting himself in a certain Mlle d'Arans:

Jugez-en par le sort que vous fait éprouver cette provinciale que vous avez sans doute trouvée jolie, mais que ses grands sentiments, ses sots préjugés devraient l'enlaidir à vos yeux; à moins toutefois que vous n'ayez formé, le projet de la mettre dans de meilleurs principes, et de la mener au bonheur par la route du plaisir. Ce serait une œuvre méritoire qui vous ferait honneur dans le monde.[19]

The provincial is a derisory object for the Parisian's attentions not through her ignorance but through her purity. Mlle d'Arans is only worthy of a Parisian's interest if she is to be seduced for prestige in the 'monde'. Her innocence can be regarded as a useful testing ground for the trainee seducer: 'Si vous entreprenez d'instruire cette belle idiote, ne vous rebutez pas des difficultés qui sauraient arrêter un novice. Elle est toute fraîche sortie de son couvent; sa jeune tête est remplie du radotage des nonnes; cela croit aux revenants, à la vertu, à mille sornettes reléguées dans quelques cloîtres, et dans un coin de la province.'[20] The quest for 'bonheur' through the deprivation of 'vertu' and 'préjugés' is part and parcel of the critical depiction of the Parisian in the later fiction of our period. Instead of appearing ridiculous to all reasonable people, the provincial is now only ridiculous to the depraved Parisian.

The contrast between the views of Paris and the provinces is constantly underlined in the works of Restif de La Bretonne. His attitude to Paris is complex but he is keen to point out the Parisian's blinkered outlook on his compatriots: 'tel Parisien qui n'ignore pas les usages des Iroquois, des Hurons, des Anabaquis, ne sait pas un mot de nos usages français dans les villages et les campagnes'.[21] Life in the provinces is unworthy of consideration for the sophisticated Parisian who regards titbits of information on exotic lands of more consequence.

We have outlined the changing attitude to the provincial and the Parisian in eighteenth-century fiction. In the early period the provinces were disdained and Paris was merely subjected to jibes at particular abuses. In broad terms, post-1760 fiction presented a reversal of these roles; the provinces were lauded and Paris received general condemnation. In addition, we contended that the realism of the early period was a fictional transcription of social life while that of the later was aimed at a critical examination for transcendent purposes. The following chapters will clarify our assertion and lead, we trust, to a greater understanding of the development of the novel.

2. The appeal of Paris

WHAT are the reasons which prompt provincials to 'monter à Paris' in prose fiction? This question needs to be answered from a thematic rather than chronological standpoint since the movement of characters to the capital is constant throughout the century. Whatever motives they may ascribe to them, many eighteenth-century authors present their provincial characters paying at least one visit to Paris in the course of their narratives.

A significant factor in deciding the provincial to leave for the capital is the picture presented to him in his home environment. He might, for example, be cajoled into abandoning domestic security by the persuasive tongue of a Parisian. Mme de Menneval has just lost her son and is urged by his tutor to adopt a peasant as a substitute. Their choice falls on Bazile who, after much flattery, agrees to the suggestion and confesses: 'Vous m'inspirez, monsieur, un désir ardent de voir ce Paris dont, à nous autres villageois, on raconte tant de merveilles.'[1]

The city's reputation is also spread by those provincials who have already spent some time there. Before her marriage, the mother of Mouhy's Jeannette had been employed by a noblewoman, served in the capital and is well qualified to satisfy her daughter's curiosity. Her tales of wealth and splendour arouse Jeannette's desire to shed her rustic garb as she later remembers: 'J'avais le cœur élevé, et je ne pouvais m'accoutumer à être paysanne. Il pétillait lorsqu'on me parlait de la ville, et toutes les fois que ma mère me contait l'histoire de quelqu'une de mes semblables qui y avait réussi, il me semblait qu'il devait m'en arriver autant.'[2] In the *Paysanne pervertie* of Restif, Ursule feels a similar urge which is stimulated by the poise and elegance of Mme Parangon. In a letter to Fanchon, she relates that she has accepted a proposal to take her to Paris: 'Je pense que le voyage de Paris me serait avantageux; je le vois aux grâces de la chère Mme Parangon, qui, dit-on, le doit au temps qu'elle a passé à Paris.'[3] Here Ursule's vanity has been awakened by the prospect of future graces.

Arigène the hero of a cautionary tale of the abbé Compan, likewise hears the praises of the capital sung around him.[4] However he is only spurred to uproot himself on reading the paeans of a friend. The latter, Acanthe, had settled in Paris some time previously and had begun sending glowing reports to his compatriot. This correspondence had increased Arigène's discontent, especially as: '[Acanthe] finissait toutes ses lettres par le plaindre d'être obligé de végéter tristement dans une province où l'on ne connaissait ni le bon ton, ni les belles manières'.[5] Arigène is induced into thinking something of incomparable value is missing in his surroundings and leaves them forthwith.

An important reason for moving to Paris is the expectation of a happy existence. With a view to enhancing his daughter's prospects of an advantageous marriage, a nobleman from Nîmes proposes to escort her to the capital. The thought of her impending journey causes Adélaïde to adumbrate her conception of the city: 'le portrait attrayant qu'on m'avait cent fois fait de Paris me faisait regarder cette capitale comme un lieu enchanté où les femmes régnaient despotiquement, comme un séjour où l'ennui, le chagrin étaient ignorés, et où les plaisirs de toutes sortes de nature renaissent sans cesse'.[6] This almost Utopian vision of Paris is a fair portrayal of the impact of tales on an immature mind. Tales, which may have been balanced at the outset, became magnified out of all proportion in constant retelling, with the result that their reality has been exchanged for an elaborate pattern of illusion.

A further motive for the exodus to the capital is to search for wealth or advancement. Ambitious provincials will be depicted as yearning for the great city through the pages of eighteenth-century fiction. With luck and perseverance, a man or woman may forge a path of worldly success and acquire both prestige and riches. After the death of her father who had squandered the family fortune, Victoire Ponty was raised by a devout but impoverished aunt. Meeting Montlui- son, a man who has seen the error of his ways, she is given a glimpse of the 'grand monde'. Though infatuated with the young girl, Montluison is strong enough to restrain his feelings, and obtains a post for her with a marquise in Paris. The marquise is much taken with the girl's solid sense of values and provincial modesty, so Victoire prospers in society without straying from the paths of virtue.[7]

Often people drift to the capital as the result of being orphaned or after the death of a guardian. Of unknown parentage, Alexis is brought up in a village in Picardy by the incumbent 'curé'. When the cleric dies, Alexis finds he has no binding ties with the local community, and, judging himself a man of some ability, sets off to 'me pousser dans le monde'.[8] From Burgundy we have de Billi with a few sous in his pocket eager to 'tenter la fortune'.[9] Provence, the servant of an English lord, explains his origins at his master's request. Born at Riez of bourgeois stock, stage-struck at an early age, he absconds from school to walk the boards. After a couple of years as an actor, characterised principally by disorderly living, he determined to 'venir chercher fortune à Paris'.[10] These aspirants seem to come from insecure backgrounds, yet this was not the case with all fortune hunters.

Given a solid education and a respectable upbringing, a young man could be encouraged to seek advancement in the capital. In Prévost's *Le Monde moral* a widower tells his son of his plans to remarry and advises him to go and try his luck in the metropolis; the son recalls the interview: 'En me faisant l'ouverture de cet étrange dessein, il y mêla adroitement ses idées pour ma fortune, qui languissait dans l'obscurité d'une province; et, ce que le plaisir de m'avoir continuellement sous ses yeux lui avait fait éloigner jusqu'alors, il me proposa de faire le voyage de Paris, où mes propres soins feraient naître les occasions de m'employer, que nous attendions inutilement du zèle de nos amis.'[11]

At this point let us glance at another group of hopefuls who strike out for the capital, those issuing from large families. In *La Jolie bourgeoise et la jolie servante* Restif presents the case of a country lass who has come to the capital to enter domestic service. At her mistress's request Madelon explains her motives: 'j'ai d'honnêtes parents, chargés d'une nombreuse famille [...]; mon bon père et ma bonne mère, en m'envoyant à la ville, m'avaient bien recommandé de ne me jamais fourvoyer du chemin de la vertu'.[12] It is evident from the tone of this reply that Madelon left her home on account of her parents' fertility rather than through any wish 'to see the world'.

Yet even wealthier families were confronted by the difficulties of maintaining excessive numbers of children. Since the older children were favoured, it was the youngest who bore the brunt of the misfortune. Younger daughters often found themselves dispatched to convents to save the parents paying ruinous dowries. As for younger sons, this was a different matter. If all the normal avenues of a military or ecclesiastical career were closed to them, they were frequently left to their own resources. Striving to make their way by personal initiative, their thoughts turned to the capital and its imagined promise of salvation. In *Paris ou le mentor à la mode* Mouhy introduces us to such a fortune-seeker, the Chevalier d'Elby, who declares: 'Je suis de Bordeaux, et le cadet de onze enfants, tous vivants. Me voyant inutile et de trop à la maison, j'ai pris, il y a quinze jours, le parti de venir à Paris chercher fortune, comme beaucoup d'autres' (Paris 1735, p.6). It is significant that he has deemed it expedient to leave even a city as large and prosperous as Bordeaux to search for a livelihood.

The Chevalier de Présac is another young nobleman who experiences the need to secure a position to maintain his social standing. Contrary to d'Elby, his misfortune does not stem from belonging to numerous progeny but solely from his position as a 'cadet'. Born in Périgord at the cost of his mother's life, he hardly reaches maturity before his father dies too. At this point his sister is incarcerated in a nunnery, the succession having fallen to his elder brother. Présac is bitter about his predicament and contests the justice of the 'droit d'aînesse'. At this stage he finds no other course of action but to follow the well-trodden path to the capital in the hope of procuring some means of subsistence.[13]

Paris also attracts those involved in litigation. Marivaux writes in *Le Spectateur français* of meeting a girl who had journeyed to the capital to settle a dispute; she informed him: 'Nous sommes venues à Paris, ma mère et moi, après avoir vendu tout ce qui nous restait, pour hâter la décision d'un procès dont le gain nous rétablirait.'[14] In Diderot's *Jacques le fataliste* we have the example of Mme and Mlle d'Aisnon: 'Mme de La Pommeraye avait autrefois connu une femme de province qu'un procès avait appelée à Paris, avec sa fille, jeune, belle et bien élevée.'[15]

The Marquis de Télème has to marshall all the funds at his disposal to re-claim an inheritance from an impostor who impersonates his wife's elder brother: 'M. de Télème ne balança pas, il réunit tout ce qu'il put trouver d'argent, et décida sa femme à aller elle-même à Paris plaider cette importante affaire en l'assurant que rien ne déterminait des juges dans ce pays-là comme les sollici-tations d'une jolie femme.'[16] The Marquis is a rather antiquated 'gentilhomme de campagne' who has never served in the army and has no credit or protection in the capital; yet he is convinced his spouse's charms will win the day: 'Quoiqu'il en soit, le marquis de Télème nullement connu dans la capitale, et ne voulant pas s'abaisser à demander des lettres de recommandation à l'intendant de sa province, imagina que sa femme avec une jolie figure, un beau nom et de l'argent, avait tout ce qu'il fallait pour réussir' (p.231). It is significant in terms of the pride of the provincial nobleman that he would not demean himself to enlist the aid of an 'intendant' to facilitate his wife's manœuvres in Paris, his 'titres de noblesse' are sufficient guarantee.

One of the main lures of residence in the capital is the variety and abundance of its pleasures. Their renown is widespread in the provinces and exercises a magnetic attraction for both men and women. Saint-Gory for instance is the son of a merchant in Lyons. He receives a desultory education at the hands of an incompetent tutor, a frequent case in the novel of the day. At the age of twenty he is orphaned, receives a large legacy, and judging even Lyons too constricting a place for his projected wild oats, his thoughts turn to the capital. Years later he recollects his intentions: 'J'étais venu à Paris dans la saison des plaisirs pour en profiter, et pour voir les beautés qu'offre cette grande et superbe ville.'[17] A similar desire was experienced by Restif's Edmond. Just like his sister, he had been impressed by the qualities that Mme Parangon had acquired in the capital and was longing to see it: 'Oh! je veux la voir cette capitale si vantée, où les femmes enchantant, même sans beauté, font des passions sans être fidèles [...], font adorer jusqu'à leurs défauts les plus décidés; je veux la voir bientôt, j'en brûle d'envie.'[18]

To be sure the capital's pleasures do not merely consist in wanton dissipation, they can be of a gentler nature. Besides the obvious pastimes of the theatre, the opera, the balls, there is the congenial intercourse of Parisian society. It is to establish contact with the latter that the Baron de Murcy agrees that his son should leave home:

je consens volontiers que vous passiez quelques mois à Paris; j'espère que vous profiterez de l'occasion qu'elle vous offre de voir bonne compagnie; c'est l'école du bon goût, et des usages qui vous sont nécessaires; mais je vous invite à faire attention au choix de vos connaissances; il en est qui ne serviraient qu'à vous décrier parmi les honnêtes gens, ce serait pour vous une tache que vous parviendrez difficilement à effacer.[19]

It is indeed essential to gain admittance to the ranks of the 'bonne compagnie', the 'in crowd' of the day.

Paris is equally a cynosure for the woman who yearns for greater diversion than the provinces can offer. Born in the Isle de l'Amérique, a daughter of well-to-do merchants, the future Mme de Vilfranc comes to Paris as a young girl. She then experiences many romanesque adventures; seduction at the age of fifteen by Derville, then abduction by her lover, followed by incarceration in a convent; marriage to M. de Vilfranc, his death at Derville's hands; loss of a lawsuit and the devastation of her property in Martinique; remarriage to the unattractive Dervaux and a subsequent judicial separation. As the result of this separation, she is in a position to move from her provincial confinement and recalls: 'Je me trouvai libre et riche de plus de dix mille livres de rente; fortune assurément trop considérable pour végéter dans le fonds d'une province. Aussi je songeai bientôt à revoir Paris, ce séjour charmant des plaisirs et de la galanterie.'[20] There she leads a life of dissipation before recognising the error of her ways; this entails a rejection of loose living, but is, at bottom, a rejection of fickle men!

Mme de Vilfranc is not alone in fleeing a provincial husband. A short story of Sade, *Le Cocu de lui-même*, contains a cameo of a married woman in this predicament. She has become Raneville's mistress and is delineated as: 'séparée d'un mari plat et ennuyeux, elle était venue de province chercher fortune à Paris, et n'avait pas été longtemps à la trouver. Raneville, naturellement libertin, à l'affût de tous les bons morceaux, n'avait pas laissé échapper celui-là, [...] et faisait oublier à cette jeune femme tous les chagrins que l'hymen avait autrefois pris plaisir à semer sur ses pas.'[21] If, on the other hand, the bored wife finds it either impossible or injudicious to desert her spouse, she can always employ her guile to persuade him of the benefits of a trip to Paris. In *Le Mot et la chose*, Valmigni, the narrator's guide in society, points out a certain Mme de Colbale. This lady coaxed her husband into transplanting their household from the security of the provinces to the maelstrom of the capital. Valmigni pities the old man and explains:

Il eut pour elle la faiblesse de troquer l'opulence dans laquelle il vivait en province contre une situation médiocre dans cette ville. L'événement a bien justifié sa complaisance. Ce pauvre M. de Colbale ne connaissait point les usages de Paris; et étant d'un âge à ne plus apprendre, il trouvait mauvais que sa femme allât tous les jours au bal, aux spectacles, qu'elle ne rentrât qu'à deux ou trois heures du matin.[22]

Mme de Colbale takes a succession of lovers, which her husband finds difficult to tolerate. There ensues a separation which leads to the abused spouse returning to his native town regarded by his wife's friends as a boor.

It is not just husbands who are inveigled into uprooting themselves to satisfy female whims, lovers are so entreated by their mistresses. In Marmontel's *La Mauvaise mère* the elder brother maintains Fatime, an actress, as a status symbol. She persuades him to abandon his wife and go away with her. Once in Paris, he rents an apartment near the Palais Royal. Soon they are embarked on a life of prodigality which leads to his ruination. Now the cupboard is bare, Fatime tires of his company and is off to richer pickings.

Dissipation may sometimes be viewed as a salutary exercise as in the case of a novel by Longchamps. Alexis came into the world a mere six months after his parents' wedding, an event which disconcerted his 'father' and caused him to renounce any interest in the child. His mother ruined her figure weaning him, and later his education was entrusted to a brutal country priest. Understandably discontented with his lot, he wanders from his home and happens upon a former playmate, Lubin. After sowing some wild oats, Lubin is now an upright shepherd who resides with the venerable Philemon and his virtuous daughter, Lyse. Alexis is persuaded to stay with them and immediately falls in love with Lyse. However he is assured by Lubin that she would only be capable of returning sisterly affection. Shattered by this disclosure, Alexis once more takes to the road only to come back later and discover Lyse has died. She had of course loved him all the time.

Lubin, a true servant and friend, advises Alexis that he urgently needs distraction, and a journey to the capital is proposed:

La vie champêtre, [...] offre mille loisirs que vous donneriez à votre mélancolie, et c'est ce qu'il faut éviter. Dans les circonstances présentes, la vie active et dissipée est la seule qui puisse vous convenir. C'est dans le tourbillon d'une grande ville que vous arracherez le trait qui vous déchire. C'est dans ce chaos immense, que vous perdrez de vue les objets de douleur qui vous suivraient partout ailleurs. Ne craignez pas d'y rencontrer l'image de la vertueuse Lyse. C'est à Paris que je vous mène.[23]

It is significant that, at least in Lubin's eyes, one is unlikely to find such paragons of virtue in Paris.

Those who seek to parade themselves also find the capital an ideal milieu. We noted previously how much Mouhy's Jeannette disliked the idea of being buried alive in her village and longed for Paris. In Gaillard de La Bataille's rehashing of the theme, *Jeannette Seconde ou la nouvelle paysanne parvenue*, the heroine feels a comparable longing. Not for her the monotony of the countryside; she senses her superiority at an early age: 'Ma taille au-dessus de l'ordinaire est finie; et dans le temps que je n'étais qu'une simple paysanne, j'avais des grâces naturelles dans toutes mes notions, qui feraient honneur à la fille de Paris la mieux élevée.'[24] After a series of adventures, facilitated by the concealment of her origins, she succeeds in reaching Paris. There she is able to make the most of her pulchritude and ensnares a duke into matrimony.[25]

This desire to show oneself off to advantage is sometimes fostered by a flatterer or would-be seducer. In François Béliard's *Rézéda* a marquis uses this tactic to capture the affection of the heroine. He contrasts her present situation with the one she ought to be enjoying in Paris:

adorable comme vous êtes, il est affreux que vous soyez anéantie, enterrée dans un misérable village, avec un tas d'originaux qui ne ressemblent à rien. Quelle perte pour la capitale et pour ce minois ravissant que vous n'y paraissez pas avec l'éclat brillant d'un ajustement de goût! Vous êtes charmante, vous seriez divine; on vous idolâtrerait. Quelle maussade façon de se mettre dans les provinces![26]

Nevertheless, by virtue of her excellent provincial upbringing, Rézéda is strong enough to repel the marquis's advances and keep her vanity in check.

Others will not be so steadfast, especially Marmontel's Laurette. Amidst festivities in the village of Coulange, she stands out as the local beauty. She receives praise from all quarters, particularly from some visiting noblewomen. These ladies insist her exceptional endowments are meant for better things. Their blandishments are reinforced by the Comte de Luzi who tells her: 'il ne tient qu'à vous d'avoir à Paris un petit palais brillant d'or et de soie, une table servie selon vos désirs, les meubles les plus voluptueux, le plus élégant équipage, des robes de toutes les saisons, de toutes les couleurs, enfin tout ce qui fait l'agrément d'une vie aisée, tranquille, délicieuse'.[27] When she compares her hard-working existence – which had seemed natural to her until then – to a life of ease in Paris, her vanity is aroused. At a dance for the peasant community, Laurette tells Luzi that his propositions are enticing but her father must be consulted first. Presently there is a storm which destroys the harvest, plunging the village into dire distress. In a manner foreshadowing Valmont, Luzi makes a spurious gesture of largesse to Laurette's father which touches her deeply. He arranges a meeting with her the following morning, a secret tryst before his departure. In vain he urges her to flee with him to Paris. Realising the failure of this strategy, he puts on the tragic lover act; Laurette conveniently swoons. She is immediately seized by the Comte's servants who transport her inert body to Paris. Such is the fate of a girl whose vanity is tempted, even temporarily, by the splendour of the capital!

Another visitor who is attracted by the chance to parade herself and possibly make a fortune is the prostitute. Mlle Florival is a strumpet from the south of France who changes her zone of operation: 'Me voilà décidée à me fixer à Paris. Je vois bien qu'il n'y a qu'ici où l'on peut faire fortune par le libertinage. Bordeaux n'est rien en comparaison.'[28] A noteworthy feature of this influx of whores is the frequency with which they are conducted to Paris by a chaperon. In Boufflers's tale, *La Reine de Golconde*, Aline finds herself in trouble after her seduction by the narrator. Her pregnancy discovered, she is chased from the parental home and taken in by an old woman in a neighbouring town. The hag's motives are anything but charitable for she prostitutes her charge. Appreciating the potentialities of Aline, she decides that a new field of business is required as Aline recalls: 'Ma tante espérant que ma beauté lui serait encore plus utile dans une grande ville, me mena à Paris, où après avoir passé par plusieurs mains différentes, je tombai dans celles d'un vieux Président.'[29] After the death of her 'tante', she is wealthy enough to cover up her past, invent a false lineage and wed the Marquis de Castelmont before embarking upon the series of romanesque adventures which conclude the tale.

In Aline's case, she is debauched by a money-grubbing stranger, in others it will be a relative. Having spent an indolent childhood in the provinces, Julie is looking forward to a life of ease. However her aunt and guardian, Daigrement, wishes to profit from her niece's endowments as Julie recounts:

Ma bonne tante qui raisonnait assez juste sur ce qui tendait à me faire valoir un jour, prévoyait sagement qu'il n'est qu'un Paris pour toutes sortes d'entreprises; la sienne demandait effectivement un lieu où le théâtre de la volupté pût fournir l'occasion d'exposer avantageusement les talents de son élève pour la coquetterie: ainsi notre départ fut conclu.[30]

After a certain acclimatisation to the ways of the capital, Julie is introduced to a hideous lecher, M. Poupard. The latter showers gifts on Julie and her aunt and despite her aversion, Julie finally yields to his advances.

Yet aunts are not the sole corruptors of youth; even mothers are capable of exploiting their offspring. Thérèse has been raised on the French frontier in Alsace by a promiscuous mother. In adolescence she is taken to Metz to advertise her attractions, but business is not brisk. Removal to a more lucrative arena is called for, so the mother 'tourna les yeux vers Paris; ce qu'elle en avait entendu dire réveilla ses espérances; il fut conclu que c'était dans ce séjour que nous devions essayer de captiver la bienveillance du sort'.[31] The mother surveys their new environment and conducts a piece of market research: 'Ma mère connaissait à peu près la carte de Paris; différentes relations l'avaient mise au fait des mœurs de ses habitants; elle savait le cas que l'on y faisait de tout ce qui venait de loin. Cette raison la porta à me faire conserver mon habillement d'étrangère, c'était en quelque sorte m'afficher par le côté le plus séduisant.'[32] Thérèse strikes up relations with a musketeer, an old roué, and is also guided by Dame G., an 'entremetteuse'. So experienced and brazen does she become that she is eventually able to do her own soliciting.

Not all mothers, however, deliberately set out to prostitute their daughters.[33] In relating her childhood Sara emphasises her unhappy upbringing. Her profligate father kept on abandoning his family whilst her mother was continually striving to rejoin him. In desperation she came to Paris and being unable to find any other means of support is obliged to become a 'femme du monde'. Having sunk herself to mercenary love, she has less qualms about debauching her elder daughter as Sara remembers: 'Ma mère, qui prévoyait la fin de son argent, [...] tenait une conduite que je veux croire forcée par la nécessité [...] Mon infortunée sœur fut livrée malgré elle à un vieux libertin.'[34] Later on she will attempt to sell Sara's services in the Palais Royal.

Mme d'Aisnon after losing her lawsuit felt obliged to take advantage of her daughter's attractions.

J'étais presque résolue à mettre ma fille à l'Opéra, mais elle n'a qu'une petite voix de chambre, et n'a jamais été qu'une danseuse médiocre. Je l'ai promenée, pendant et après mon procès, chez des magistrats, chez des grands, chez des prélats, chez des financiers, qui s'en sont accommodés pour un terme et qui l'ont laissée là. Ce n'est pas qu'elle ne soit belle comme un ange, qu'elle n'ait de la finesse, de la grâce; mais aucun esprit de libertinage, rien de ces talents propres à réveiller la langueur d'hommes blasés.[35]

The daughter hates her sordid existence and she and her mother are eager to accept Mme de La Pommeraye's scheme of vengeance.

The motives which prompted people to strike out for the capital can often be related to a general perspective of freedom. Paris by its very size and diversity was regarded as a privileged site for those seeking shelter or independence.

We have shown how discontented wives sought amusement in the city and hinted at the appeal of dissipation for young men. The lure of diversion was increased for the latter by the accompaniment of heady freedom. Recollecting his youth, the Comte de Comminville reveals that his father was the incumbent of one of the 'premières charges de la Province', an office which wielded no appeal for him. Consequently upon his father's death, Comminville had no wish to follow his footsteps but, inheriting a sizeable fortune, resolved to leave Franche-Comté: 'Pour être plus libre dans tout ce que je voudrais entreprendre, je vendis tout mon bien et sans trop me soucier de ce qu'on dirait d'une pareille conduite, je sortis de ma province et vins m'établir à Paris.'[36] In Paris he was free from the bonds of his native society, and could sample new experiences at will.

The Vicomte de Barjac is also bent on widening his experience of life. Luchet paints him as a young blade eager to enjoy every variety of pleasure within his means: 'Le premier usage de sa liberté fut en faveur de Paris, ce vaste et tumultueux asile des vices et des plaisirs. Ses moyens bornés ne lui permettaient pas de tenter les aventures d'éclat dont la cour est le Théâtre; il fallut partager son temps entre les spectacles, les soupers qui les suivent, et les nuits qu'on y prépare.'[37] Where else would he find comparable pastimes and savour the freedom to enjoy them?

In this connection the capital possessed another enviable attribute, its anonymity. The possibility of movement without recognition, dissipation without identification, provided an enormous temptation. A 'cadet' from Brittany makes his way to Paris for this very reason, having understood the duality of the capital's function: 'Il vint à Paris, le seul endroit du monde où l'homme puisse briller ou être ignoré.'[38] One may 'briller' in the sense of parading oneself or in terms of self-advancement, but others will travel to the capital principally to be 'ignorés'.

After an eventful life Fanfiche determines to spend her last days in the capital: 'Je partis de Toulouse comblée de richesses, pour en venir jouir à Paris, le séjour de cette ville me paraissait plus propre que tout autre pour quelqu'un qui veut vivre ignoré.'[39] The city is perfect for her purpose because it will not interfere with her desires or question her past. It will be enough for her to demonstrate her solvency to lead an unhindered retirement.

Moreover Paris is not just an abode for the idle rich, it is also a sanctuary for the poor. *Victorine* contains an intercalated episode relating the history of Sœur Marotte who, orphaned at a tender age, becomes acutely aware of her misfortune. Luckily an uncle and aunt come to her rescue and suggest she accompany them to Paris. Her saviours are a pretentious couple whom she disdains, yet she agrees to their offer for, as she confesses: 'J'aimais mieux aller cacher ma misère à Paris que de la montrer dans mon village.'[40] Her penury will be unnoticed amidst a legion of fellow sufferers in the capital, her misery will be anonymous.

Young couples are a conspicuous example of people who need to flee their homes for the freedom to pursue their love. One thinks of Manon Lescaut and Des Grieux in their escape to the capital; it was the obvious place of refuge. In the *Mémoires du chevalier de* *** a flight is necessitated by the problem of 'mésalliance'. The hero is of noble lineage whilst his beloved is of merchant stock. At first there appears to be no solution to their dilemma but soon he proposes a clandestine marriage in Paris, assuring Clarice: 'Je vous l'ai juré mille fois, quelle que soit la différence que le ciel a mise entre nous, je suis prêt à la réparer; et si vous voulez consentir à me suivre, je vous enleverai, et nous irons à Paris où je vous épouserai en arrivant.'[41] Promises of a wedding-ring have a strong pull on young girls' hearts and Clarice is not long in succumbing to his entreaties.

Nine hails from Dôle in Franche-Comté. She is just fifteen years old when her impoverished parents decide it is high time to get her off their hands. A suitable match presents himself, M. Toulet. However, Nine has no appetite for marrying a sexagenarian and so resolves that the time is ripe for her departure. Accordingly she leaves home and wanders destitute in the countryside. She is espied by a rich young man who is immediately smitten with her charms. At his request she agrees to accompany him to an inn. There she is passed off as his sister and allocated a separate room. Far into the night Florville creeps into her room, seduces her and proposes marriage before outlining his plans: 'mon dessein est d'aller à Paris; j'y pourrai jouir sans trouble du plaisir de vous voir toutes les fois que je ne vous importunerai pas'.[42] She yields to his blandishments and he gives up thoughts of entering the Jesuit order.

Amorous encounters furnish the capital with other fugitives, especially the pregnant woman. Chevrier tells the tale of a girl from Lorraine who related the following saga. She came from a well-to-do family for her father was a 'procureur' in the Parlement of Metz. She was regularly attended by a hairdresser who encouraged her to accept the advances of the Marquis de Valban. Their illicit union leads to her pregnancy and they have no recourse but to make haste to the capital.[43]

On account of her father's losing a lawsuit Justine spends much of her youth moving from town to town. Nonetheless she manages to strike up a friendship with a neighbour, Lucide, who gives her an inkling of the rudiments of love. Armed with this scrap of knowledge, Justine sets her cap at Clairval whose affections she eventually captures. However all conquests demand a price, and hers is not surprisingly what the Victorians called an interesting condition. Being a young lady of some determination, she takes stock of her predicament and decides: 'Le seul moyen de prévenir ma honte fut de le [Clairval] suivre à Paris, où nous pourrions rester quelque temps cachés, et obtenir le consentement de ses parents pour conclure notre mariage.'[44] In fact her removal to Paris did not solemnise their relationship nor did her lover live with her for a long period.

In *La Paysanne philosophe* of mme Robert (Amsterdam 1762) we are confronted with a variation on this theme. Here a marquis has wed surreptitiously and needs to conceal the deed from his family. The arrangement is pursued felicitously until his bride conceives a child. Realising the embarrassment his wife will have to endure in her outwardly unattached state, the marquis: 'pour la rassurer et remédier en même temps aux inconvénients que les suites de sa grossesse pouvaient occasionner, lui proposa de l'envoyer à Paris, pour y faire ses couches' (p.49).

Restif de La Bretonne offers a case history of an unmarried mother presented in his inimitable fashion. *Monsieur Nicolas* carries the tale of the hero's relationship with the virtuous prostitute, Zéphire. The latter's downfall has been laid fairly and squarely at her mother's door. This bawd is suddenly unveiled as Nanette, the village lass who had deflowered Nicolas at the age of ten! Yet more shocks are in store for Nanette reveals all the ramifications: 'Quand je m'aperçus que j'étais grosse par les suites d'un enfant de dix ans, j'en fus si honteuse, que je quittai le pays sans parler à personne. Je vins à Paris [... et] me donnai aussi pour une nouvelle veuve.'[45] Nicolas is therefore the father of his mistress and Restif can indulge his incestuous fantasies.

Pregnant girls did not always succeed in escaping to the freedom of Paris and were frequently left in the lurch, their gallants were sometimes quicker off the mark. In order to avoid paying for his pleasures the 'porteur d'eau' who deceived Restif's Ursule deserted his mistress and took flight. Revealing his unsavoury past, he confesses: 'Une aventure galante, et qui eut des suites, avec une fille que je n'aimais pas assez pour l'épouser, m'a fait quitter mon village et ma famille. Je suis venu à Paris, où je ne tardai pas à me trouver dans la plus profonde misère.'[46] A similar expedition is undertaken by M. Gritan, though his motives are more diverse. Dolmeuil says of him: 'M. Gritan [...] jouissait d'une fortune assez passable en Province; en partie ses dépenses superflues, en partie sa négligence pour ses affaires, sa mauvaise conduite en un mot, le mirent dans le cas de fuir la multitude de ses créanciers en quittant la province. Il vint à Paris [...]'[47] There he would be able to dodge his creditors and cultivate a new circle of acquaintances.

There is a last category of refugee we wish to consider in this chapter, the nun. In the *Histoire de mademoiselle de la C****, the heroine had been immured in a convent at the age of twelve as the result of belonging to an over-large family. There she meets Adélaïde who has been incarcerated because of a love affair. They both yearn to escape, but the heroine is more fortunate. As the result of a romanesque *quiproquo* she is abducted by the servants of Saint-Léger instead of her companion. Despite the mistake, Saint-Léger determines to make the best of things and is prepared to take her to Paris, seducing her en route![48]

Monsieur Nicolas has a short liaison with Claire Morize from Angers. She too has experienced the confinement of the cloisters and fled them: 'Elle avait été novice dans un couvent, où elle avait été mise parce qu'elle ne voulait pas épouser un riche vieillard. Elle avait escaladé les murs et s'était enfouie à Paris, où elle se cachait en service.'[49] Once again the fugitive has no hesitation in choosing the best hideaway.

Whether they travelled there for litigation, advancement, dissipation, prostitution, refuge, the capital catered for a whole range of desires. Throughout the eighteenth century authors used these motives to justify their characters moving to Paris, the main arena for fictional portrayal. What, then, was the impact of Paris on the provincial? This is the question we shall treat in the following chapters.

3. The initial impressions of Paris and Parisians

THE provincial who travels to Paris for the first time is struck by its physical aspects, indeed his original impressions are recorded in a multitude of works in the eighteenth century. Approaching the outskirts of the city the stranger experienced excitement at the prospect of entering a fabled land. Here was the capital of his country and its greatest glory, and everything about it must be examined. Jeannette affords us a general perspective of the city:

Dès Saint-Germain j'avais observé mille choses qui m'annonçaient la proximité de cette capitale, et du séjour des Rois de France. Tout occupait mes yeux, et les surprenait en les amusant. Chemins vastes et entretenus, sur lesquels roulaient fréquemment des voitures diverses, et d'une composition qui m' était étrangère, forêts peignées, chevaux superbes, et montés par des hommes; dont les habits me paraissaient d'une bizarre magnificence; maisons de campagne ou palais, que je croyais plutôt l'ouvrage de l'enchantement que de la main des hommes; jardins admirables et décorés par les efforts les plus heureux de la nature et de l'art, rien n'échappait à mon attention.[1]

Jeannette is overwhelmed by the visual splendour, amazed at the variety and brilliance of both people and houses.

Yet when the traveller enters the city, will his expectations be realised? The answer is probably no since the entry into the city was anything but enchanting. A letter sent from Restif's Edmond to Pierrot contains a note from Ursule which declares: 'Il faut pourtant avouer qu'en entrant dans Paris, du côté de la Bourgogne, je vis de très vilaines rues, toutes remplies d'un peuple sale et misérable: mais dans le faubourg Saint-Germain que nous habitons, ce n'est pas la même chose; et ce fut bien mieux encore l'autre jour que Mme Canon nous mena aux Tuileries.'[2] Restif returns to this theme later in the novel through the medium of Edmond. His hero underlines the heterogeneous nature of the city's buildings and streets (ii.158):

Paris est un vaste assemblage de bâtiments irréguliers, qui forment quelques belles rues, d'autres qui ont l'aspect le plus désagréable, et l'air le plus malsain: on voit d'un côté la profusion sans nécessité, de l'autre la mesquinerie la plus incommode: telle rue, dans un quartier désert, où il ne passe pas trois carrosses par jour, a quarante pieds de large; tandis que telle autre (comme celle de la Huchette, un des passages les plus fréquentés) n'a pas cinq pieds, et que l'on risque à tous moments d'y être écrasé.

Paris is not the uniquely beautiful capital that the provincial may dream of. The contrasting aspects are capable of shocking the unsuspecting stranger.

A critical attitude like that of Restif is even more manifest in Contant d'Orville's *Sophie*. The heroine is staggered to discover that her preconceptions of the capital shattered by its reality:

Je l'avouerai, l'idée que je m'étais faite de cette ville unique, était bien au-dessus de la réalité; ma surprise augmenta à même que nous avancions. En effet, quel contraste entre ces hôtels immenses et magnifiques qui annoncent la grandeur, le luxe et les concussions de leurs maîtres, et ces humbles forêts qu'habitent la misère, et quelquefois le désespoir! entre ces vastes et riches magasins qui recèlent les chefs-d'œuvre des arts agréables, et ces sombres boutiques où l'ouvrier nécessaire et exténué de fatigue, trouve à peine, après un travail de quinze heures, de quoi fournir à sa subsistance, entre ces places qui annoncent les talents des vitruves modernes, et ces cloaques infestés, dont on ne peut trop promptement se détourner! entre ces équipages élégants, dont les superbes chevaux font étinceler les pavés, qui promènent le vice, et ces haillons que traîne la vertu, qui se sauve à pied! Ce sont, pourtant, me disais-je à moi-même, ces contrastes révoltants qui font de Paris la première ville du monde.[3]

Sophie expresses horror at the poverty and exploitation of the labouring classes by juxtaposing the ease and comfort of the rich. The author is anxious to underscore the iniquitous inequality of contemporary society and uses his novel as a vehicle. Existing conditions are exposed in economic and moral terms in his critical portrayal of reality.

Louvet is another author who devotes space to an examination of social abuses. On his arrival in Paris, the Chevalier de Faublas is dumbfounded by what he sees:

Ce fut en octobre 1783 que nous entrâmes dans la capitale, par le faubourg Saint-Marceau. Je cherchais cette ville superbe dont j'avais lu si brillantes descriptions. Je voyais de laides chaumières très hautes, de longues rues très étroites, des malheureux couverts de haillons, une foule d'enfants presque nus; je voyais la population nombreuse et l'horrible misère.[4]

He is so disconcerted that he asks his father if this is typical of the whole city. The latter replies that other districts are more salubrious and promises to take him sight-seeing the following day. True to his word, he has them transported to the Place Louis xv, now the Place de la Concorde. There they alight from their carriage and Faublas views the obverse of the previous day's surprises:

le spectacle qui frappa mes yeux les éblouit de sa magnificence. A droite, *la Seine à regret fugitive*; sur la rive, de vastes châteaux; de superbes palais à gauche; une promenade charmante derrière moi; en face, un jardin majestueux. Nous avançâmes, je vis la demeure des rois. Il est plus aisé de se figurer ma comique stupéfaction que de la peindre. A chaque pas, des objets nouveaux attiraient mon attention; j'admirais la richesse des modes, l'éclat de la parure, l'élégance des manières. Tout à coup je me rappelai ce quartier de la veille, et mon étonnement s'accrût; je ne comprenais pas comment il se pouvait qu'une même enceinte renfermât des objets si différents: l'expérience ne m'avait encore appris que partout les palais cachent des chaumières, que le luxe produit la misère, et que de la grande opulence d'un seul naît toujours l'extrême pauvreté de plusieurs.[5]

The presence of fine buildings cannot dim the memory of human misery but only show it in starker relief. The future Girondin uses Faublas's youthful sense of justice as a means of criticising society.

In Marchand's *Le Véridique* we encounter a passage on the contrasts of the capital: 'il était difficile en moins de temps de voir tant de richesse et tant de gueuserie, tant de faste et tant de mendicité, tant de magnificence et tant de saleté, tant de politesse et tant de grossièreté, enfin tant de beauté et tant de laideur rassemblées'.[6] Saint-Preux also notes the tremendous disparity between the lot of the rich and the poor and tells Julie: 'c'est peut-être la ville du monde où les fortunes sont les plus inégales, et où règnent à la fois la plus somptueuse opulence et la plus déplorable misère'.[7] It is evident then, that many of the post-1760 novelists in bringing their provincials to Paris were quick to seize the opportunity of highlighting and censuring social inequalities. Their portrayal of the extreme contrasts was not motivated solely to display their narrative technique but to elucidate a contemporary evil.[8]

Dolbreuse, on the other hand, establishes a happy relationship on his arrival. Loaisel's hero has spent some time at the court and is now eager to imbibe the atmosphere of the capital:

> Toutes les choses qui sont en possession de séduire les yeux et de surprendre l'admiration, les embellissements de la sculpture et de l'architecture prodigués au-dedans et au dehors des palais, qui, dans Paris, se multiplient sous les yeux de l'étranger; les scènes riantes de la campagne, et les faits intéressants de l'histoire retracés sur la laine et sur la soie, sur les étoffes et les ameublements; le génie de l'homme respirant dans les édifices et les jardins publics, les grands mouvements de son âme exprimés avec autant de délicatesse que d'énergie, sur le marbre, sur la toile, comme dans les chefs-d'œuvre de l'éloquence et de la poésie; la matière modifiée, vivifiée pour ainsi dire de cent façons diverses; le spectacle de l'industrie occupant un vaste horizon, cet air de magnificence et de fécondité qu'elle donne, le coup d'œil brillant, le doux tumulte d'un peuple empressé de jouir; la mise des femmes, l'élégance et le goût de leur parure, jusqu'au parfum qu'elles laissent sur leurs traces, et qu'on dirait l'encens de la volupté même, ou plutôt l'appât invisible qu'elles jettent à l'envi dans tous les lieux où elles passent, pour captiver tous les cœurs; cette image enfin des beaux jours d'Athènes et de Rome, tous ces tableaux, tous ces objets réalisèrent à mes yeux les merveilles de la féerie.[9]

Here indeed is someone who is under the spell of Parisian enchantment, who appreciates the fascinating diversity of people and places, albeit the better to stress the dangers of the capital. The whole tone of the passage is almost sensuous, conveying effectively the ease and magnificence of the capital.

Some features of the capital invite merely factual transcription. The lively pace of Parisian life is brought out by almost every writer: what a change of tempo for a provincial: 'Au premier coup d'œil que l'on jette sur le peuple de Paris, il paraît tout le contraire de nos citadins de province: chez nous, c'est l'apathie, la nonchalance, le goût de la tranquillité; ici, l'on voit une activité, un air d'affaire; on ne marche pas, on court, on vole; nulle attention les uns pour les autres.'[10] The very density of the population makes this fact even more startling, witness Mlle Derville's reactions: 'Elle fut si frappée de la grandeur de cette superbe ville, qu'à chaque pas tout lui semblait prodige. Les richesses, la beauté des édifices, le fracas des carrosses, leur multitude, leur magnificence; et cette affluence innombrable de citoyens qui semblent partout où passe un provincial, tant il a peine à concevoir que tant de monde habite un même lieu.'[11] Equal astonishment is conveyed in the *Lettres de Montmartre*. In this work of Coustelier, probably a parody of *Le Paysan parvenu*, Jeannot has become bored with watching the family mill revolving endlessly and sets off to make his fortune. In Paris he writes to his godfather in the 'poissard' style: 'Je sis arrivé à Paris, mon Guieu la grande ville! Queu de monde! Je croyons, Guieu me le pardonne, que c'est comme ça la vallée de Chaussefat, et que tous les morts qui étaient morts dépis que les hommes vivaient s'y étaient rassemblés itou.'[12]

The masses of people are only to be balanced by the superabundance of carriages. After a coach trip, Julie reaches the capital. Once again we are treated to a compilation of first impressions:

Nous arrivâmes enfin dans Paris, dont le tumulte me surprit avec raison: occupée à regarder les embarras, la quantité prodigieuse des carrosses, la circulation de l'infanterie, et pour tout dire ce chaos général, je ne pouvais croire qu'on pût s'y reconnaître. Pour achever de m'étonner, le hasard nous fit rencontrer un brillant et leste équipage, accompagné de jeunes cavaliers uniformes, qui, tombant à coups de fouets sur notre humble voiture, crient au cocher de se ranger.[13]

The preoccupation with the number and variety of coaches is common in eighteenth-century fiction. Louise is an ingenuous country lass who has been obliged to come to the capital as the result of her marriage. Straightway she is struck by the hustle and bustle of the streets and the dangers for the pedestrian: 'Bon Dieu! quel bruit, quel vacarme dans les rues: des carrosses, des voitures qui menacent d'écraser les passants, ou qui les couvrent de boue; une foule perpétuelle qui s'agite et se pousse.'[14] Traffic jams were a frequent feature of the Parisian scene; even in an early work of the century we are offered a vivid account of such an occurrence:

[Des Frans] se trouva arrêté dans un de ces embarras qui arrivaient tous les jours au bout de la rue des Gesvres. Et malheureusement pour lui, les carrosses venaient à la file de tous les côtés, il ne pouvait se tourner d'aucun. Un valet qui le suivait était dans la même peine; et tous deux en risque d'être écrasés entre les roues des carrosses, s'ils avaient fait le moindre mouvement contraire.[15]

Perils indeed! Moreover they were often increased by careless and querulous drivers; Marivaux's famous cabman was not alone.

What of the amenities and the amusements of the capital? The various public gardens were a 'must' on any visitor's itinerary. A character of Mouhy newly arrived in the city can think of no better outing than to the Tuileries: 'ne sachant que devenir, ne connaissant encore personne à Paris, je me fis conduire aux Tuileries. J'avais tant entendu parler de ce beau jardin en province, que je voulus en juger par moi-même.'[16] Once in the garden let us hear the testimony of Mme de Bonval:

J'allai le lendemain aux Tuileries. Dieux, que j'en fus enchantée! J'y vis le plus beau jardin de l'Univers [...] J'y vis des statues d'une perfection exquise, et qui semblent enchérir sur la nature; mais ce que je ne puis croire, malgré le témoignage de mes yeux, je n'y vis personne que des nouvellistes, quelques rêveurs, et cinq à six femmes qui marchaient comme des divinités.[17]

Yon is a mediocre writer whose aim is to pass a few carping remarks in the framework of a traditional narrative. In 1759 a hack was not affected by the increasing critical realism which was to be evidenced in the works of a Restif or Louvet.

One genre of Parisian entertainment drew throngs of provincial spectators, the theatre. The eighteenth century was infatuated with the stage and the Parisian theatre was the greatest in the land. Dorine is a discerning young lady who recognises this superiority as one of the main attractions of the capital: 'Dorine semblait préférer le Théâtre Français; c'était un des premiers avantages qu'elle trouvait à Paris sur toutes les autres cités. Son goût éclairé, formé par la fréquente lecture des historiens et des poètes ne lui avait fait trouver que de l'ennui dans les spectacles de province.'[18] Inside the playhouse, what were the reactions of the newcomers? They exhibited above all a lack of etiquette; when they were moved by a piece they were not afraid to show their feelings, much to the scandal of their hosts or neighbours. On account of the poignancy of a tragedy, Thérèse weeps copiously, an outburst which brings a rebuke from her maid: 'Eh! Mademoiselle, vous allez vous perdre d'honneur. Vous faites acte de villageoise en plein public. S'amuser à écouter une pièce avec assez d'attention pour en être émue! Quelle honte!'[19] This extract is mildly satirical and we have to wait for a work such as Nougaret's *La Paysanne pervertie* for serious intent. In spite of the endless chatter around her, Jeannette manages to follow the play and gives vent to an abundance of tears. This display of emotion provokes a sarcastic comment from a fellow spectator: 'Voyez comme elle pleure, s'écria l'un d'entre eux assez haut, c'est quelque provinciale.'[20] Provincials are ridiculously unaware of the way to behave in such instances, manifesting again the disparity between Parisian and provincial manners. In addition there is the suggestion that provincials are capable of truer feelings than the inhabitants of the capital, that they express individual emotions rather than stereotyped responses, a point which will be developed later.

Provincials consistently maintained their spontaneity, or ignorance in the eyes of Parisians, in that breath-taking spectacle, the Opera. In a work of Bricaire de La Dixmerie, Laure writes to Emilie: 'Vous autres gens de province, vous n'avez presque aucune idée d'un pareil séjour. C'est l'Opéra [...] Je vous dirai seulement que c'est le plus brillant spectacle que l'industrie humaine puisse offrir à l'œil humain. C'est un ensemble magique.'[21] Magic indeed is the impression conveyed to the majority of unprepared spectators. It is a far cry from the lack-lustre entertainments of Normandy to the splendour of the Parisian stage. Witness the enthusiasm of mme Robert's heroine who has come to the capital to live with an uncle and aunt when she is taken to the Opera: 'J'avoue que lorsque je vis lever la toile, je crus d'abord être transplantée dans les siècles de Féeries où les enchanteurs ne coûtaient qu'un coup de baguette.'[22] Thérèse is yet another member of the Opera audience who cannot conceal her stupefaction at the spectacle:

Le premier coup d'archet avait déjà frappé la mienne [son âme], mes sens suspendus, balancés vaguement, par les efforts de l'harmonie j'avais perdu toute considération étrangère au plaisir qui m'occupait; j'avais oublié jusqu'aux petites précautions de ma vanité provinciale contre la suffisance parisienne qui m'observait pour jouir de mon trouble.[23]

One may therefore assert that the distinguishing feature of the provincial's reaction to the theatre is consistently revealed as an unencumbered spontaneity, a significant contrast with the Parisian's.

The theatre was an excellent place in which to parade oneself, in fact it was the major reason for attendance. Clémentine is a coquettish adolescent who typifies the Parisian attitude: 'Clémentine aimait beaucoup le spectacle: non qu'elle eût l'esprit assez pénétrant pour démêler dans les pièces de théâtre ce qu'il y avait d'instructif et de vraiment agréable. Elle aimait le spectacle parce que, chaque fois que sa mère l'y menait, tous les regards se tournaient sur leur loge, et qu'on s'écriait de tous côtés: qu'elle est jolie! qu'elle est belle!'[24] The light tone of this passage is unusual for such a late work though the observation was commonplace. The theatre was obviously a place for any provincial who wished to be noticed.

The whore who made her way to the capital in search of success would be advised to station herself there as a means of self-advertisement. Counsel of this order is purveyed in the anonymous *Histoire de Gogo*: 'Sachez que ce qu'il y a de plus aimable à Paris rampe misérablement faute d'être placé dans un point de vue avantageux, et le théâtre est de tous le plus favorable: c'est là qu'un reste de laquais devient un ragoût de Seigneur [...] En entrant dans l'Opéra, c'est s'afficher comme cherchant des amants.'[25] A young singer enters the Opera where she thrives not through her fine voice but through the attentions of a lord. She writes home to her mother in the provinces: 'J'ai suivi l'exemple de mes compagnes; je me suis fait des amis, et je me trouve à présent fort à mon aise; j'occupe un grand appartement meublé tout au mieux; j'ai un buffet rempli de belle et bonne argenterie, avec un contrat de rente, dont m'a fait présent un riche et généreux Seigneur.'[26] Bret's Thérèse has also heard of the benefits to be derived from an appearance amidst Parisian audiences and resolves to do the rounds (*La Belle Allemande*, p.43):

Je débutai par l'Opéra, où j'étalai dans une première loge mes charmes, relevés de tout le piquant que leur pouvait donner mon habillement d'étrangère.

Dès que je fus placée, je devins le but de tous les lorgneurs de profession. Ils sont communs dans ce lieu où le plaisir des sens est la seule divinité qu'on y révère.

These works are all composed in the manner of the early social realism, recasting a contemporary situation for explanatory and not critical comment.

What were the feelings of provincials toward the capital as they envisaged their stay there? Were they full of expectation or beset by disquiet? As for Marianne the pulsations of hope beat steadily in her breast:

Je ne saurais vous dire ce que je sentis en voyant cette grande ville, et son fracas, et son peuple, et ses rues. C'était pour moi l'empire de la lune: je n'étais plus à moi, je ne me ressouvenais plus de rien; j'allais, j'ouvrais les yeux, j'étais étonnée, et voilà tout.

Je me retrouvai pourtant dans la longueur du chemin, et alors je jouis de toute ma surprise; je sentis mes mouvements, je fus charmée de me trouver là, je respirai un air qui réjouit mes esprits. Il y avait une douce sympathie entre mon imagination et les objets que je voyais, et je devinais qu'on pouvait tirer de cette multitude de choses différentes je ne sais combien d'agréments que je ne connaissais pas encore; enfin il me semblait que les plaisirs habitaient au milieu de tout cela.[27]

Marivaux's heroine senses she is entering the perfect milieu for her own personality, it is as if she belongs to the capital. The subtleties of Marivaux's style were not matched by his contemporaries, yet Marianne's intuition of the pleasures of Paris has numerous echoes.

Perrin illustrates his heroine's demand for pleasure as Julie realises at once that Paris is the theatre where her aptitudes and endowments will find a most satisfactory outlet: 'rien ne fut plus prompt que l'impression que je reçus en arrivant dans cette ville enchantée; ma petite vanité, aussi folle que ridicule, m'offrait une perspective des plus riantes, et me persuadait que je n'avais qu'à paraître'.[28] None experiences a more agreeable foretaste than the Jeannette of

Gaillard de La Bataille. Until this time, she has spent her life in the wings in preparation for her entrance on to the proper stage for her talents (*Jeannette Seconde*, ii.195):

Jeannette, voilà votre séjour, me disais-je en secret; c'est ici le théâtre où vous allez paraître: c'est d'aujourd'hui que vous commencez à vivre; le temps passé n'était que l'insipide préparatif de votre élévation et de vos plaisirs. Séjour heureux, que vous me promettez des charmes! Un embarras de carrosses nous força d'arrêter un moment dans la place du Palais Royal; c'était l'heure de l'Opéra. Je vis des femmes superbement parées, qui dans des équipages où l'or brillait de toutes parts, arrivaient à ce spectacle. C'est avec cette pompe, continuais-je à me dire tout bas, que l'on me verra bientôt paraître.

This sentiment of future enjoyment and success is by no means confined to female characters.

For an example of a male who has comparable feelings let us return to Marivaux and *Le Paysan parvenu*. As the result of his brother's marriage, Jacob is entrusted with the task of transporting the family wine to its Parisian destination:

L'année d'après le mariage de mon frère, j'arrivai donc à Paris avec ma voiture et ma bonne façon rustique.

Je fus ravi de me trouver dans cette grande ville; tout ce que j'y voyais m'étonnait moins qu'il ne me divertissait; ce qu'on appelle le grand monde me paraissait plaisant.[29]

His realisation of the benefits of life in Paris develops more slowly than that of the women recently discussed, but nevertheless emerges steadily during the early part of his stay: 'J'étais fort content du marché que j'avais fait de rester à Paris. Le peu de jours que j'y avais passé m'avait éveillé le cœur, et je me sentais tout d'un coup en appétit de fortune' (p.12). The proposed marriage to Geneviève fills him with an even sharper sense of what the future may hold in store for him (p.26):

Je voyais que du premier saut que je faisais à Paris, moi qui n'avais encore aucun talent, aucune avance, qui n'étais qu'un pauvre paysan, et qui me préparais à labourer ma vie pour acquérir quelque chose (et ce quelque chose dans mes espérances éloignées n'entrait même en aucune comparaison avec ce qu'on m'offrait), je voyais, dis-je, un établissement certain qu'on me jetait à la tête.

It is true that Jacob did not become immediately aware of his potentialities, but without the impact of the capital his latent talents would never have been awakened, never mind realised.[30] It will be noted that these characters who anticipate a happy future in Paris are portrayed in works of the earlier period. Subsequently they will all benefit in varying degrees from their stay.

However not all provincials experienced a sense of exultation and anticipation upon their arrival in the capital. Just like Jeannette, the Chevalier de Présac is struck by the contrast between bustling streets and rural tranquillity. Yet his perception of the disparity transcends the physical aspects to encompass a comprehension of the moral differences:

Elevé dans le calme de la solitude, loin des plaisirs tumultueux, n'ayant jamais connu d'autres amusements que ceux d'une vie innocente: figurez-vous ma surprise en arrivant à Paris: je ne vis de toute part qu'agitation et que trouble; ici le crime se montrant avec hardiesse, parce qu'il est assuré de l'impunité, là se couvrant des dehors de la vertu mais pour se rendre plus dangereux encore; l'avarice et la volupté se disputent le droit de régner sur les cœurs, mais l'avarice obtenant toujours la préférence, toutes les passions soumises et rangées pour ainsi dire autour d'elle; l'amour même, cette passion et si noble et si belle faite pour épurer nos cœurs, j'ai vu l'amour avili, profané, venir encenser les autels de la fortune.[31]

This is not just a censorious commentary on the ethics of Parisian life, but also hints at a certain unease of the stranger before a different world. Rousseau too illustrates this malaise when he has Saint-Preux write from Paris: 'J'entre avec une secrète horreur dans ce vaste désert du monde. Ce chaos ne m'offre qu'une solitude affreuse où règne un morne silence' (*La Nouvelle Héloïse*, p.231). Laure likewise senses a certain disquiet during her initial contact with the capital. Bricaire de La Dixmerie's character feels alienated by a milieu in which she cannot integrate herself and writes ruefully to Emilie:

Vous restez en province; on m'entraîne dans la capitale. Je l'ai vue cette ville qui fait peur, cet horrible amas de palais et de masures. Je me trouve au milieu de ce peuple, qui ne ressemble à rien, et qui dédaigne tout ce qui ne lui ressemble pas. Je dois lui paraître bien gauche. Une petite personne qui n'a pour elle que ses dix-sept ans, des yeux, comme on dit, de province, et les grâces du couvent, a tout-à-fait ici l'air de tomber des nues.[32]

She is not equipped with the manners of high society and is unable to accept or be accepted into its life. She would far rather return to the peace of the provinces and the comforting presence of her correspondent. Writing of herself in the third person, we are shown the abrupt nature of her dealing with Paris (pp.5-6):

On la jette, on la précipite au milieu d'un monde absolument nouveau pour elle. Paris est un séjour aussi dangereux qu'il est brillant et séducteur. Il m'effraie encore plus qu'il ne m'éblouit. Je regrette notre solitude. Est-ce embarras de figurer dans ce monde que je ne connais pas encore? Est-ce la crainte d'y figurer mal? Je ne puis vous le dire. Ce que je sais le mieux, c'est que je voudrais me soustraire à cette épreuve.

From the security and simplicity of the provinces she has been thrust into the ambiance of a highly sophisticated society.

The last few quotations are taken from novels published in the period after 1760 and mirror a changed attitude to Paris. Mistrust and unease have replaced hope and expectation. No wonder, then, that these characters will fare badly in the capital.

Gradually we have been moving from an account of the physical aspect of Paris to consider the impact of its society. How did the Parisian and his way of life impress the provincial during the early stages of his visit? As for Nine, she is not a little mortified to discover that her illusions about the capital's citizens are dashed at first blush. The time-honoured opinions bruited in her home wither before reality as she admits: 'Enfin nous voilà dans la capitale du Royaume: j'y trouvai les gens faits comme partout ailleurs, quoiqu'il fût reçu généralement à Dôle et à Besançon, que les Parisiens avaient quelque singularité dans la figure.'[33] The future Mme Bonval has an adolescent conviction that her elders are generally stupid and sets great store on 'esprit'. Her idea of Paris is stimulated by the visit of a Parisian cousin. Consequently when she departs for the capital with her husband she is brimming with expectations:

J'avais plus d'impatience que lui d'arriver dans cette ville célèbre. Quelle agréable nécessité pour une femme de province! Nous partîmes, nous arrivâmes après dix jours de marche. Je vis enfin cette capitale de l'Europe. Ah combien il me fallut rabattre des idées que je m'étais faites sur le récit de mon petit cousin! J'avais imaginé toutes les femmes des modèles de beauté, des Grâces, des Vénus, et les hommes de la taille la plus noble, de la figure la plus élégante. Quelle fut ma surprise de ne voir dans ce sexe que des poupées, et dans la nôtre que des masques enluminés.[34]

The Parisians fail lamentably to live up to her idealisation of them as almost magical beings. Yon again strikes a mocking note but has no general axe to grind.

Given contact with the 'Tout Paris' of the day, the provincial was able to form his own estimate of that society. The description of the entry of such a stranger into the social life of the capital is contained in Prévost's novel, *Mémoires d'un honnête homme*. When its hero goes to the capital as a young man he has already some experience of polite society in his province. Nevertheless he immediately notices differences in the tone and subject matter of the conversations he hears:

Les dames me parurent aimables; la plupart des hommes étaient des gens de robe ou de finance, qui ne manquaient ni d'esprit ni d'usage du monde. Je trouvai à tous les convives plus de facilité et de chaleur que je n'en avais vu dans la province. L'attention que j'étais obligé de faire sur moi-même pour entrer dans le sens de mille choses que j'ignorais, ne me permit pas d'autres réflexions. J'appris les histoires courantes de la ville, les modes et les plaisirs, le caractère des nouvelles pièces de théâtre et des livres nouveaux.[35]

As the result of this initial incursion, he is invited to various suppers. A welcoming hostess gives him cameos of the previous evening's guests, thereby affording him further insight into Parisian society. Despite the scandal-mongering and badinage he has to admit that he enjoys his soirées: 'Je ne pouvais désavouer néanmoins que ceux à qui je trouvais tant de légèreté et d'injustice avec si peu de sens et de raison, n'eussent bien des qualités aimables. J'y étais même sensible, et rien ne m'avait paru moins ennuyeux que mes deux premiers soupers' (p.27). Amidst the malicious gossip he is chided for his strong sense of justice, but is excused on the grounds of being a recent arrival in the capital. A later hero world rarely be so indulgent.

The frivolity which was the staple ingredient of so much conversation in Parisian society found a doughty antagonist in Jean-Jacques Rousseau. When Saint-Preux encounters the great 'socialites' he is repulsed by their insincerity. Offers are not made from the heart but from an artificial concept of social practice, and literal acceptance would often betray a lack of the proper accomplishments. He writes to Julie: '[il y a] mille manières de parler qu'il ne faut pas prendre à la lettre, mille offres apparentes qui ne sont faites que pour être refusées, mille espèces de pièges que la politesse tend à la bonne foi rustique' (p.232). Appearances are ever deceptive among the élite, and Saint-Preux is dismayed at the attitudinising and fashionable vagaries. So refined is the art of varnishing that even blatant wrongs can be concealed under the veneer of truth. Nonetheless Saint-Preux is prepared to attend the suppers, spectacles, parties, which constitute its daily diet, albeit without any real appreciation. The variety of these activities does possess a superficial attraction as he confesses (p.245):

Ce n'est pas que cette vie bruyante et tumultueuse n'ait aussi quelque sorte d'attraits, et que la prodigieuse diversité d'objets n'offre de certains agréments à de nouveaux débarqués; mais, pour les sentir, il faut avoir le cœur vide et l'esprit frivole; l'amour et la raison semblent s'unir pour m'en dégoûter: comme tout n'est que vaine apparence, et que tout change à chaque instant, je n'ai pas le temps d'être ému de rien, ni celui de rien examiner.

The so-called pleasures have a hollow resonance for Saint-Preux, an impression supported by other visitors.

The Marquis de Murcin is a young provincial who anticipated universal gaiety in the capital and is bewildered to discover the general air of boredom around him: 'La magnificence des maisons et l'élégance des voitures me faisaient toujours croire que c'était chez les personnes à qui elles appartenaient qu'habitait le plaisir; mais jusqu'aux domestiques, rien n'était gai.'[36] Neither can he find anything to recommend the theatre and Opera. Below the glittering appearances, Paris is devoid of any worthwhile values.

Nougaret's Jeannette likewise repines at the empty pursuit of pleasure during her early days in the capital: 'Quel est en effet la vie que l'on y mène? On n'y songe qu'à varier les plaisirs, qu'à satisfaire toutes ses passions, qu'à passer dans l'oisiveté et les festins des jours qui paraissent s'écouler trop lentement. Je parle des gens qui composent la bonne compagnie.'[37] The 'bonne compagnie' was the supreme promoter of this merry-go-round and exercised the vapid offices of social despotism.

We may say therefore that the impact of Paris and its society was certainly not uniform. Many provincials in the later novel expressed shock at the disparity between opulence and misery on their arrival in the city. Nevertheless most agreed that the better quarters contained many fine buildings and gardens which lived up to their expectations. Characters in the pre-1760 novel viewed their entry on to the Parisian stage as a prelude to success and happiness, whilst their successors experienced a malaise before a society marked by inequality and clamouring for pleasures. Whereas Marivaux, Gaillard de La Bataille etc., offered a representation of contemporary society, Rousseau, Louvet and their like presented a critical appreciation. Nonetheless one and all illustrate the importance of the provincial's initial impressions of Paris as a literary theme.

4. The trials of inexperience

AN immediate effect of contact with Paris is a feeling of 'dépaysement'. As we showed in our introduction, the provincial was a traditional figure of fun in French literature. A common way of provoking this laughter was the highlighting of the gap between Parisian and provincial manners. In ignorance of metropolitan usage, the newcomer would display his inadequacy by committing successive blunders. To what extent did this tradition survive in eighteenth-century fiction?

Having satisfied himself with the layout of the city, M. de Fillerville ventures forth to a relative's house where he is introduced as a 'gentilhomme pauvre et Normand'. When he is inside his lack of experience overcomes him:

Je fus introduit, et je demeurai pétrifié. Les lanternes des rues m'avaient frappé d'étonnement. Que devins-je à la lueur d'une illumination des plus éblouissantes, au milieu de laquelle je remarquai une immensité de diamants, de broderies, et de louis d'or dont ma vue fut offusquée! Les jambes me manquèrent, ma parole fut interceptée, et en voulant faire une révérence, je pensai culbuter sur une jeune dame qui était à côté de moi.[1]

The luxurious residence leaves at a loss someone who is used to the primitive amenities of the provinces.

This same feeling of helplessness afflicts Jacob at the end of Marivaux's version of *Le Paysan parvenu*. He has come to the aid of a man being attacked in a street, drives off three assailants and wins the gratitude of the Comte d'Orson. The latter is a man of repute who takes charge of his saviour and conducts him to the theatre. There, in spite of his enhanced knowledge of good manners, Jacob is unable to merge into such elevated company: 'Les airs et les façons de ce pays-là me confondirent et m'épouvantèrent. Hélas ! mon maintien annonçait un si petit compagnon, je me voyais si gauche, si dérouté au milieu de ce monde qui avait quelque chose de si aisé et de si leste!' (p.265). He is sufficiently aware to recognise the superior qualities of those around him and the need to maintain his poise, but the gulf between rational appreciation and emotional response is too wide to be bridged in immediate self-control.

This absence of self-assurance inhibits a stranger in an alien situation. Marivaux makes use of it again in his *Lettres sur les habitants de Paris*. To support his thesis that the capital's 'marchandes' have most engaging manners, he recites the tale of a hapless visitor: 'Un jour, un provincial, nouvellement débarqué dans Paris, entra dans la boutique d'une de ces marchandes pour acheter quelque chose de considérable. D'abord salut gracieux, étalage empressé; la marchandise ne lui plaisait pas, il mâchait un refus de la prendre et n'osait le prononcer.'[2] The customer has seen nothing which suits his requirements, yet such is the presence of the assistant, he walks out of the shop with an unwanted article.

It is the constant dread of the provincial to exhibit his naivety in Paris. Bridard de La Garde's Thérèse fears stupid mistakes and the subsequent wounds to her vanity. Bearing this in mind, conversation was a veritable torture:

Je crains de parler, je ne sais sur quel ton je dois le prendre avec tous ceux que je vois ici. Les uns sont guindés à l'excès; les autres rampent si bas, que l'on craint de se baisser trop pour les examiner. Lorsque j'entendis parler mon oncle, j'imagine quelquefois que ses façons de s'énoncer, si familières, sont des pièges tendus à la simplicité d'une jeune provinciale, pour lui faire hasarder quelques expressions ridicules.[3]

In like manner, the Marquis de Murcin trembles at the prospect of making a fool of himself before the Comtesse de Rouvigny. He confides to the Commandeur de Saint-Brice: 'je craignais de ne lui paraître qu'un provincial très gauche et très ridicule, et de ne lui inspirer que du dédain'.[4] The provincial's self-esteem is in evidence in these situations, and he experiences an inferiority complex.

The ignorance of the unwritten rules of Parisian society is a stumbling-block too. The marquis in Nougaret's *La Paysanne pervertie* offends this code. A scurrilous abbé persuades him that a liaison with an actress or dancer is a necessary ingredient in his 'éducation sentimentale'. Accordingly a rendez-vous is arranged with a 'danseuse d'Opéra' at which he arrives too early and earns a reproof from Julie: 'Elle m'a raillé sur l'heure à laquelle je venais la voir, et m'a dit malignement, qu'on s'apercevait bien que j'étais nouvellement débarqué de ma province puisque j'ignorais qu'à Paris les dames ne sont visibles qu'à midi, au plus tôt' (iii.6). An error of a comparable nature is perpetrated in Nougaret's *Les Astuces de Paris* (Londres 1775). Mitouflet and his sister decide to pay a visit to a cousin. The relative is still enjoying his slumbers. Mitouflet misunderstands a servant's remarks and has to suffer the humiliation of a sneering comment: 'Vous êtes donc bien provincial, puisque vous ignorez qu'il est d'usage à Paris de faire entendre que quelqu'un dort, en disant *il n'est pas encore jour*' (p.33). This formula must have been in constant use for the devotees of Parisian society were not renowned for their early rising![5]

The provincial male is deemed to expect modesty from his female counterpart and is perturbed when confronted with the women of the capital. Saint-Preux informs Julie: 'Depuis le faubourg Saint-Germain jusqu'aux halles, il y a peu de femmes à Paris dont l'abord, le regard, ne soient d'une hardiesse à déconcerter quiconque n'a rien vu de semblable en son pays; et de la surprise où jettent ces nouvelles manières naît cet air gauche qu'on reproche aux étrangers' (p.268).

That a provincial would expect to employ a chivalrous code of conduct is stressed in a novel of the marquis d'Argens, the *Mémoires du Comte de Vaxère*. In Paris primarily to study, the hero later joins the army. He falls in love with the widowed Mme de Dorset, but cannot think of a decent way to further his desires: 'Je connaissais si peu le monde et surtout le caractère des femmes que je me figurais qu'une déclaration d'amour était une offense pour celle à qui elle s'adressait. Je regardais comme une témérité des plus punissables l'audace d'avoir osé lever les yeux sur une personne que je devais respecter.'[6] Despite his timidity, his wishes are eventually fulfilled, but only as the result of the advances of Mme de Dorset who had recognised his 'gaucherie'. In Louis d'Ussieux's *Alexis*, the hero has a series of misadventures before his qualities are rewarded. On his way from his village in Picardy he succours a lady whose coach has become embedded in a ditch. In recognition of his services, she offers him a post as her secretary which he readily accepts. Endowed with provincial frankness, he expresses his opinions too freely, and is promptly dismissed. The author accords him a similar fate in the employment of a writer whose works he dares to criticise even when invited to do so. Furthermore in the payment of a financier, he learns once again that truth is a commodity which needs to be seasoned with a large dose of tact. However, after a spell in gaol, he is befriended by a kindly minister and set on the road to riches.

A more serious hazard for the unwary provincial is the Parisian 'filou'. When Nougaret's gullible brother and sister arrive in the capital they decide to hire a carriage to convey them to their lodgings. The driver realises their naivety and takes them for a ride, literally and figuratively: Mitouflet later discovers his treachery: 'On m'a depuis informé que son dessein était de gagner du temps: manèges, m'a-t-on dit, pratiqués de tous ses confrères, lorsqu'on les paye à l'heure, et singulièrement quand ils s'aperçoivent qu'ils ont affaire à quelque provincial.'[7] There follow numerous occasions when the couple purchase worthless goods at exorbitant prices, the sister being the main sufferer for: 'L'œil observateur s'aperçoit enfin que sa timidité, que son maintien gêné, est le fruit des mœurs simples de quelques villes de province' (p.23). They are innocents at large since their ingenuous air reveals their origin immediately.

A visitor from Noyer in Burgundy is injudicious enough to talk about his finances in a cabaret. Overhearing these remarks, a friendly Parisian approaches him, offers him hospitality, and subsequently robs him – all within twenty-four hours of his arrival in the capital.[8] This theft affords the author an opportunity to pass warning comments through the medium of Laurent's host (p.11):

vous êtes ici dans le pays des braves gens et des escrocs, et autant il y est avantageux de contracter des liaisons honnêtes autant l'on doit craindre de se laisser duper par les apparences de la probité et de la vertu [...] jugez des risques auxquels s'expose un jeune étranger, qui, comme vous, croit dès la première nuit pouvoir impunément inventorier tout un quartier. Il n'est sorte d'adresse, de ressorts, d'expédients auxquels n'aient recours cette espèce d'aventuriers connus ici sous le nom général de filoux.

Lying in a pitiable state in a Paris street, a youngster from Bordeaux draws the attention of some passers-by. They transport him to a hostelry where he tells them his tale of woe: 'Je suis un jeune homme qui, en débarquant à Paris, ai donné dans le panneau que m'ont tendu des malheureux.'[9] Mouhy has him explain that while journeying to the capital he struck up acquaintanceship with an abbé. This is the start of a stock fictional device. At the abbé's request, the Chevalier d'Elby accompanies him to the house of a 'cousine' and her daughter. D'Elby cannot believe his good fortune and, feeling rather weary, begs to retire for the night. He is conducted to his room, consumes some drugged tea and dozes off immediately. Thereupon he is robbed and stripped of his valuable garments; the next thing he remembers is waking up in the street. The 'filoux' were able to deceive him and get off scot free since he was unacquainted with the city. One of his benefactors, M. d'Orneville – a provincial himself – promises to look after him and guide him on a safe tour of the capital.

A heroine of Sade experiences a similar mishap. From her home in Rouen, Rosette plans to visit her uncle Mathieu in Paris. Even before she arrives we are given an inkling of subsequent events: 'elle allait dans une ville bien dangereuse pour le beau sexe de province y débarquant avec de l'innocence et beaucoup de vertu'.[10] As a stranger to the maze of streets around her, she asks for directions. Unfortunately she addresses herself to a 'filou', feeling sure her destination, the rue de Quincampoix, will be quickly accessible. The rogue discovers she has never met her uncle and cousins before, and therefore has little difficulty in persuading her of his friendship with them. By temporising he manages to send word to his associates to form a plan to deceive Rosette. He escorts her to the supposed home of her relatives where she is received familiarly. Rosette is slightly suspicious about her 'relations' but yields pitifully to their dupery. As the result she is inebriated, robbed, raped and dumped in the street. Eventually she summons help, establishes her identity and her father hastens to fetch her before she returns to Rouen vowing never to venture to the capital again.

Coustelier's peasant meets with a comparable fate. Jeannot had enjoyed some success during his stay in Paris, both socially and financially. Chance has bestowed on him a winning ticket in a lottery. The proud possessor of recent wealth and a new name, Laribalandière, he deems his trip most worthwhile. However, he has had his share of luck, and a reversal is in store. A whore and her accomplices get him intoxicated, rob him, and abandon him naked in the gutter; he can only reflect: 'Ah, que ses gens de Paris étaient des dénicheux de merles et de bourses!'[11] The provincial with money would seem to have had the utmost difficulty in retaining it.

Another victim of Parisian trickery in the literature of the period is the woman involved in a lawsuit. The inordinate delays of the legal system seemed to be designed to extract the last sou from a litigant. We have already mentioned a mother and daughter who came to Paris to expedite an important dispute. The daughter explains her problems:

On néglige de travailler pour nous, parce que nous n'avons de quoi payer; enfin, monsieur, la misère où nous sommes tombées, le chagrin, le mauvais air, et l'obscurité du lieu où nous logeons; la douleur de me voir souffrir moi-même, et le grand âge, ont entièrement abattu ma mère; elle est malade, tout lui manque, et moi, qui suis au désespoir de la voir dans cet état-là, il faut, monsieur, que je combatte encore mon amour et ma compassion pour elle. Si je les écoute, je suis perdue. Un riche bourgeois m'offre tous les secours possibles; mais quels secours, monsieur! ils sauveraient la vie à ma mère; ils déshonnoreraient éternellement la mienne.[12]

The tortoise process of law has placed her in a dilemma, for neither of the alternatives is acceptable. The allusion to a willing suborner is indicative of a breed of men we shall have occasion to discuss in due course.

A variation on this theme of the unfortunate litigant is to be encountered in *Le Financier*. The Marquis d'Osambeuil proposes to the financier's elder son that they seduce two girls from Rennes whose mother is in a sorry plight:

Madame de Cermeil, épuisée par la perte d'un procès, est venue aujourd'hui chez moi avec ses deux filles qui n'ont que quatorze ou quinze ans, et qui sont des miracles de beauté [...] éblouies par le ton de magnificence et de grandeur qui règnent dans ma maison, et par une somme d'argent dont je feindrai de les secourir, ces personnes étant actuellement dans le plus grand besoin, elles céderont à la nécessité [...] je ne connais point de beautés à Paris qui les égalent. Trouvez-vous ce soir chez moi [...] Nous unirons nos soins et nos intérêts pour lier une connaissance intime avec elles. A l'égard de la mère, on lui fera un sort honnête, et nous la renverrons dans sa province.[13]

Penniless, friendless, helpless, they should be easy prey for the two young men. However they are spared what seemed at first an unavoidable outcome through an anonymous act of 'bienfaisance' by d'Argicourt.

Not all will be as lucky as Mme de Cermeil and her daughters, and certainly not a heroine of Sade. We left the Marquise de Télème on the point of setting out for the capital in high hopes of preserving her inheritance. Her choice of lawyer is injudicious, for Saint-Verac is unscrupulous and immediately connives at her downfall with an old lecher, M. de Fondor: 'il lui confia naturellement que cette provinciale, facile à mettre à l'aumône en huit jours, était un morceau délicieux que le sort n'amenait à Paris que pour lui' (*La Marquise de Télème*, p.232). The Marquise is ignorant of legal formalities and is as putty in Saint-Verac's hands. To facilitate her seduction, it is imperative to whittle away her finances because: 'on ne fait rien d'une femme qui a de l'argent: la vertu de ces dames se règlent assez communément sur l'état de leur bourse, elle n'est pas plus tôt dégarnie qu'on les trouve plus douces que des agneaux'. This exercise is well within the Parisians' capabilities as the maid is corrupted to further her mistress's ruin. The Marquise is consequently in an abject state and cannot escape her pursuer's lust. She is not to be blamed for the occurrence and is offered the following words of consolation: 'venue à Paris sans crédit, sans ressources, sans protection, à peine âgée de dix-sept ans et une trop jolie figure, vous deviez nécessairement être dupée, ce n'est pas votre faute' (p.236).

We have seen how the trials of provincials at the hands of 'filoux' led to material rather than moral consequences. With the possible exception of the characters in the works of Sade, we are presented generally with financial losses which entail limited moral repercussions. However the capital held far more serious hazards for the stranger than we have hitherto recounted.

A serious pitfall for the provincial was gaming. This pastime was greatly enjoyed by eighteenth-century society and never ceased to strike the visitor during his stay in the capital. The Swiss traveller, Muralt, commented: 'Il [le jeu] est fort du goût de leur nation, et c'est peut-être celle où il y a le plus de joueurs; au moins est-il sûr que c'est la nation où il y a le plus de joueuses.'[14]

As the above extract suggests, gaming particularly attracted women. Campan remarks that it is the only thing that will divert women from the cultivation of their good looks: 'Le jeu est peut-être la seule occupation où les femmes se permettent des distractions sur leur beauté. L'air d'application et de cupidité altère un peu les grâces du plus joli visage, l'humeur le défigure totalement.'[15] Such was the universality of this pastime that it took place amidst a considerable aura of respectability.

Bridard de La Garde's Thérèse notes its position in the daily round, and realises it is not just a disinterested activity (*Lettres de Thérèse*, i.71-72):

Le jeu est ici un commerce fort décent, ou reçu comme tel, d'injures presque grossières, de querelles, de mauvais procédés, et souvent même de petites ruses tant soit peu friponnes entre les plus honnêtes gens, dans lequel on met tous ses soins à se gagner amicalement, et pour s'amuser, le plus d'argent qu'il est possible! étrange manie! usage tyrannique et fâcheux.

The players do not maintain the decorum associated with a casual amusement and she goes on to portray the style of play: 'elle exerçait la plus sérieuse fonction d'une femme riche, c'est-à-dire, faisant sa partie de jeu'.[16] Thérèse is a spectator of, rather than a participant in, society and she is therefore untouched by the magnetism of this activity, unlike many of her fellow provincials who will be discussed shortly.

However let us first consider gaming establishments. Besides the low class gaming dens there were arenas owned by people of social standing who hoped to replenish sagging fortunes.[17] An example of one of these in the novel is found in Rutlidge's *Alphonsine*. A widowed baroness and her children leave Lyons and settle in the capital. They are installed in a fine house through the auspices of the late husband's correspondent and his wife. Monsieur P...t, the correspondent, hoodwinks the baroness's daughter into an unsatisfactory marriage. Accordingly Alphonsine is united with the outwardly respectable Comte de Valvain. The comte shows his true colours when he invites guests to his mother-in-law's home, as Alphonsine recollects:

Valvain avait eu soin de pourvoir notre appartement d'un nombre très considérable de tables à jouer. Durant les premières soirées il ne désemplit plus de personnes toutes titrées, qui s'accoutumèrent en assez peu de temps à entrer, à sortir sans gêne et sans cérémonie, et de qui les manières devinrent bientôt plus libres que l'accueil plein d'effusion provinciale de la Baronne n'eût dû les provoquer à l'être.[18]

One gains here the idea of the free and easy access of the gaming establishment and the consequent mingling of a varied clientele.[19]

What was the atmosphere like in these 'tripots'? Falconnet describes the activity of a group of players: 'une assemblée de frénétiques tourmentés tour à tour par la crainte, l'espérance et le désespoir [...] L'un déchire les cartes, l'autre les mord: celui-ci tord les bras, celui-là grince les dents.'[20] Such was the scene for many a provincial who often felt drawn to the gaming table. Mitouflet is soon under its spell and cannot sustain the role of onlooker. In an 'académie de jeu' he follows the fortunes of one player and then decides to back him:

Entraîné par un mouvement dont je n'étais pas le maître, et voulant suivre l'exemple de quelques-uns des spectateurs, je me mis à parler pour mon joueur adoptif [...] Alors la fortune changea tout-à-fait; mon joueur perdit vingt parties de suite; on aurait dit qu'il s'entendit avec celui dont nous désirions la défaite: je me ressouviens même actuellement de m'être aperçu de certains signes d'intelligence.[21]

It is all too late when he discovers that Providence is not in control of the cards. Nougaret's tone is mildly satirical but with Restif the critical realism of the later novel is paramount.

Ursule and Edmond have been corrupted by Paris and add gambling to the list of their vices. Having suffered at the hands of cardsharpers, they try to learn the ruses themselves as Ursule explains in a letter to Laure: 'Edmond et moi, nous avons horriblement dépensé: Il a joué, moi aussi, et nous avons été la dupe d'escrocs. Edmond est furieux: il voudrait pour le double de la perte savoir le secret de ces honnêtes messieurs, seulement pour qu'ils ne pussent s'applaudir de leur adresse à mes dépens.'[22] Ursule seduces one of the 'filoux' to acquire the craft of cheating. Notwithstanding this initiative, when they play again, they are utterly robbed of their money – Ursule even consents to stake her charms! Restif is stressing the demoralising features of gambling and its individual and social repercussions.

In the *Histoire de Laurent Marcel* (1779) a young man from Montluçon in Bourbonnais wanders in the Tuileries gardens. His distress is observed by some passers-by who manage to persuade him to tell them of his troubles: 'C'est un coupe-gorge que cette ville, et maudit soit mille et mille fois le jour où il me prit fantaisie de quitter ma famille pour venir ici chercher des plaisirs que j'ai payés si cher.'[23] He has been another victim of the card-tables and the crooks that operate them. He has not only lost his wherewithal but been confronted with all he voluntarily renounced, the comforts and security of his home life. In a rare psychological insight for an obscure writer, Bardou has recognised that adversity stimulates nostalgia.

Many provincials who find their finances dwindling as the result of the expenditure required by their stay resort to gambling as a means of re-establishing them. M. de l'Etang has been alarmed to see his wealth diminish and hopes to recoup his losses by playing with a few 'friends':

Le jeu est une ressource. L'Etang prétendait exceller au picquet. Ses amis, qui faisaient bourse commune, pariaient pour lui, tandis que l'un d'eux jouait contre. A chaque fois qu'il écartait: Ma foi, disait l'un des parieurs, c'est bien jouer! On ne joue pas mieux, disait l'autre. Enfin M. de l'Etang jouait le mieux du monde, mais il n'avait jamais les as.[24]

Here there is still a comic tone but, as the century advances, gaming is the subject of increasing condemnation.[25]

To illustrate this general trend let us look at Perrin's *Henriette de Marconne* (1763). The Chevalier de Présac wishes to pursue a military career and mixes with soldiers on his arrival in Paris. Ignorant of worldly pleasures he follows his new acquaintances anywhere. The latter escort him to a gambling den:

Le désœuvrement nous conduisit dans une académie de jeu. J'ignorais ce qui se passait dans ces assemblées; séduit par l'exemple, et plus frappé du bonheur de ceux auxquels je voyais la fortune favorable, que des pertes qu'essuyaient ses victimes, je risquai aussi une partie de ce que je possédais: d'abord je fus heureux, mais la chance tourna bientôt, et mes pertes se suivirent avec rapidité. Loin d'être rebuté de ces premiers échecs, je n'en devins que plus ardent et plus animé; ma ruine entière fut le fruit de mon opiniâtreté.[26]

Gaming is depicted here as producing a demoralising effect on its victim. Présac had no experience of it in his native province and he is pitifully unable to resist its ravages. Both money and integrity are lost in pursuing an activity which Perrin introduces for critical exposure.

The most outspoken and virulent critic of this cancer is Dolbreuse. Just like l'Etang, Loaisel's hero has lived above his means in the capital and has recourse to the card-tables. Nevertheless he is quite nauseated by what he sees: 'Il n'est pas selon moi de spectacle plus affligeant pour la raison, et même pour l'humanité, que celui d'une assemblée de joueurs. Une triste sévérité règne sur leur visage; la pâleur de l'envie, le travail intérieur de la cupidité, se manifestent dans leurs traits.'[27] He recognises that it is the moral rather than the financial deprivation which is ruinous.[28] However he himself became addicted before he regained his self-control. He had gambled away both his fortune and his honour, a circumstance which leads him to assert:

Que de bonnes qualités, que de vertus changées en passions basses, en vices de toute espèce! Que de sujets nés avec les dispositions les plus heureuses pour servir leur patrie, par de grand talents, par d'utiles travaux, sont devenus une charge inutile à l'état, et souvent l'opprobre de l'espèce humaine! Les gens du monde n'attribuent jamais ces changements et ces malheurs à la véritable cause; mais le philosophe qui remonte à la source du mal, considère le jeu, surtout aujourd'hui, comme un des principes les plus destructifs de l'amitié, de l'honneur, de la bienfaisance, et de tous les sentiments qui sont faits pour tourner au profit commun de la société.[29]

Dolbreuse sees it not only as destructive of the imprudent provincial's virtue but as noxious to society as a whole. It sweeps aside social values to replace them with a passion for personal gain. Moreover he is inclined to view its debilitating effects as irreversible in some cases: 'De toutes les passions déréglées, celle du jeu, portée à un certain excès, est la plus funeste, et peut-être la seule qui donne des remords sans fruit.'[30] He has been fortunate enough to recover from this vice which constituted in his eyes one of the most evil activities of the capital.

From being for the most part an acceptable distraction in the first decades of the century gaming provoked increasing hostility as the years went by.[31] If Voltaire launches an occasional assault on this activity, it is normally conducted on a comic level satirising a particular abuse. In the works of Loaisel de Tréogate and Restif de La Bretonne, however, it is portrayed as a vicious attribute of an over-sophisticated society, as a sinister threat to the virtue of the provincial in Paris.[32]

A different danger for the provincial was prostitution in one form or another. As in every epoch in the life of the capital, venal love had a role to play. Prostitutes occupied varying ranks in their own hierarchy, from the 'femme entretenue' through the 'fille d'Opéra' to the humble 'péripatéticienne'. These ladies were a familiar sight in Paris and their presence is noted by many a writer.

Where would they be seen? The rue Saint-Honoré was a favourite hunting-ground. Restif provides us with a general description of this street and its ambiguous glories: 'Je passai par la rue Saint-Honoré: superbe rue! assemblage du luxe, du commerce, de l'éclat, de la boue, de l'Opéra, des filles, de l'impudence, de l'urbanité, de la débauche, de la politesse, de l'escroquerie, de tous les avantages et de tous les abus de la sociabilité.'[33] The Palais Royal was a splendid shop window for those who wished to advertise their wares. Margot claims that the garden was the time-honoured preserve of her colleagues:

Le Palais-Royal étant un territoire dont la propriété semble nous être acquise par une prescription aussi ancienne que l'établissement de l'Opéra: c'est dans cette espèce de Jardin de franchise que nous sommes en toute liberté, du droit de faire les femmes de conséquence, et de braver impunément l'œil du spectateur par nos grands airs et notre orgueilleux étalage.[34]

So great is their luxury that they could enjoy prestige in fashionable circles.

The attraction of these women was often enormous for the 'nouveau débarqué'. The provincial had never seen the like; easy women of such splendour were unknown in his village or small town. Edmond is enthralled by the actresses and longs for riches in order to sample their company. In a letter to Gaudet d'Arras he admits: 'J'étais hier à l'Opéra: l'enchantement de ce spectacle fortifie mes idées ambitieuses: en y voyant briller tant d'actrices charmantes, j'ai senti doublement le prix des biens de la fortune, pour les dissiper avec elles.'[35] The Lyonnais Saint-Gory likewise experiences an inclination for an actress, temporarily forgetting his devotion for the spotless Sophie. He recalls the appeal of being 'charmé des grâces de la nymphe théâtrale, je ne désirais plus que de la captiver, je me fis informer de son nom, et je résolus dès le lendemain de faire ma cour à la charmante Duprex, après avoir fait à Sophie une visite plus courte qu'à l'ordinaire'.[36] He succeeds in capturing his quarry but finds that it entails an immense outlay of money: 'Pendant un mois que cette intrigue dura, je me crus le plus heureux des hommes: mais la dépense excessive qu'une maîtresse de si bon ton exige m'effraya.'[37] As a result he has to abandon an idol who has merely filched his wealth. Just as in gaming, the money earned in the provinces flows into the coffers of the capital.

Similarly a mistress can ruin a weak lover. Rosalie is a hard-headed whore who delights in the prospect of bankrupting her paramour: 'J'ai fait la connaissance d'un jeune homme de province qui est fou de moi. Il sera ruiné avant peu. Il ne cesse de me faire des affaires; aussi m'apporte-t-il journellement des montres, des pendules, des étoffes de toutes espèces etc. Tant pis pour lui; quand il n'aura plus de rien, je le quitterai; c'est l'usage.'[38] When he is destitute, she carries out her promise. However the author has him wreak vengeance by murdering her in the Bois de Boulogne. The spurned and penniless provincial then puts an end to his own wretched existence. This novel is frankly licentious and is of thematic rather than chronological interest.

One of the most intriguing encounters between a provincial and a prostitute is related by the abbé Prévost. His 'honnête homme' has been introduced to Parisian society by an old marquis, a friend of his father. Wishing to acquaint the young man with all the pleasures in vogue, the marquis invites him to a party in a 'petite maison'. Although by no means priggish, the newcomer is disgusted by the debauchery and the three nymphs who are the principal purveyors: 'Malgré l'éloignement naturel que je me sentais pour trois créatures qui faisaient un si indigne usage de leurs charmes, je ne pus me défendre d'une certaine compassion pour leur âge, et pour la pauvreté qui les forçait peut-être de s'abandonner avec cet oubli de toutes les lois' (p.40). He succeeds in obtaining an interview with one of them named Fanchon. He is not seeking sexual indulgence but would like to learn the girl's history. Accordingly he asks her to talk of her origins and her involvement in such an abject life (p.42):

elle me fit l'histoire d'un vieux major de cavalerie qui l'avait débauchée dans une ville de province, et qui l'avait amenée à Paris. Il y était mort depuis peu, sans lui avoir assuré une pension qu'il lui avait promise; et dans la crainte de ses parents qui la faisaient chercher, elle avait accepté les offres d'une dame qui lui avait promis de la faire vivre heureuse et tranquille, en ne sortant que la nuit pour les partis de seigneurs.

He is touched by her tale and offers to help, but he only becomes her dupe. Yet this confidence trick has no lasting effect on him in this novel of 1745 other than a deeper knowledge of worldly living.

Germeuil has come to Paris with a stout heart and a sound mind. Unfortunately Baculard d'Arnaud's hero befriends Blinval, an unscrupulous schemer who introduces him to Mme de Cérignan. The latter is a compound of whore and adventuress who plots the provincial's downfall. Torn between the lure of Mme de Cérignan and his duty towards his wife, Germeuil all but maintains his conjugal fidelity. Nonetheless he falls victim to an abuse of his better feelings. Blinval convinces him that Mme de Cérignan is mortally ill. Out of compassion Germeuil visits her and views with anguish her 'death-bed'. On a table lies the money she owes him, a ploy to gain his sympathy. When she 'miraculously' recovers he becomes more and more attracted to her and squanders his wealth on her: 'Ses prodigalités sont suivies de dettes qui entrainent le désordre de sa fortune; les créanciers l'assiègent; sa maison ne tardera pas à offrir le spectacle humiliant de la misère.'[39] In this tale of 1777, Germeuil suffers both moral and financial ruination through his affair with Mme de Cérignan. Baculard sets out not merely to present a dupe of Parisian 'filoux' but to illustrate the perverse aspects of the capital. Germeuil's liaison with a courtesan is not used as a particular step in an 'éducation sentimentale' but as a critical exploration of a corrupt society. Whereas the 'honnête homme's adventure was an end in itself, Germeuil's was a *means* to an end.

There is obviously the reverse of this picture, the provincial girl who comes to Paris and ends up willingly or unwillingly as a prostitute. We dealt in a previous chapter with those who deliberately set out to sell themselves in the capital, so we cite merely one example here. The principal character of the *Aventures de trois coquettes* was born into a middle-class family in Dijon. Whilst still young, Lucile realises the power of her attractions and enters into a liaison with a lodger, de Berville. Soon she is pregnant and subsequently deserted by her lover. Thereupon she strikes up with another lodger, Gerbois, and they go off to Monbelliard. This is followed by a flirtation with a certain de Brene before she resolves to break her family ties irrevocably. Acting on this decision, she states: 'Je jugeai qu'il n'y avait que Paris qui pût me dérober aux recherches de ma famille. Mais je n'y ai nulle ressource, nulle protection, nul appui; à quel genre de vie me destinerai-je? je n'en sais en vérité rien; or que peut annoncer une pareille incertitude, sinon que me voilà abandonnée à jouer le rôle d'aventurière?'[40] On her way to the capital she meets Julie from Metz. A friendship develops, and when they reach their destination, they take rooms together in the rue Saint-Honoré. Having dressed in all their finery, they stride out to tempt fortune (p.96):

Nous étions allées produire nos petites figures provinciales aux Tuileries [... et] quel sujet de triomphe pour notre amour-propre; à peine paraissons-nous que nous fixons tous les regards. De combien de soupirants dont nous eussions eu à entendre les tendres déclarations, si nous eussions été moins novices dans le métier que nous allions exercer; mais loin de paraître sensibles aux hommages qu'on rendait à nos appas, nous en paraissions embarrassées.

Despite their previous intrigues, they find themselves out of their element amidst the knowing stares of the Parisians. Here is an early narrative with no critical intent.

But what of the girls who are unfortunate enough to be in the capital without friends or finances, plunged into a world of anonymous faces? In *Thérèse philosophe*, the work attributed usually to the marquis d'Argens, the heroine leaves Toulon in the company of her mother. The mother soon dies causing Thérèse to reflect: 'Me voilà donc au milieu de Paris, livrée à moi-même, sans parents, sans amis, jolie, à ce qu'on me disait, instruite à bien des égards, mais sans connaissance des usages du monde.'[41] Alone in a hostile environment, this is an experience common to many women in the works of the period.

An actress and her lover take flight from a town in Burgundy and seek refuge in Paris. They are pursued by both sets of parents but only the lover is captured. The girl envisages her future in the blackest terms: 'à Paris, sans asile, sans connaissance, avec peu d'argent, à la veille d'être réduite à la plus affreuse misère, ou à la plus honteuse débauche'.[42] Poverty or prostitution would seem to be the only alternatives for someone in her position. However she is lucky since a Parisian acquaintance comes to her rescue: 'Il avait ce ton d'aisance qui en impose à de jeunes gens nouvellement arrivés de province' (p.48). He takes care of her, lodges her, and eventually goes off with her on an acting tour of the provinces and the continent. Once again we are presented with a social situation to further the plot and not to invite critical analysis.

One recourse for the destitute female was the Opera, indeed Chevrier describes it as the only one: 'Une fille sans parents, sans amis, sans talents, n'a d'asile que celui de l'Opéra.'[43] This was the solution of La Vilers who, having been a lady's maid in Toulouse, left for Paris and eventually joined the troupe of the Opera. There her attributes are admired by a financier who panders to her needs: 'Un financier, qui avait soin d'elle depuis qu'elle était à Paris, lui conseilla de quitter l'Opéra. Il lui fit un sort et l'a marié à un commis, qui a pris tout sur son compte.'[44] She has been preserved from future penury, but only through conduct which is far from edifying. Furthermore, we do not receive moralising comment from the author.

The young provincial left destitute in the capital may resort to prostitution through the advice of an acquaintance. Magny's Justine is an example. After the death of her baby and the desertion of her lover, she becomes friends with her neighbour, Hortense. She relates a turbulent account of her life and her present difficulties. Hortense is a sympathetic listener and an active friend who arranges a liaison with a foreigner to ease Justine's troubles. This relationship is disrupted by a meddlesome abbé but she soon secures the attentions of a financier who dispels her mortal coils.

D'Argens's Thérèse likewise seeks solace in the arms of a neighbour, Mme Bois-Laurier. The latter had been a foundling, understands Thérèse's predicament and is portrayed as 'une femme que la nécessité avait contrainte, pendant sa jeunesse, de servir au soulagement de l'incontinence du public libertin, et qui, à l'exemple de tant d'autres, jouait alors incognito le rôle d'honnête femme, à l'aide d'une rente viagère qu'elle s'était assurée de l'épargne de ses premiers travaux' (*Thérèse philosophe*, p.137). Bois-Laurier fixes Thérèse up with a financier; this results in a disastrous encounter where the ravenous wolf fails to devour the unsubmissive lamb. Indeed Thérèse retains her virginity for a remarkable period of time, only to succumb to an adoring count after he has let her view some licentious books and pictures!

Some decide there is no avenue open to them save selling themselves. The heroine of another of Des Boulmier's tales is the daughter of a hurdy-gurdy player who works a season in Paris during the winter months. In the course of the trip the musician dies leaving his widow and daughter to fend for themselves. As is frequent in these plots the mother's death soon follows. The orphan realises that there is only one course of action within her capabilities, that of prostitution: 'J'avais treize ans, j'étais grande et bien faite, et l'on eût dit que l'amour m'avait donné une dispense d'âge pour jouer de ses plaisirs; c'était le seul patrimoine que je possédais; aussi avais-je résolu de le bien faire valoir.'[45] After affairs with a chevalier, a président, and others, she succeeds in accumulating sufficient funds to live in easy circumstances. Here again her predicament has been used to provide a basis for a series of adventures rather than to exploit the iniquity of Paris.

Up to this point, the forlorn girls we have discussed have either decided upon prostitution themselves or have been so counselled by a friend. Let us now consider those who are induced to take up the profession through the persuasion of a stranger.

We left Lucile and Julie strutting somewhat self-consciously in the Tuileries. Their gaucherie is espied by another stroller, La Monrive, who begins a conversation with them. She herself had travelled to Paris in the past and immersed herself in the city's pleasures. She is now a naturalised Parisian and offers them her experience and protection, whilst advising them that: 'il faut une fois dans la vie porter ses vues dans l'avenir, c'est sur votre intérêt que vous avez à régler l'amour que vous voulez inspirer ou que vous voulez prendre'.[46] Thereafter she acts as their 'tante' and shows them off at the Opera, the Comédie-Française, the various gardens, all the advantageous sites where men seek female attachments. In the long run Julie weds a rich old financier while Lucile marries a sexagenarian from Auxerre. They have indeed regulated their love to self-interest in accordance with La Monrive's guidelines. Lambert's novel was first published in 1740 and manifests none of the didactic tendencies so frequent in post-1760 literature.

La Monrive is an example of a stock character in eighteenth-century fiction, the procuress or amorous intriguer. When Desbief's Nine is separated from her lover, Florville, she is cast into prison. There she learns from a priest – in reality the Comte de Terline – that Florville's parents intend to keep her confined for the rest of her days, initially in gaol and then in a convent. Her informant promises to obtain her release, and offers her the post of maid to a cousin whose arrival from the country is imminent. The cousin is imaginary and she soon realises that her domestic position is a complete fabrication. She is not long in discovering the identity of her saviour and immediately flees the trap.

Wishing to collect her thoughts, she enters a church. Her lachrymose countenance interests a kindly lady who offers to take her back to her own home.[47] The enquirer is a 'maquerelle' who, after taking care of Nine for the day, introduces her unwitting pupil to a 'nephew' in the evening. Locking the door behind her, she leaves the girl and the young blade alone. Alert enough to realise his designs, Nine fights desperately with her assailant before grabbing his sword and running him through. The 'tante' is terrified by the fracas and its possible consequences. Somehow or other she gets in touch with the Comte de Terline who calms Nine's fears and arranges a stay in Normandy for the distraught girl.

Perrin's Julie has enjoyed many amorous escapades but on her return to Paris falls into dire straits and is forced to rent a shabby room in a lodging-house. Whilst out for a stroll one day, she is knocked down by a careering coach and is aided by Mme Mont-Louis who guides her back to her home. The outwardly respectable Mme Mont-Louis is a bawd at her hypocritical best. Julie is, in the romanesque tradition, unaware of the real functions of her benefactress's house. While contemplating her condition, she is snatched from her reverie by the sudden intrusion of an agitated man. He is in hot pursuit of Mimy who refuses to be thrashed by his 'poignée de verges'. Upon seeing Julie he hopes to have discovered a more sporting accomplice. She will have none of it and soon realises she has been conducted to a brothel.[48] Furthermore she discovers that Mont-Louis is a celebrated pimp 'qui, par le bon ordre avec lequel elle administre les plaisirs publics, s'est fait une réputation, et est parvenue à se faire tolérer, et à attirer chez elle les gens les plus distinguées'.[49] Julie is of course quite used to mercenary love and accepts Mont-Louis's advice to profit by her talents. After several affairs, including one with her old suitor, M. Poupard, she settles down to married life with a neighbour, M. Gerbo. This novel again illustrates the prevalence of the procuress as a character and the brothel as an unsuspected refuge in the literature of our period.

Cécile arrives in Paris on account of her pregnancy and is deserted by Valban, her lover. She is taken in by Mme Duban, a midwife, but her child is still-born. La Duban is running a house of ill-fame and wishes to profit from her charity. Cécile is presently introduced to her first customer who, believe it or not, is none other than Valban! She flees in horror! Undaunted, La Duban encourages Cécile onto the slippery path of prostitution in a manner her protégée later recalls:

elle me mit en chambre garnie dans la rue neuve Saint-Eustache, quartier réservé aux demoiselles de mon état; le séjour que j'y fis ne fut pas long; Mme Duban, qui mesurait ses bontés sur les quarante écus que je lui devais, me conduisit le quatrième jour à la barrière du Roulle. L'intendante de cet hôtel me reçut avec une joie que tout le monde partagea, à la réserve des demoiselles qui devenaient mes camarades; tout Paris, informé de ma demeure, courait à la belle Lorraine. J'ai resté cinq mois dans cet hôtel, comblée de plaisirs et d'argent.[50]

Her loss in moral stature is enormous, yet Chevrier is concerned with the fabrication of a tale and not the statement of a moral. In fact the most chastening part of the story is Cécile's being cheated out of a large proportion of her earnings by the proprietress of the Roulle; subsequently she has no other recourse than to return home to receive paternal mercy and a place in a convent.

In one of Restif's feeblest productions, *Lucile ou les progrès de la vertu*, the heroine is the sole surviving child of a rich merchant and his wife. Being an attractive match in all senses of the word, she is much sought after. Her favoured suitor, Fisioman, is odious, and she prefers her father's clerk, Dangeot. Lucile deceives her parents into thinking that she will marry the man of their choice, thereby acquiring money and jewels. In possession of this wealth, she and Dangeot elope to Paris. There virtue is preserved since the couple sleep in separate rooms, and it is obvious that Lucile ran away more out of loathing for Fisioman than for love of Dangeot. Now there is a 'péripétie' as the clerk is captured by the jilted suitor. Lucile, on the other hand, manages to escape her father's clutches and seeks refuge in the anonymous streets. As she wanders aimlessly she wins admiring comments from the 'petits-maîtres' before strolling into the Palais Royal.

Once inside the garden she is noticed by La Courton who starts a conversation with her: 'Elle aperçut Lucile, et lit dans son cœur. Elle l'aborde, en affectant un air de bonté. – Mademoiselle me paraît étrangère? – Hélas oui. – Mademoiselle cherche apparemment quelqu'un, ou s'est égarée dans un quartier qu'elle ne connaît pas? [...] Je vous offre mes services.'[51] Lucile is duped by the unctuous tones of the kindly lady and accepts an invitation to her home. La Courton is delighted with her acquisition; a virginal creature who can dance divinely, sing graciously and yet is merely fourteen and a half years old. She teaches Lucile various feminine skills such as lace-making, and generally pampers her. Moreover she ensures that the girl has no contact with her other experienced pupils. She starts the process of corrupting her protégée by glorifying the pleasures of worldly existence: 'On lui parle des spectacles, de ces délicieuses assemblées qu'on nomme bals, où les jolies femmes deviennent des divinités; on tâche de lui faire naître l'envie d'y briller' (p.39). In addition her 'nouvelle maman' allows her to read licentious works which stimulate her imagination. The time is now ripe for her initiation and her introduction to her proposed 'amant', M. Durichement. With this in mind, La Courton proffers advice: 'ma chère Lucile, pour conserver un amant, il faut de l'adresse et de la prudence: N'aimez jamais si vous voulez être toujours aimée: ne prenez jamais avec un amant le ton de la candeur et de la bonté' (p.44). Durichement reveals himself to be a most superior rake who still possesses estimable qualities. Upon seeing Lucile's beauty he mysteriously apprehends that she is not the usual type of strumpet he exploits. Accordingly he pays La Courton handsomely for the privilege of taking her away with him – the bawd had pretended that Lucile was her daughter. Henceforth he embarks on a programme of reviving her fundamental virtue with the aid of his tutor; she has been saved on the brink of perdition. Restif has transformed the procuress of the early novel who often ensures her charge's fortune into one who embodies the corruption of the capital.

A variation on this theme of a provincial accosted by a procuress is the situation where the victims are handed over to the 'lupanar'. Julie is an orphan from Périgueux, seduced and abducted by a rake who abandons her near Poitiers. Thereupon she resolves to travel to Paris and takes the coach. One of her fellow passengers is a monk who engages her in conversation and later visits her in the capital. He persuades her to change her lodgings and move to the home of one of his 'relatives': '[il] la détermina à préférer pour sa demeure la maison d'une soi-disant dévote sa parente qui logeait près de son couvent. C'était une de ces dévotes qui n'ont de la piété que l'extérieur propre à masquer une vie licencieuse et infâme; c'était enfin la surintendante des menus plaisirs du béni père.'[52] Despite the attentions of the 'entremetteuse' and the lecherous monk she succeeds in evading their clutches, and lives happily with a count for a number of years before he marries, leaving her in comfortable circumstances.

Dolbreuse, perverted by his stay in Paris, becomes a corrupter himself. Crossing a park one day, he glimpses an innocent-looking young lady who turns out to be a countess recently arrived in the capital. The latter is escorted by a baroness well known to Dolbreuse who is described as follows: '[elle] était une de ces femmes dont Paris offre des modèles, qui ont vieilli dans les intrigues, dans la turpitude de la galanterie, et fini par être chassées de la bonne compagnie dont elles firent le déshonneur' (*Dolbreuse*, i.158-59). By virtue of her imminent senility, she hates the youth of her own sex and has become increasingly vindictive and callous. She is always searching for fresh prey and has a predilection for provincials (i.159-60):

elle cherchait à se lier avec toutes les femmes qui débutaient dans le monde et avaient le malheur de ne le pas connaître, s'emparait surtout de celles qui arrivaient de province, leur donnait des règles de conduite à sa manière, combattait leurs scrupules, détruisait leurs préjugés lorsqu'elles en avaient, et leur cherchait des amants. Dans l'occasion même, elle produisait des filles; sa maison servait à des parties de plaisir, à des soupers libertins. Elle donnait la main à toutes les perfidies, à tous les projets de séduction, et par ces basses complaisances, et mille autres soins officieux, cent fois plus vils encore, se rendait supportable, et même nécessaire aux hommes, et surtout aux jeunes gens, dont elle recherchait toujours la société, n'osant et ne pouvant plus en attendre autre chose.

What more natural, then, that she should regard the countess as a choice morsel for her trade. Similarly for the countess, acquaintance with such an experienced member of Parisian society must have seemed a stroke of luck (i.160):

La jeune Comtesse, séparée de son époux depuis quelques mois, tirée par des événements du fond d'une province où elle vivait heureuse, et jetée, comme des nues, dans le sein de la capitale, était tombée dans les mains de cette Baronne méprisable. Sans défiance sur les dangers de sa jeunesse et de sa beauté dans cette ville dangereuse, elle s'applaudissait de la rencontre d'une femme qu'elle jugeait respectable par son nom, par son âge, et qui lui promettait les ressources d'une société agréable et les conseils de l'expérience, dans une ville immense où elle était inconnue.

Dolbreuse approaches the two women in the park and the baroness at once appreciates his intentions.

Visiting her the next day she has sufficient experience to penetrate his motives and tells him: 'Monsieur se lasse des beautés de la capitale, il lui faut un cœur neuf, des appas tout frais pour réveiller ces appétits languissants' (i.162). Dolbreuse's desires are physical and are not the cerebral quests of Valmont. His senses may be jaded but he confesses his attraction for the countess. He plots with the baroness to accomplish the provincial's downfall. Their plans succeed and the countess is seduced in an enchanting garden. Just like Restif, Loaisel has recreated the role of the 'entremetteuse' to symbolise the capital's corruption.

It will be seen from the preceding pages that prostitution played a prominent role in the lives of many provincials who came to the capital. For the inexperienced male the prostitute represented a hazard of some proportions with her insidious charms and skilful play-acting; she was a siren who showed his naivety and ignorance in stark relief. On the other hand, prostitution was for the female a profession she was forced to adopt either through treachery or poverty. A tendency to condemn the corruption of Paris is manifest in the later novels. The heroines of Perrin, Magny, Lambert, are usually quite ready to accept the consequences of their predicament and subsequently to profit by them. However in the works of Restif, Loaisel, Baculard, we are struck by the authorial intent to point out and blame the evil influences of the capital. In *Les Egarements de Julie* (1755) Perrin, for instance (in contrast to his stance in his later novel *Henriette de Marconne*), makes no attempt to pass a moral judgement on his heroine, indeed she ends up quite happily and unrepentant after her vicious youth. With the second group of authors such infamy would never go unpunished, nor would it escape moralising digressions. Furthermore, Restif, Baculard and Loaisel would not attribute such sexual depravation to any innate propensity to vice as would many of their predecessors, but rather to the deficiencies of society. The destitute girl should not be in a position where vice is the only means for survival. Let the reformed Dolbreuse be their spokesman: 'Il est un sentiment que l'honnête homme, que le philosophe ne peut refuser à cette classe de femmes, c'est celui de la pitié qu'inspire leur état, et que fait naître l'injustice de ceux qui, causant et partageant leur déshonneur, les condamnent à un mépris exclusif' (ii.138). It is men who should receive the moral vituperation. The exploiters are always more reprehensible than the exploited. Following the above extract is a long, imaginary harangue from a harlot; it bemoans the whore's situation and berates society for turning a blind eye to male waywardness while lacking compassion for their victims. In addition it illustrates the typical downfall of the future prostitute: 'Délaissées d'un séducteur, d'une famille respectable qui nous rejette de son sein, comment ne pas céder à notre affreuse destinée.'[53] The provincial girl in particular, unaccustomed to Paris and Parisians, is almost doomed to depravation unless society adopts a more liberal and less hypocritical attitude to her problems.[54]

We have seen in this chapter the treatment of major pitfalls for the provincial. They are presented in the early novel to convey facets of Parisian life and thereby to authenticate the actuality of the narrative. In the case of gaming, for instance, we find the *Lettres de Thérèse* commenting on the social importance of this pastime. As for prostitution, it is employed merely as a framework in which to incorporate a succession of characters and situations. In post-1760 fiction, however, the same activities are depicted for a different purpose. Loaisel denounces them as economically, morally, and thus socially destructive. He does not introduce them as particular abuses but as concrete examples of general corruption. Descriptive intent has been transformed in the later period into critical function.

5. The disintegration of provincial virtue

NOTWITHSTANDING the girls who travel to Paris with a view to prostitution and the men who long for dissipation, by and large writers present the provincial as arriving in the capital imbued with both virtue and integrity. The question increasingly treated in the literature of the eighteenth century is, what happens to these qualities in the city? In the social realism of the early period, we are rarely presented with a clear-cut answer. Yet in the works of Marivaux there are already the seeds of critical evaluation. After his master's death and his troubles with Geneviève, Jacob determines to return to his village. On entering a 'gargote', however, he is disturbed by the gross manner of some carters: 'Ils me dégoûtèrent du village. Pourquoi m'en retourner? me disais-je quelquefois. Tout est plein ici de gens à leur aise, qui, aussi bien que moi, n'avaient pour tout bien que la Providence. Ma foi! restons encore quelques jours ici pour voir ce qui en sera; il y a tant d'aventures dans la vie, il peut m'en échoir quelque bonne' (*Le Paysan parvenu*, p.40). Even though his contact with Paris has been short it has still given him an insight into a more refined life. His disgust at the vulgarity of the carters is a disgust at the worth of his former existence, a life which had seemed natural until his stay in the capital. Moreover, since he regards Paris as a worthier site for his endeavours, he decides to lose his rustic accent to accelerate his integration (p.85):

Jusqu'ici donc mes discours avaient toujours eu une petite tournure champêtre; mais il y avait plus d'un mois que je m'en corrigeais assez bien, quand je voulais y prendre garde, et je n'avais conservé cette tournure avec Mlle Habert que parce qu'elle me réussissait auprès d'elle; mais il est certain que je parlais meilleur français quand je voulais. J'avais déjà acquis assez d'usage pour cela, et je crus devoir m'appliquer à parler mieux qu'à l'ordinaire.

An accent is identified immediately with a provincial background and erects a social barrier. Jacob's progress at self-improvement is a rapid process as Mme de Ferval testifies: 'Mais est-il vrai qu'il n'y a que quatre ou cinq mois que vous arrivez de campagne? on ne le croirait point à vous voir, vous n'êtes point hâlé, vous n'avez point l'air campagnard' (p.135). He still shows many traits which reveal his country origins; in fact Mme de Fécour advises him to acquire more self-assurance if he wishes to 'succeed': 'j'ai un conseil à vous donner; vous venez de province, vous en avez apporté un air de timidité qui ne sied pas à votre âge; quand on est fait comme vous, il faut se rassurer un peu, surtout en ce pays-ci; que vous manque-t-il pour avoir de la confiance? qui est-ce qui en aura, si vous n'en avez pas, mon enfant? vous êtes si aimable!' (p.186). As the result of his marriage and his acquaintance with society ladies, his confidence is ever waxing. Yet another hurdle is in store.

M. de La Vallée, as he now calls himself, loses his composure in the company of the Comte d'Orsan and his friends at the theatre. When questioned about his family, he feels obliged to be evasive: 'Mon père demeure à la campagne où est tout son bien, et d'où je ne fais presque d'arriver dans l'intention de me pousser et de devenir quelque chose, comme font tous les jeunes gens de province et de ma sorte' (p.264). This slanting of the truth is not just perpetrated through 'dépaysement' but more through vanity and shame at his origins. To suggest that Jacob was corrupted by Paris would be a gross exaggeration, yet would it be correct to claim that such vanity would never have come to the surface had he remained in his village? It is not Marivaux's intention to sermonise but to analyse nuances of emotional response to different situations, hence he chooses the strange world of Paris to act as a stimulant to an awakening self-consciousness. Yet there is an ambiguous and disquieting depiction of some Parisians in this novel which hints at the author's unease.

This unease is patent in the presentation of another provincial in Paris in the *Quatorzième feuille* of *Le Spectateur français*. In this instance a son does not merely invent a spurious background for himself but actually disowns his father. As a young man, he had been dispatched to Paris to train for the bar and subsequently becomes a successful lawyer. His father, who has come to live at his home, is looked upon as an embarrassment. The demands of social prestige in the capital make the son callous enough to inform him (p.191):

vous avez presque toujours vécu dans une petite ville de province, et vos idées, vos manières de faire, vos usages sont si différents de ce qui se passe dans le monde, que vous auriez dû vous dégoûter le premier de la compagnie de ceux qui viennent ici: mais vous ne sentez pas cela, et je le sens moi. Le bel agrément pour votre fils de vous voir converser avec gens d'un certain rang, polis et délicats, que vous faites rire, et à qui votre simplicité donne la comédie!

He is humiliated by his father's manners and feels acceptance into Parisian society is impossible while it can mock the old man. The father is sent off to a lonely existence in a country house, savage repayment for someone who had endowed his son with all his worldly wealth. What we wish to emphasise in this tale is the stifling of natural instincts by the artificial code of the capital. To achieve social eminence, the son casts aside filial duty in a nonchalant and hard-hearted manner. Nevertheless Marivaux is deploring a particular effect of Paris which he does not generalise into a total condemnation.[1]

A similar situation arises in Voltaire's *Jeannot et Colin* (1764). During his early school days in Issoire, Jeannot had shared a close friendship with Colin. Due to his father's financial speculations, the former is taken to Paris to benefit from the family's improved fortune. There Jeannot rises to the status of Marquis de La Jeannotière and assumes highfaluting attitudes. He no longer replies to Colin's letters, such correspondence is beneath his dignity. Here we are shown in comic vein the would-be superiority of the naturalised Parisian and its contrast with provincial sincerity. Voltaire is not denouncing Paris but pointing out one of its less attractive effects. Jeannot's personality is affected but not perverted by the capital. Yet the date of the tale would seem to indicate that even Voltaire was possibly reflecting the growing disenchantment with Paris in literature.

If Jeannot is not really corrupted, his experience is rare in post-1760 fiction. An example of a man who does suffer as a consequence of moving to the capital is M. Dorsan. While young he pursues a military career of some distinction, though his services go unrewarded. After the death of his parents he inherits considerable wealth, leaves Brittany, and arrives in the capital at the age of twenty-five. He bewails his choice from the vantage point of experience: 'Habiter Paris, dans cette situation, c'est s'exposer au danger de la mauvaise compagnie; c'est se lever à une dissipation perpétuelle, que le désœuvrement rend nécessaire, et qui mène toujours à la débauche la plus outrée. On devient bientôt la proie des courtisanes, le jouet des coquettes et la dupe des fripons.'[2] As a rich young man he is flattered into squandering his money and is lionised by a parasitical society. In due course he marries the delectable Mlle Morinval and all would seem to be rosy. Nonetheless his inability to manage his resources leads to his moral and financial bankruptcy. He realises the pernicious effect of Paris too late to save himself.

Dorsan exemplifies a common theme in the eighteenth-century novel, the entry of a young man or woman into Parisian society. The portrayal of their initiation affords an excellent opportunity to describe the worldly society and register its impact on the 'débutant'. Within the framework of this situation there appears a recurring character, the 'déniaiseur'. He who has little knowledge of social requirements is most vulnerable to the 'déniaiseur's' insinuations.

Since he is attracted, almost in spite of himself, by the luxurious ambiance of the capital, Dolbreuse falls into the hands of the 'men about town'. They manage to make him forget his marital duties and natural virtues. So rapid is the tempo of his life that he has no time for reflection in their company (*Dolbreuse*, i.124-25):

j'avais affaire à des hommes qui ne donnaient pas le temps à la réflection de mûrir dans mon esprit. J'étais tombé entre les mains de ces agréables de la capitale, qui érigent la scélératesse en système, et la font passer en amusement; qui se disant les dispensateurs des réputations, les maîtres de la renommée, s'emparent de tous ceux qui débutent dans le monde, les endoctrinent, les forment, et se dépêchent à les associer à tous leurs vices et à tous leurs travers. Au plus petit nuage, à la plus petite altération visible sur mon front, ils opposaient la proposition d'une partie brillante chez quelqu'une de ces beautés fameuses que tout le monde court, dont personne ne fait cas, et qui cependant donnent le ton au plus grand nombre. Ils me menaient chez les femmes galantes, chez les femmes coquettes, et dans tous les cercles assez à plaindre pour s'amuser de leur fadeur et de leur impertinence, c'est-à-dire, dans les assemblées où les sottises brillantes font fortune, où l'on déchire les amis faibles, le mérite indigent, les grands disgraciés et les beautés passées. Ils allaient chez les marchands s'émerveiller de tout, avoir envie de tout, demander le prix de tout, sans jamais rien acheter; dans les ateliers des peintres et des sculpteurs, admirer des choses médiocres, critiquer des chefs-d'œuvres, donner des avis aux artistes, et afficher partout leur ignorance et leur fatuité. Enfin ils me traînaient péniblement de maison en maison, de boutique en boutique, de fête en fête.

His 'friends' cast him into a maelstrom of frivolous activity,[3] as they are consumed by a corrupt mode of life which they take delight in foisting on all around them. Dolbreuse must lose his prejudices to conform to a hedonistic existence. Sensual satisfaction replaces moral integrity and the provincial is unable to salvage his conscience from this frenzied atmosphere.

Dolbreuse becomes a noted participant in the social round (i.135):

Bientôt je tins un rang distingué parmi les agréables du jour. J'avais déjà tous les ridicules en crédit, tous les travers qui réussissent dans le monde. J'étais de tous les conseils où se décide la grande affaire des modes, de toutes les parties extravagantes, de toutes les débauches où l'on se ruine sans s'amuser. Je donnais des concerts, des soupers délicieux dans de petites maisons. J'y rassemblais des libertins choisis, des femmes décriées, des beautés faciles.

What he regarded formerly, and indeed will regard after his rehabilitation, as inconsequential minutiae of an inconsequential existence hold all his attention and stimulate all his deliberations. He has become a womaniser who can no longer sate his appetite in the arms of harlots but must seek the conquest of society beauties instead: 'Ennuyé des courtisanes, je cherchai des intrigues parmi les femmes des conditions brillantes de la societé. En prenant du goût pour elles, je crus épurer mon cœur, que je venais de souiller par des passions viles. Mais mon cœur, en se polissant par l'usage du grand monde, se blasa davantage' (i.148-49). He laboured for a while under the illusion that noble affairs would somehow purify if not legitimise his infidelities and cleanse him of the taints of mercenary love.

Not only were the sexual mores of Parisian society instilled into him but he was also driven to adopt the wit and badinage of the 'homme aimable': 'J'appris à débiter joliment des choses frivoles, et à leur donner un tour précieux: à faire valoir des idées sans consistance, à disserter sans raisonner, et à parler longtemps sans rien dire. J'appris à persifler avec sel, à médire avec politesse, à mêler la grâce à la malignité, à intéresser par beaucoup de vices, et à plaire sans aucune vertu' (i.149). It is at this juncture that he embarks on his seduction of the countess already related.

The outcome of his debauched activity is penury and incarceration in a debtors' prison. Here at last he has time to ponder on his frenetic routine and is confronted with the stark reality of his situation: 'je vis mon corps souillé par des liens! De quelle flétrissure mon âme fut atteinte quand on me conduisit à travers les flots d'un peuple empressé de me voir. Le cachot où l'on me fit descendre me causa moins d'horreur que la curiosité barbare de cette populace affamée de tous les spectacles de l'humanité souffrante' (ii.40). His moral degradation is matched by his abject surroundings, loss of wealth has meant an end to vice with impunity. His wife obtains an order to release him from his dungeon, arranges to erase his debts and sets him on the road to moral recovery. Loaisel has passed Dolbreuse through the sieve of Parisian vices to illustrate his thesis that the capital depraves the honest provincial. Contemporary vices such as gaming and prostitution lend themselves to critical scrutiny as representing the ethos of Paris and its suffocation of natural virtue.

Justine de Saint-Val is an orphan who travels to Paris to meet a relative. During the journey an officer's wife informs her of the perils of the city for an innocent beauty: 'elle voit des pièges, des séductions, des poursuites; ma figure met mon honneur en danger, et mon innocence même conspire contre; je n'ose la prier de s'expliquer mieux, et quoique je ne la comprenne guère, elle me communique des frayeurs. L'approche de Paris me donne une espèce de délire'.[4] On the outskirts of the city she is met by M. de Melsieux who offers a more reassuring synopsis of Parisian life (i.77-78):

Il [Melsieux] m'a fait une peinture riante des plaisirs séducteurs de la ville, à laquelle je ne voulais pas croire davantage; et lorsque je lui ai opposé ce que j'ai entendu dire si souvent à mon père et à ma mère, il m'a répondu avec un peu d'humeur, que si les grandes villes recèlent beaucoup de vices et non moins de crimes, elles sont aussi l'asile des vertus; que pour être moins gothique, on n'est pas moins homme de bien.

Melsieux fancies the seventeen-year-old girl, while his country cousin is flattered by the Parisian's attentions.

Henceforth Melsieux tries to 'form' her, to turn her aside from her virtuous upbringing. He broadens her knowledge of books, music, dancing, drama. With aspirations to membership of the Académie française, Melsieux is also a friend of the 'philosophes', hence the insidious nature of his instructions! Letters from her aunt express alarm at the blossoming of their relationship, and upbraid Justine for now ranking 'esprit' and 'connaissance' above 'vertu'. By constant coaxing, Melsieux makes Justine forget her aunt's misgivings. To speed up his seductive overtures and reinforce the already effective results of 'philosophie', he enlists the help of Mme Urbain. At his request, she gives Justine the first volume of *La Nouvelle Héloïse* which is designed to encourage her to imitate Julie to his Saint-Preux. As expected she admires Julie. However she reads of Rousseau's heroine only in the context of the love affair, for Melsieux is careful to conceal from her the last sections of the work illustrating Julie's reformed mode of life. Now the stage is set for her seduction where Melsieux calls her resistance cruel and feigns illness to gain her sympathy. Finally she succumbs and lives only for him and through him, substituting her provincial virtue for a blind adherence to life as embodied by her lover.

Melsieux's triumph was motivated by a cerebral campaign rather than by instinctive love or desire. His vanity is satisfied and his interest dwindles proportionately. Justine has lost her integrity and can write to her grief-stricken aunt only of her total submission: 'Mon cœur, ma vie, ma personne, tout est au pouvoir de Melsieux, mes charmes sont flétris, mon cœur corrompu' (ii.144-45). She has not merely yielded her body but also her 'selfness' to her conqueror.

Pregnancy ensues yet Justine is more troubled by her lover's diminishing attentions. Melsieux is presented as a blackguard with no redeeming features who gloats over his victim's distress and informs Mme Urbain (ii.166):

S'il est fort agréable d'avoir par-ci par là des cousines jeunes et gentilles, il serait fort incommode de ne pouvoir plus s'en débarrasser. D'ailleurs, elle est trop jolie pour avoir besoin de compassion. Pour peu qu'elle le veuille, sa fortune est faite, car je la mettrai dans la bonne voie, et il suffit qu'elle m'est appartenu pour que sa réputation soit faite. Plaisanterie à part, elle pourrait aller loin.

His prognostications, however, are not fulfilled. In an attempt to induce an abortion, he gives her a potion which kills her. On her death-bed, Justine shows a resilience typical of the eighteenth-century heroine in penning a letter of contrition to her aunt. Through the loss of 'prejudices', she gained an ephemeral bliss, but finished as another exemplar of Parisian corruption, morally and physically degraded.

In *La Paysanne pervertie* Nougaret has the Comte de C*** set out to corrupt the Marquis de F***. The Comte chides his young friend for being under his mother's thumb and not pursuing his own interests. In a series of insinuating letters he undermines the Marquis's principles by painting glowing pictures of

Parisian life and criticising the monotony of the provinces. In urging his correspondent to enjoy a freer existence he eulogises the capital's amusements (ii.248-49):

Ma foi! vive Paris! c'est le séjour de la liberté, le centre de la joie et de la bonne compagnie; la raison n'y est pas lourde, pédantesque; elle est gaie, vive et charmante; on végète partout ailleurs; on ne jouit de la vie que dans cette capitale des arts et des amours badins: avisez-vous en province d'entretenir avec éclat une beauté docile; comme l'on criera! comme vous serez honni et détesté! Eh bien, à Paris, la chose paraît si simple, si naturelle.

Eventually the marquis comes to Paris and agrees to attend a supper party. Contrary to his expectations he enjoys his evening and admits to his mentor: 'Je ne puis songer aux plaisirs que j'ai eus sans éprouver la plus douce émotion. C'en est fait, je me livre entièrement à vos conseils, je me prête avec docilité à tout ce que mon ami voudra prescrire' (ii.264). The Comte's efforts to 'déniaiser' his pupil are immediately supplemented by the contagious air of the capital. A debauched routine is now set in motion, though his provincial virtues do provoke the occasional pangs of conscience. The inordinate expenditure demanded by his new life leads to a degrading visit to a usurer. In addition he is prompted by the Comte to sample the pleasures of a brothel. Not even this encounter can halt the disintegration of his morals: 'je craignais de mettre les pieds dans ces maisons consacrées au culte de l'amour, et que l'on m'avait dépeintes avec les couleurs les plus affreuses. Mais que je les ai trouvées différentes de l'idée que s'en forment les gens trop scrupuleux' (iii.284). He has no more qualms about his libertine pursuits and cares not a jot for his former 'prejudices'.

To crown his wanton career he embarks on the seduction of Jeannette, herself a victim of the coquettish air of the capital. He relates the triumphal conclusion of his adventure to his mentor and goes on to show the transformation in his character: 'Peut-être qu'avant de venir à Paris, j'aurais été incapable d'une dissimulation; mais l'usage du monde que je commence à connaître, et surtout vos judicieuses leçons, m'ont appris que la première vertu est de ne se fier à personne, et qu'on doit même se refuser à la douceur d'épancher ses plaisirs ou ses peines dans le sein d'un ami' (iv.147-48). Paris and the Comte's counsel have worked together to impose artificial reactions on the provincial's behaviour. He has learnt to conceal his intuitive feelings and lost the capacity for worthwhile friendship. Instead of being frank, he is now on his guard and ever ready to exploit the weakness of others. Whereas his upbringing moulded him for virtue, he has become both personally and socially reprehensible.

Another puppet for the Parisian corrupter is Baculard d'Arnaud's Germeuil. Blinval is an excellent example of someone who can inveigle his way into the company of a provincial: 'Blinval cachait sous cet extérieur séduisant, une âme infectée de tous les poisons. Son unique objet était de jouir; de cette source corrompue découlaient tous ses principes; il avait dissipé sa fortune par de folles dépenses; il s'agissait de réparer ses pertes; les moyens lui paraissaient légitimes, s'ils lui procuraient des ressources' (*Germeuil*, p.10). Blinval is governed by a hedonistic philosophy while Germeuil has arrived in Paris imbued with all the good qualities of a provincial upbringing: 'le goût invariable pour l'honnêteté et le vrai, l'exactitude à remplir ses devoirs, la sobriété dans ses désirs, la sage retenue dans ses plaisirs, un esprit droit, un cœur extrêmement sensible, des vertus modestes, des connaissances utiles, tout ce qui forme le citoyen également aimable et estimable' (p.5). To realise his aims, Blinval has to undermine Germeuil's strict conception of morality.

Besides being a 'déniaiseur', Blinval is also intent on acquiring financial reward from his enterprise and is not like Crébillon fils's Versac, someone who receives a perverse pleasure from 'forming' his pupil. Accordingly he engages Germeuil in a riot of worldly amusements: '[Germeuil] osait avoir des mœurs, une âme dirigée vers le bien; il fallait donc corrompre son cœur pour l'amener à ce degré d'égarement qui ne permit plus de réflechir; c'était par l'attrait du plaisir qu'on se proposait de l'attirer dans le piège' (p.11). Just as for Dolbreuse, the tempo of the pleasures envisaged is intended to remove the occasions for reflection so as to involve Germeuil unthinkingly in a succession of disruptive circumstances.

We have previously mentioned Blinval's accomplice, Mme de Cérignan, and her 'deathbed' deceit of Germeuil. Let us now record the events that led up to that trap. She was introduced to Germeuil by her partner and ingratiates herself with the provincial through an affectation of melancholy and 'sensibilité'. She is even presented to her prey's pious wife who intuitively experiences misgivings on her account. Adélaide's forebodings are not ill-conceived for Germeuil is increasingly under Blinval's domination. The latter employs the arguments of 'philosophic' to sap the foundations of Germeuil's beliefs, attacking monogamy by claiming that a man needs more than one woman to fulfil a true life of pleasure. Moreover, he affirms that there is no room for sentiment in human relationships, since life is a dynamic process which demands change and novelty as prerequisites for the highest good, individual happiness. Despite this indoctrination and his growing love for Mme de Cérignan, Germeuil is still strong enough to confess his guilty secrets to his wife. She overwhelms him with her understanding and pardon, and he vows to have no more dealings with his seductive friends.

The predatory couple have no intention, however, of allowing Germeuil to escape their clutches. They know he is on the threshold of submission and it is at this point that they invent the trick already described. The upshot of this plot is the ruination of Germeuil: 'Germeuil s'était ruiné pour cette méprisable Cérignan; le perfide Blinval avait partagé le fruit de l'intrigue criminelle' (pp.67-68). The erosion of Germeuil's finances was of momentous consequence, yet it was far outweighed by the destruction of his self-respect. So corrupted has he become, that his 'sensibilité' is scarcely aroused by a touching letter from his wife.

Blinval and Cérignan are on the point of washing their hands of the impoverished Germeuil when a chance meeting with an American causes them to revise their plans. He informs them that Adélaide is to benefit from a large inheritance. Acting on this information, Mme de Cérignan plays a 'larmoyant' scene before Germeuil, protesting that she must give him up for the sake of his wife and family – if only he were her husband! The depraved Germeuil, aware of Adélaide's deteriorating health, offers to wed his mistress should he be left a widower. Taking into account this new development Mme de Cérignan has Adélaide's medicine poisoned. Cérignan's chambermaid learns of the deed and immediately informs Adélaide's servant. The latter hastens to apprise her mistress of this murderous attempt, but Adélaide resolves to drink the draught since her husband no longer loves her. Germeuil, also warned by Cérignan's maid, rushes to his wife's side and saves her from her deadly intent. This incident shakes Germeuil out of his degenerate attitude, he recognises his errors, mends his ways, and they live happily ever after! To emphasise this victory, Baculard shows both the villains perishing ignominiously, Cérignan in poverty, and Blinval on the scaffold.[5] Just like Dolbreuse, Germeuil is used as a tool to explore the iniquities of the capital. The confrontation of provincial virtue with Parisian vice is born of critical realism in which the former is shown in this instance to be ultimately victorious.

César de Perlencour and his tutor, the abbé Roussin, come to the capital from Lyons. On their journey, they pass through Auxerre and are reminded of Restif's *Le Paysan perverti*. This brings forth an ominous warning from Roussin to bear in mind Edmond's downfall. Once in Paris, their troubles begin. César picks up some whores in the rue Saint-Honoré and insists his tutor accompany them to a brothel. On leaving this establishment the cleric is arrested for behaviour unbecoming someone in holy orders and locked up in Saint-Lazare. With his independence, César sets out to enjoy every experience within his grasp. He ventures into an 'académie de jeu' and is accosted by the Chevalier de Marqué. César is delighted with his new acquaintance and writes to his correspondent in Lyons:

Je mène toujours la même vie. Rien de plus régulier. Je me partage entre mes exercices, les spectacles, le jeu modéré, Levrette [his mistress] et la philosophie. J'ai fait une trouvaille. J'ai un autre guide à présent que le pauvre Roussin. C'est un homme du monde. Il n'aura point le titre assommant de gouverneur; on ne sera pas obligé de lui en payer les gages, et il me dirigera dans la carrière du monde qu'il connaît parfaitement.[6]

Marqué promises his protégé an enormous social success whilst flattering his vanity. To gain entry into the 'monde' César has to shed his prejudices, a sloughing which brings joy to Marqué's heart. Here again we are presented with this perverse enjoyment of a provincial's 'déniaisement', though robbery was the principal objective.

César's mistress is an example of the virtuous prostitute who warns him of the influence of Marqué whom she knows to be an 'échappé de Bicêtre'. In addition César is subject to the attentions of Marqué's accomplice, Frédégonde. Through their pressure he signs numerous 'billets' and borrows from a usurious Jew. He has been deluded into believing he is to become 'l'homme du jour' and agrees to all the demands made of him as he writes to Dumoulin:

Me voilà jeté dans le tourbillon, mon ami. Je suis entraîné dans le torrent des plaisirs. C'est une ivresse. On n'a pas le temps de se reconnaître. Il est vrai qu'il m'en coûte gros; mais il ne faut pas penser à cela. On répand l'argent comme de l'eau, dans les compagnies que je fréquente. C'est celui qui en a qui paye. C'est à présent mon tour, parce que j'arrive, et je suis un peu en fonds.[7]

Nevertheless his spendthrift existence takes its toll and he finds himself a prison inmate rather than a social success. Upon his release he is as depraved as ever and engages in several nefarious activities, including the rape of Laure de Lysange, the daughter of a family friend. His demoralisation at the hands of Parisian corruptors is complete and after many romanesque adventures he perishes 'roué'.

Men were obviously not the sole victims of Parisian 'déniaiseurs', as the tragedy of Justine de Saint-Val illustrated. When we last wrote of Rutlidge's Alphonsine, she had been tricked into marriage and been forced into organising a gambling den. This was not the least of Valvain's skullduggery, for he had prostituted his wife to a superannuated duke. She was horrified at this abuse of her body but her mind was still intact. This was the signal for the cajoling power of Mlle P…t to bring about her complete corruption. Her glib tongue is employed to addle Alphonsine's sense of virtue:

Chère et raisonnable amie! les usages de ce grand monde absolument nouveau pour vous peuvent bien heurter vos préventions, et effaroucher votre candide inexpérience… et si dans les provinces on ne s'en est point encore aperçu, au moins dans la capitale, et surtout à la cour, les femmes sont aujourd'hui assez complètement déniaisées pour qu'il ne puisse plus leur échapper que messieurs les hommes, en s'arrogeant toutes les prérogatives, sont grossièrement en contradiction avec eux-mêmes; et que, dans la bonne réalité, c'était à de vraies momeries qu'ils avaient tâché de nous asservir.[8]

The arguments of Mlle P…t soon overturn Alphonsine's principles, her 'pré-ventions' are crushed under the onslaught of such a devious 'philosophie'. How could one expect a provincial to survive an alluring re-education on the rights of sensual pleasure contrasting with the abstinence of virtue? The innocent provincial is also ignorant and has no defence against the sophisticated indoc-trination of the capital's inhabitants.

Mlle de Vasy is the daughter of a nobleman who marries M. d'Auranges. The latter has journeyed to the provinces in search of an artless girl for a bride and thinks he has found one. After the wedding ceremony, the couple make their way to the capital where the new marquise cements a friendship with Mme de Lorevel. A woman of some forty years, with an ambiguous past, Mme de Lorevel relishes her role as the young bride's adviser and counsels her to take a lover to secure an honourable place in the 'monde'. Moreover Lorevel chooses the object of the Marquise's future joy: 'Parmi l'essaim brillant qui aspirait à l'honneur de détruire en elle toute façon provinciale, Dorival, jeune mousquetaire, était le plus de son goût.'[9] She should harbour no scruples at such an attachment for Paris now sanctions liaisons of this type. Lorevel is eager to put her on the right road by claiming that the capital has decreed that marriage is an outmoded institution in terms of strict fidelity, in fact it is merely a springboard for sexual licence: 'Autrefois le jour de notre hymen commençait notre esclavage; dans ce siècle raffiné et ingénieux, il commence le règne de notre liberté.'[10] The Marquise soon espouses these principles and puts them into practice by effecting an early rupture with Dorival. There follows a succession of lovers, including Trenel, another musketeer. She particularly savours his attentions since he gives enor-mous satisfaction – after all, according to her newly acquired philosophy, it is pleasure and not love that counts. The poor husband who had sought virtue in a wife by taking a provincial bride had not reckoned on the vicious influence of Mme de Lorevel and is shocked by his wife's misconduct.

At this point we are introduced to the Chevalier de Soudris who, at Lorevel's behest, embarks on the corruption of a certain comte d'Angely. The marquise is by this time totally depraved and desires d'Angely's downfall to vitiate his relations with the virtuous Mlle de Rosbel. Soudris manipulates d'Angely into becoming his helpless pupil. With his new ideas, d'Angely scandalises Mlle de Rosbel and henceforth attaches himself to the Marquise. She toys with him and only after a considerable time does she render him 'heureux'.

Finally, however, d'Angely realises the despotic nature of the Marquise's hold over him, he knows he has been duped. He returns to Mlle de Rosbel, explains the reason for his untoward behaviour, and begs forgiveness. In a manner befitting the Marquise de Merteuil, Barthe's heroine is furious at this reversal of fortune, a change in which she had no controlling hand. One thought springs at once to her mind, revenge. To pursue this aim, she ingratiates herself with the Chevalier de Saint Georges and incites him to challenge d'Angely to a duel. After the combat, which ends with no grievous injuries, d'Angely convinces his opponent of their mutual deception by the Marquise. Saint Georges is not a man to be taken lightly and arranges his own savage vengeance. Since he cannot fight the Marquise with the sword, he resorts to the pen by engaging a professional hack to write a vaudeville which mocks the Marquise and makes her the laughing-stock of the town. Beside herself with rage, the Marquise decides to leave for the provinces at the suggestion of her 'friend', Mme de Lorevel. She has travelled a twisted road since her departure from her home, though the fruits of her corruption are perhaps less moral degradation than ostracism from the milieu she has come to love most. Retribution is social rather than moral.

In Baculard d'Arnaud's 'nouvelle', *Julie* (1767), the heroine and her brother are brought up in a provincial town. When the brother is old enough, a lucrative post is obtained for him by a family friend, away from the parental home. As a result M. and Mme Courville redouble their affection for Julie. Despite their joy at Julie's presence, they decide it would be in her best interests to go to Paris, for: 'sa vertu et sa beauté lui procureraient à Paris un parti avantageux'.[11] Their concern at the separation is soothed in the knowledge that Julie will reside with a relative. It is therefore with high hopes that the young girl sets off with the family retainer after a tearful farewell.

Once in the capital Julie is soon in the custody of her relation, Mme de Subligny. This lady is a widow, middle-aged, childless, yet still in vain pursuit of pleasure. Julie is shown the sights of the city and introduced to Mme Sauval, her aunt's boon companion and supposedly a 'bonne créature'.

Mme Sauval exercises a strong influence over the life of her friend and at once senses that Julie possesses a latent coquetry which she could encourage:

Elle saisissait toutes les occasions d'égarer sa faible amie; la coquetterie de la jeune personne, son désir extrême de plaire, de briller, de fixer les yeux, n'avaient point échappé à la vue pénétrante de cette femme, que semblait humilier l'honnêteté, et qui aspirait à s'en venger: c'était un génie corrupteur attaché aux pas de Julie, et impatient d'entraîner sa perte.[12]

Here is another Parisian who takes delight in corruption for corruption's sake, she is gleeful at the prospect of 'forming' Julie. In a manner reminiscent of Mlle P...t, she instructs her pupil in the 'philosophical' manner (pp.214-15):

Apprenez qu'il n'y a que l'opulence et le plaisir qui soient recherchés, et tous les deux se donnent la main [...] ni vous ni moi n'aurons le privilège de corriger les hommes: il faut donc vivre avec eux tels qu'ils sont, et se borner à les faire servir d'instruments à notre bonheur et aux agréments de la vie; que ce soit là notre unique objet; tout le reste n'est que pure rêverie.

To advance her plans, she arranges a 'chance' meeting with the Marquis de Germeuil (no connection with Baculard's hero of the same name). He is the embodiment of all the treacherous characteristics of the 'homme aimable': '[il] était un de ces séducteurs à la mode, qui possèdent tous les artifices du métier ridicule et criminel de tromper un sexe sensible, en sachant lui plaire, et qui cachent sous des dehors attirants un cœur perfide, et un système suivi de scélératesse' (p.218). Now begins the gradual, systematic seduction of Julie. The demoralising advice of Mme Sauval has not stifled all the principles instilled in the provincial by her devoted parents. She struggles to retain her virtue and only yields to Germeuil in the intoxicating surroundings of a 'petite maison'. Though Germeuil was the author of her downfall, he was only the tool of Mme Sauval who had plotted the circumstances with military precision – Mme de Subligny was but a feckless onlooker.

Through Mme Sauval's scheming Julie is squarely on the road to perdition. To add to her misfortunes, Germeuil makes a bogus promise of marriage and Mme de Subligny dies. Negligent though she may have been in caring for her charge, Subligny nonetheless represented a vital link with Julie's virtuous past and a tenuous hope of redemption. Her death signals the utter depravation of the heroine (pp.223-24):

Germeuil [...] promena sa maîtresse de spectacle en spectacle: elle fut suivie dans les jardins publics, appelée à toutes les fêtes; elle fit l'admiration des hommes et le désespoir de ses rivales; son déshonneur, en un mot, comme son triomphe, fut complet; la richesse, le luxe, tous les plaisirs cherchaient à réveiller ses goûts [...] sa vie était une dissipation continuelle.

Next ensues the predictable rupture; with his vanity satisfied, Germeuil deserts his mistress.

Julie who had genuinely loved him begins to feel remorse for her conduct. In short she may have returned to the paths of virtue had it not been for Mme Sauval. The latter fosters the young woman's desire for jewels and rich finery and introduces her to Dorival. A man of some substance, he supplies Julie with all the adornments she has ever coveted. One day at the Opera, however, she hears herself called a 'fille' for the first time, and is stunned at the realisation of her status in society. The voice of her long muted conscience is suddenly heard and she thinks of her loving parents. Spurred by this resurgence of her true sentiments, she manages to break free from the domination of Mme Sauval. Her life is in tatters and only ascetic repentance will save her soul. Once again Baculard employs a 'nouvelle' to point out the dangers of contemporary life in the capital.

A supreme example of the moral disintegration of a provincial through contact with the capital is Restif's Ursule. Since she and her brother have parallel destinies we have decide to concentrate our attentions on Ursule so as not to duplicate Restif's arguments. As a country lass Ursule showed an inkling for frivolity which was restrained in the narrow community of her village. It is therefore with an air of expectation that she arrives in Paris. She is pleased by the city's architecture but disturbed by the attentions and comments of men who follow her. Nevertheless she is quick to appraise the benefits of urban living and tells Fanchon: 'les manières des villes sont trop agréables pour qu'on puisse ensuite trouver supportables celles de la campagne; outre qu'à la ville la vie est bien plus douce, et surtout qu'on y connaît des plaisirs que rien ne peut compenser au village'.[13] Ursule is convinced even at this stage that children destined for rural occupations should never be allowed contact with the easy life of the towns.

An advantage which she hopes to derive from her removal to Paris is a better marriage – one recalls that Julie's parents in Baculard's tale had the same expectations. Openings are more common in a large city: 'les partis se trouvent à la ville plus facilement qu'au village; peut-être la corruption des mœurs en est-elle cause; on regarde ici davantage à la figure, et on sacrifie plus volontiers l'intéret au plaisir' (i.132). She is sought after by a 'conseiller', a financier, a page, even a veteran enters the lists. Furthermore, she receives letters from a marquis which should outrage her virtue, but Paris has provoked a certain coquetry which prompts her to respond to his overtures. It was Gaudet who had instigated this marquis's pursuit. Ursule is presently on speaking terms with the marquis who proposes a clandestine marriage and, as an increased inducement, a lieutenantship in the army for her brother, Edmond. She writes: 'Le marquis trouve souvent le moyen de me parler: avec de l'argent, on fait tout dans ce pays-ci' (i.329). Whereas her peasant instincts would have recoiled from this misuse of money, her acclimatisation to Parisian mores has atrophied her natural reactions and replaced them with an acceptance of customs devoid of ethical motivation.

At this point Ursule has a premonition or rather a dream of her imminent abduction. This dream is materialised for, before long, she is ravished by the Marquis. The trust in her new life has been shattered and she describes her fall in a letter to Laure. This event marks the real beginning of her moral disintegration, until this moment she had been coquettish and vain yet still cherished a fund of good qualities from her provincial upbringing.

Gaudet cajoles her into signing a letter exonerating the Marquis's behaviour. This is another fateful step for while she had lost her purity in a state of considerable innocence, she has now consented to make a financial transaction of it. Notwithstanding this compensation, she experiences remorse as she informs Fanchon: 'Quel triste sort m'attendait à Paris! et quel a été le terme de mes trop mondaines espérances! j'ai perdu [...] ce qu'on ne recouvre jamais, et j'envie le sort de filles que je regardais comme bien au-dessous de moi, mais qui sont à présent au-dessus; elles ont l'honneur, et je ne l'ai pas' (ii.42). Dishonoured and deflowered though she may be, Ursule still prefers life in the capital to that of the village. Now the stage is set for a philosophical lesson from Gaudet (ii.155):

Cette piété naturelle et vraie est ce qu'il faut à une famille de village pour être honorée, considérée, en un mot, pour être heureuse avec des gens bonasses, et qui si quelquefois ils sont impies, n'ont pas assez de lumières pour l'être par principes. Mais à la ville, c'est tout autre chose! votre piété, telle qu'elle existe dans la maison paternelle, ne serait qu'un ridicule.

Gaudet makes here a damaging attack on fussy prejudices. Ignorant piety is acceptable in the village but in the town greater strength of mind is required. If people are wicked in the country, it is unthinkingly, it is not 'par principes'. For Gaudet one must intellectualise and systematise one's wickedness in order to act on other people, and fulfil one's own desires. Ursule needs to be in the 'monde' to experience true happiness, to expand her personality. She, for her part, is a most receptive pupil.

However, Gaudet's supreme interest is centred on Edmond and Ursule must be used to this end. When the child fathered by the Marquis is born, it must be wrenched from her and she is told it has died. Meanwhile Gaudet has attached another protégé to the deluded girl, Lagouache. There follows a further remarkable exposition by Gaudet to the effect that laws are social and not divine and he urges Ursule to retain her former air of frankness as a mask for society. Gaudet's plans run smoothly and she becomes infatuated with Lagouache. Upon receipt of a parental refusal to this match, Ursule resolves to be abducted by her new lover. This project is executed promptly, though only to her eventual chagrin, as soon Lagouache reveals his true colours as an unprincipled rogue.

She is now the complete debauchee, suffering no constraint or compunction and demanding above all to be entertained: 'Il faut pourtant que je m'y amuse: je suis lasse des réalités, je veux un peu exercer mon imagination' (iii.170). Pleasure is the *summum bonum* and it is variegated by a series of amorous escapades. Prodigality has become the key-note of her existence as she luxuriates in her apartments and relishes the perks of a kept woman. In a missive to Laure she expatiates on her conduct and then reveals the next victim of her attentions: 'c'est un gros Américain, bête, brutal, et fort laid; mais qui doit me valoir une tonne d'or. Il ne faut pas laisser échapper cela' (iii.245). Nonetheless mercenary love requires its amusements and relaxations too. She has grown tired of an importunate Italian and sets in motion a scheme to dupe him by substituting a repugnant negress for her wholesome self. Discovering the deception, the Italian knifes the negress and will later wreak a terrible vengeance on Ursule.

Vice has asserted itself as the norm in Ursule's routine as she confides to Gaudet (iii.259-60):

Me voilà dans une situation qui m'aurait fait horreur, si on me l'avait prédite à mon village, ou bien à Au**, même à Paris dans les premiers temps. Mais je ne tardai pas à entendre dans cette grande ville des propos qui m'ouvrirent les yeux. Dès Au**, on en avait tenu quelques-uns devant moi mais je ne les comprenais pas. Il serait bien étonnant que la façon de penser des gens de ville, presque tous éclairés fût mauvaise et fausse, et qu'il n'y eût de vraie que celle des automates de village telle que j'étais; telle qu'est encore toute ma famille.

Urbanisation has produced refinements, luxury, grandeur, how could the village compete with it even in terms of morality? Ursule is content to justify her actions by comparisons with those around her. She sees the enormous wealth and prestige of Parisian financiers, yet knows that many have amassed their fortunes through shady transactions and are now dissipating them in loose living. She has exchanged the traditional, absolute morality of her rural background for the recent, relative standards of the city. Virtue is merely a meaningless façade shown by the weak and the ignorant, unless it be a clever convenience for the 'déniaisés' in their enjoyment of pleasure. As a confirmed disciple of Gaudet, she proclaims: 'Le vice, je le regarde aujourd'hui comme un écart de la routine, une licence hardie, telle que celles que font les grands poètes. La vertu, je la compare à mon rouge; cela donne de l'éclat, mais il faut que la couche soit superficielle' (iii.264-65). So wanton has her life become that even Gaudet is amazed at her excesses.

We have already noted that Ursule and her brother lose heavily at cards and that she stoops to selling herself in a vain attempt to recoup their losses. Yet this was not to be the nadir of her degradation for her Italian lover savours sweet revenge. She is deceived and brutalised by his henchmen into marrying a 'porteur d'eau' and succumbing to a negro. In addition the Italian compels her to carry out manual drudgery, a striking contrast with the luxurious ease of her recent past. In desperation she kills the negro, but this leads only to her removal to a brothel by the Italian. Eventually she escapes from this establishment but has to seek refuge in another. She outlines her existence to Laure (iv.20):

Je me suis faite amie de la P**, ma maîtresse ou maman, et j'en suis assez bien traitée: il me revient quelques charmes par le soin que je prends de moi, et surtout par le repos durant la nuit, dont j'ai si longtemps été privée. Cet état est bien vil! bien dégradant! mais comment le quitter! [...] Je m'accoutume à ma situation; j'ai tout oublié, honneur, parents, vertu, fils et moi-même! Trois années, grand Dieu! dans cet état! sans entendre parler de personne! Quoi! je ne verrai pas un visage de connaissance!

Such is her demoralisation that she no longer regards herself as a human being, she is just an organism which ekes out an almost insensate existence (iv.21):

L'Univers est devenu un désert pour l'infortunée Ursule R**! Ursule! R**! Une fille de mon état, a-t-elle un nom de famille! rayée du nombre des citoyennes, morte civilement, elle n'est plus rien! elle n'a plus ni nom, ni parents, ni sexe; elle est un monstre d'une nature au-dessous de l'humaine; elle en est sortie, et si elle y rentre, ce n'est que pour être le jouet des Brutaux qui la dégradent.

She has, as it were, excluded herself from the ranks of society, she feels a moral outcast.

Ursule's downfall has been paralleled to a certain extent by that of her compatriot, Laure. Having prostituted herself in Ursule's company, Laure spent three months imprisoned in the Salpêtrière ravaged by venereal disease. Nevertheless Ursule is our major concern and she is more and more overwhelmed by her predicament. A plaintive letter to Zéphire describes her depersonalisation: 'viens, Zéphire, viens, ma fille, viens te pénétrer d'horreur pour le vice et pour les hommes qui l'ont créé! viens frémir! viens voir au plus bas degré de la douleur et de la pourriture un corps vivant, rongé, qui n'est plus que la moitié de lui-même' (iv.94). Ursule is placed in the 'Hôpital' where she writes home to Fanchon for the first time in six years and has the courage to reveal her dreadful life. She is removed from this institution through the auspices of Mme Parangon and returns to her parents. Henceforward she devotes her energies to charitable works in an effort to redeem her past crimes. Her end is as tragic as much of her life, she perishes at the hands of her brother who is unaware of her conversion.

Ursule's moral disintegration was partially the work of Gaudet's insidious philosophy and partially that of the capital which exploited it to the limit. In the confined community of her village, virtue was a quality of inestimable value, unchanged by spatio-temporal variables; on the other hand, in the rootless society of Paris, morality was governed by the fashionable vagaries of the day. The introductory section of the novel leaves us in no doubt as to the source of Ursule's perversion, her other brother lays the blame roundly on the town:

tout ce qui a perverti et vicié ma pauvre sœur était non dans son cœur droit et simple, mais dans vos villes, o lecteurs, dans ce séjour de perdition, où l'on n'a pu souffrir que cette belle créature conservât sa noblesse active et son excellence de cœur et d'esprit; parce qu'elle aurait sans doute trop humilié les difformes d'âme et de corps, dont les villes sont pleines![14]

It is the over-sophisticated society created by man which must be indicted for the fall of Ursule, not any concept of original sin. The city would appear inherently in Restif's opinion to incarnate a vicious milieu. His argument was that, given the vices of towns, those who were accustomed to the purer air of the provinces were best advised to remain there, since they would probably be unable to cope with urban changes. Conversely, those who were inured to town life should stay in this environment being the best suited to the attainment of their happiness. In sum, transplantation from one place to another provokes hardship and unwelcome difficulties for all.[15] Restif can therefore be seen to be offering a tale designed to keep provincials away from the capital. His fictional transcription of contemporary perils has not merely a descriptive purpose but also a normative intent.

This chapter has stressed the overwhelming presentation of Parisian corruption in late eighteenth-century fiction. The provincial, and he is almost invariably a callow youth, is lamentably unable to cope with the snares of the capital. He normally arrives in Paris endowed with natural virtue and is then schooled into rejecting it as an antiquated prejudice. Not only does he lose his good qualities but somehow his 'selfness'. If, in the first decades of the century, Marianne was able to escape the clutches of a rake such as Climal, her successors in post-1760 fiction are doomed to disaster. The disintegration of provincial virtue is thus offered as a critical portrayal of Parisian life, as a means of denouncing its general corruption.

6. The indictment of Paris and civilisation

It is obvious from the foregoing pages that many writers of the late eighteenth century were disenchanted with the role of Paris in the life of their nation. In this chapter we wish to explore this disenchantment in social and political works and illustrate what we believe are the echoes in fiction.

A common complaint was that it was a head too large for the rest of its body:

Nous l'avons dit, le *plus ultra* est la devise de l'homme: ses désirs le déplacent au physique, ainsi qu'au moral. Le villageois habiterait un bourg, s'il pouvait perdre son champ de vue; le bourgeois n'aspire qu'à s'établir à la ville; et l'homme de ville envie le sort de l'habitant de la capitale. Ce désir universel tend cependant,[...] à faire à l'Etat la forme de pyramide pour prendre celle du cône renversé [...]

L'étymologie du mot nous apprend qu'une capitale est aussi nécessaire à un Etat que la tête est au corps; mais si la tête grossit trop, et que tout le sang y porte, le corps devient apoplectique, et tout périt.[1]

Paris, the head, is sucking the life-blood away from the body, the provinces, and depriving it of any vital existence.

Mercier is preoccupied by the same problem: 'Je vois cette ville florissante, mais aux dépens de la nation entière'.[2] Furthermore he claims that Paris attracts far more provincials than in days gone by, it is the capital's renown:

qui séduit tant de jeunes têtes, et qui leur représente Paris comme l'asile de la liberté, des plaisirs, et des jouissances les plus exquises.

Que ces jeunes gens sont détrompés quand ils sont sur les lieux! Autrefois les routes entre la capitale et les provinces n'étaient ni ouvertes ni battues. Chaque ville retenait la génération de ses enfants, qui vivaient dans les murs qui les avaient vu naître, et qui prêtaient un appui à la vieillesse de leurs parents: aujourd'hui le jeune homme vend la portion de son héritage pour venir la dépenser loin de l'œil de sa famille; il la pompe, la dessèche, pour briller un instant dans le séjour de la licence.[3]

Mercier illustrates the breakdown of traditional ties between the generations, the young no longer necessarily live and die in their native environments. Moreover this increase in social mobility promotes another noisome consequence.

The immigrants bring not only their persons but also their wealth to the capital. The draining of people and money from the provinces incurs the wrath of Rousseau. In *Emile* (1762) he complains:

On dit que la ville de Paris vaut une province au roi de France; mais je crois qu'elle lui en coûte plusieurs; que c'est à plus d'un égard que Paris est nourri par les provinces, et que la plupart de leurs revenus se versent dans cette ville et y restent sans jamais retourner au peuple ni au roi. Il est inconcevable que, dans ce siècle de calculateurs, il n'y est pas un qui sache voir que la France serait beaucoup plus puissante si Paris était anéanti. Non seulement le peuple mal distribué n'est pas avantageux à l'état, mais il est plus ruineux que la dépopulation ne donne qu'un produit nul, et que la consommation mal entendue donne un produit négatif.[4]

Money which could have served to reinvigorate French agriculture and renovate decaying buildings is lavished in the capital on luxury and idle amusement.

In a novel Delacroix underlines the same point, stressing the resultant poverty of the labouring masses. Montendre is visiting Paris and writes to his friend, Saint-Lieu: 'Est-ce celui qui cultive qui recueille? N'est-il pas démontré que la plus grande partie des terres appartient à des Seigneurs ou à des riches particuliers qui en dépensent le revenu dans la capitale et dans les grandes villes; dès lors que l'on sera convenu de ce fait, il en résultera que les campagnes ne sont guère habitées que par de pauvres journaliers.'[5] Further on Montendre sums up the effect of Paris on the rest of the nation: 'cette ville immense où tout se porte, où tout abonde, pour laquelle se dépeuplent et s'appauvrissent les campagnes' (p.198). The lure of Parisian life and luxury is impoverishing the provinces financially and demographically. Delacroix is offering a critical commentary on the contemporary situation in moral and economic terms.[6]

That the nobility thronged to the court and capital is beyond question in the eighteenth century. Let us instance this exodus from the work of the marquis de Mirabeau before citing examples from the novel:

On sait que toute la noblesse de France attirée à la capitale par l'ambition, le goût du plaisir et la facilité de réaliser ses revenus en argent, depuis que les métaux sont devenus plus communs, chassée des provinces par l'exemple de ses voisins, par la chute de toute considération dans son canton et par le dégoût d'obéir à certains préposés de l'autorité, s'est transplantée autant qu'elle a pu dans la capitale, et qu'il n'est demeuré dans l'éloignement que ceux qu'un reste d'habitude ou la pauvreté y a retenus.[7]

He goes on to expand his indignation by showing the destitution of their domains:

Il n' y a pas une seule terre un peu considérable dans le Royaume dont le propriétaire ne soit à Paris, et conséquemment ne néglige ses maisons et ses châteaux. Le même air de désertion et de décret qui règne sur les maisons principales, s'étend sur les fermes des particuliers, les murs, églises, clochers dans les villages sont pareillement en masures et couvertes de lierre.[8]

This is a bleak picture of the ravages of absenteeism and will find an echo in the writings of Rousseau.

Jean-Jacques denounces the drift from the land and apportions blame to novels, which are widely read in the provinces and addle the brains of the inhabitants. He illustrates the impact on a country gentleman and his family:

Tous de concert, ne voulant plus être des manants, se dégoûtent de leur village, abandonnent leur vieux château, qui bientôt devient masure, et vont dans la capitale où le père, avec sa croix de Saint-Louis, de seigneur qu'il était, devient valet, ou chevalier d'industrie; la mère établit un brelan; la fille attire les joueurs, et souvent tous trois, après avoir mené une vie infâme, meurent de misère et déshonorés.[9]

The father exchanges a useful role for a demoralising one, and again gaming is presented as a degrading resource.

It would be superfluous to cite the instances of noblemen and even rich bourgeois going to Paris in search of pleasure, we have already done so, yet there was another motivation often invoked in the novel, that of training. The nobility still exercised its function as defenders of the realm and the academies of Paris offered instruction in all the military arts.[10] There were also those who journeyed to the capital for academic instruction[11] or in search of an advantageous post.[12] We are therefore presented with this constant movement to Paris of wealthy provincials throughout the period. It is not, however, just the flight of rich people and nobles which causes concern, but often the uprooting of peasants that their departure provokes.

These peasants, frequently crushed by iniquitous taxation, abandoned their traditional occupations in favour of a move to the towns. There they often obtained employment as servants. Alternatively they were taken from their domains by their 'seigneurs' to be domestics in the capital. The transformation of a rural labourer into an urban servant earns Mercier's condemnation on numerous occasions. In an article he fulminates against its repercussions on the provinces: 'Quand on en voit un groupe dans une antichambre, il faut songer qu'il s'est formé un vide dans la province, et que cette population florissante de Paris forme de vastes déserts dans le reste de la monarchie' (*Le Tableau de Paris*, ii.208). Moreover a comparison between the lot of domestics and that of their country brethren produces a rude shock. Those who are furthering the well-being of the nation are in a pitiful state which contrasts sharply with the ease and comfort of useless servants:

Ce vol d'individus fait aux campagnes, à l'agriculture, n'a pas même été frappé parmi nous d'un impôt propre à punir cet égoïsme révoltant. Et tandis que le galon d'or et d'argent entre dans la livrée de la servitude, le sarrau de toile couvre à peine le laboureur et le vigneron. La classe travaillante voit les valets en habit de drap galonné, et les femmes de chambre en robe de soie, même avec quelques petits diamants. Cette malheureuse classe commence à s'estimer elle-même fort au-dessous de l'ordre domestique.[13]

Mercier is incensed at this anomaly and suggests on the same page that the imposition of a tax on their employers would be an extremely effective measure.[14]

Evidence of this transformation is produced in creative fiction. In the anonymous *Le Pauvre diable provincial* we read of Sophie who has been obliged to go to the capital by her indigent parents. A widow buys her services by giving 'au père et à la mère, une somme assez considérable, au moyen de laquelle ils ont consenti que je prenne leur fille à mon service'.[15] In Restif's *Le Pied de Fanchette* we are offered a miniature of a faithful servant who has suffered the tribulations to which her station is exposed. Néné is a retainer who takes Fanchette under her wing and is depicted thus:

Elle était fille d'un laboureur; dès sa jeunesse, elle vint à la ville, et servit. Elle apporta de son village de la pudeur, un cœur tendre, une figure appétissante, et beaucoup de bonne foi: un garçon de boutique, un clerc de procureur, un valet de chambre, un maître d'hôtel etc., la trompèrent tour à tour, en lui promettant de l'épouser, et ne lui tinrent jamais parole: elle aima le plaisir, mais elle eut toujours horreur du crime; elle devint sage à force de manquer à l'être.[16]

This depopulation of the countryside, then, not only found comment in political tracts but also in the novel.

In Barthe's *La Jolie femme*, Toinette, a strong-willed peasant, has a healthy disdain for those who come to wheedle away the village manhood. She asks Jeannot not to listen to their advances: 'Les personnes qui viennent de Paris, enlèvent comme cela tous les pauvres gens de village, tantôt c'est pour le roi, tantôt pour servir les Dames [...] Va, Jeannot, crois-moi, il est plus honorable de cultiver la terre ici, que d'être domestique galonné à Paris: ce galon n'est que la livrée de la plus basse servitude' (i.139). The peasant follows a useful occupation and Barthe claims it is odious to remove him for military or domestic service.

Diderot's *Jacques le fataliste* makes a similar point. Jacques and his master see a ploughman in difficulties with an uncooperative horse. With his usual acumen Jacques guesses the horse's origin and compares its destiny with his own:

Je devine que ce sot, orgueilleux, fainéant animal est un habitant de la ville, qui, fier de son premier état de cheval de selle, méprise la charrue; et pour vous dire tout, en un mot, que c'est votre cheval, le symbole de Jacques que voilà, et tant d'autres lâches coquins comme lui, qui ont quitté les campagnes pour venir porter la livrée dans la capitale, et qui aimeraient mieux mendier leur pain dans les rues, ou mourir de faim, que de retourner à l'agriculture, le plus utile et le plus honorable des métiers.[17]

Earlier in the work we were treated to a conversation between a poverty-stricken peasant and an innkeeper (pp.590-91):

LE COMPÈRE   Compère, tout ce que vous dites est vrai; il l'est aussi que les huissiers sont chez moi, et que dans un moment nous serons réduits à la besace, ma fille, mon garçon et moi.

L'HÔTE   C'est le sort que tu mérites. Qu'es-tu venu faire ici ce matin? Je quitte le remplissage de mon vin, je remonte de ma cave et je ne te trouve point. Sors d'ici, te dis-je.

LE COMPÈRE   Compère, j'étais venu; j'ai craint la réception que vous me faites; je m'en suis retourné; et je m'en vais.

L'HÔTE   Tu feras bien.

LE COMPÈRE   Voilà donc ma pauvre Marguerite, qui est si sage et si jolie, qui s'en ira en condition à Paris!

L'HÔTE   En condition à Paris! Tu en veux donc faire une malheureuse?

LE COMPÈRE   Ce n'est pas moi qui le veux; c'est l'homme dur à qui je parle.

L'HÔTE   Moi, un homme dur! Je ne le suis point: je ne le fus jamais; et tu le sais bien.

LE COMPÈRE   Je ne suis plus en état de nourrir ma fille ni mon garçon; ma fille servira, mon garçon s'engagera.

L'HÔTE   Et c'est moi qui en serais la cause! Cela ne sera pas. Tu es un homme cruel; tant que je vivrai tu seras mon supplice. Çà, voyons ce qu'il te faut.

Had the innkeeper not shown compassion the peasant's children would have been forced to abandon the land and take up the two careers as Jacques had done before them.[18]

In Doppet's anecdote, *Dorine, ou les progrès du vice et du libertinage*, the heroine has travelled to the capital from Langres. Her decision to leave her home is admonished by the author, a future Revolutiomary general: 'Une jeune fille, que je nommerai Dorine, des environs de Langres en Champagne, vint à Paris pour servir: elle eut comme beaucoup d'autres, la faiblesse de préférer l'état de servitude à celui de ses pères, qui étaient d'honnêtes vignerons.'[19] It is foolhardy to exchange the dignity of agriculture for the humiliation of servitude in the capital.

Louvet is another novelist expressing concern at the number of servants and their probable origins. In an affray Faublas is scathing about his opponents:

Celui de mes adversaires que je regardai le premier avait à peine quatorze ou quinze ans; je le reconnus pour un de ces petits enfants de jolie figure, un de ces jockeys élégants qui, majestueusement courbés sur le faîte menaçant d'un cabriolet colossal, font de gentilles grimaces aux passants que leur maître éclabousse, ou d'une voix douce et flûtée, crient gare à ceux qu'il écrase. Je ne donnai qu'un coup d'œil au second; c'était un de ces grands coquins insolents et lâches, que le luxe enlève à l'agriculture, que nous autres, gens comme il faut, payons pour jouer aux cartes ou pour dormir sur des chaises renversées près des fournaises de nos antichambres; pour jurer, boire et se moquer de nous dans nos offices; pour manger au cabaret l'argent de *monsieur*; pour caresser dans les mansardes les femmes de *madame*.[20]

Again post-1760 fiction reveals a critical depiction of society pointing out current abuses.

We have underlined in this chapter the evil effect of Paris in drawing both manpower and wealth from the provinces, yet, ultimately, the most damning criticism is that Paris has nothing worthwhile to offer its immigrants. As the century advances there is an avalanche of novels attacking the dangers and futility of Parisian life. Bastide can offer in a work of the earlier period a caricature of how to be a perfect gentleman when his hero confides:

j'entrai dans ce labyrinthe éternel qu'on appelle le monde. J'avais de l'esprit, mais beaucoup moins que je ne m'en trouvais; ma figure était agréable, mon humeur enjouée et complaisante, j'étais riche et généreux. Ces qualités composent tout le mérite qu'on demande à un jeune homme, et quand elles sont ornées d'un certain air de suffisance, on peut se flatter de parvenir.[21]

His mocking tone, an end in itself, will rarely be found in later fiction.

In Voltaire's *Jeannot et Colin*, however, we do find a comic tone though worldly etiquette is an object of attack. This cautionary tale of 1764 has a scene where Jeannot is told by his 'gouverneur' that academic training is of no account in social intercourse, and all he needs to learn is to be 'aimable' and to acquire 'les moyens de plaire'. Jeannot's parents are 'parvenus' who pride themselves on their son's accomplishments (pp.133-34):

Madame la marquise crut alors être la mère d'un bel esprit, et donna à souper aux beaux esprits de Paris. La tête du jeune homme fut bientôt renversée; il acquit l'art de parler sans s'entendre, et se perfectionna dans l'habitude de n'être pas propre à rien [...] il fit l'amour. L'amour est quelquefois plus cher qu'un régiment. Il dépensa beaucoup, pendant que ses parents s'épuisaient encore davantage à vivre en grands seigneurs.

Nevertheless contact with Parisian society is immediately cut off when the family goes bankrupt; to please is no longer a viable currency. Voltaire is not indulging in a wholesale critique of Parisian society but is underscoring the shallow nature of much of its behaviour.

The social round is supposedly one brimming with pleasures, yet the more perceptive provincial of the later novel is capable of piercing this charade. Mlle Prémont participates in the 'gaiety' of the capital but writes: 'Vous me demandez, ma chère tante, le détail de mes occupations depuis mon arrivée à Paris; beaucoup de brouhaha, des toilettes éternelles, des distractions, de la dissipation et point de plaisirs; voilà ce que j'y ai trouvé.'[22] Eraste, similarly, penetrates the artifice of these pleasures, the much vaunted amusements are a façade to cover up the inner emptiness: 'Dans cette immense capitale, le besoin de tuer le temps lie entre eux un million d'êtres inutiles et surchargés d'eux-mêmes, qui ont l'air d'être les meilleurs amis du monde, et qui ne se connaissent pas.'[23] For Eraste this pursuit of pleasure is little more than a ritual coconut shy where the prize is a momentary respite from general *ennui*. Human relations are conducted on a plane of superficiality which contrasts strikingly with the life of the close-knit communities in the provinces.

Concomitant with worldly etiquette is the fundamental narcissism of its adherents. In the Palais-Royal, Manon is not deceived by the strutting beaux and belles: 'je n'y ai vu qu'un visage, ou plutôt des figures enluminées qui paraissent se ressembler parfaitement. Le motif de leur promenade n'était pas équivoque; les hommes comme les femmes semblaient dire par leurs démarches: Regardez-moi bien, je possède les bons airs, je suis mis dans le dernier goût.'[24] Even compliments directed at women are in reality an invitation to return appreciative glances as Laure tells her correspondent:

Il n'y a pas encore trois semaines que j'habite notre capitale et déjà l'on m'a dit plus de cent fois que j'étais jolie [...] Je ne doute point que nos provinciaux n'aient d'aussi bons yeux que les Parisiens: en ce cas, ma chère Emilie, vous essuyez journellement bien des fadeurs. Ici, c'est un autre ton. Un jeune homme dit à une femme, vous êtes belle, je vous admire, comme il lui dirait: Je suis beau, admirez-moi.[25]

Paris is a stage where the actors demand and obtain applause from their fellow players while really applauding themselves.

If the concern with language and custom is uppermost in the Parisian social code, this attitude is mirrored by sartorial fashions. Dress is emblematic of social prestige, and appearances must be maintained at all costs. Enormous expenditure is incurred to shine on appropriate occasions, though M. de Fillerville from Normandy is not duped into forgetting the true motivations: 'En effet la vanité règne à Paris plus que partout ailleurs, et c'est surtout dans un jour d'apparat, tel qu'une fête ou une revue que l'on voit en plein son triomphe. Toute femme y fait assaut de curiosité et de vaine gloire, pour voir et être vue.'[26] A society preoccupied by externals is heedless of moral values and will pursue anything which provides a diversion from ordinary reality. It is not surprising, then, that this 'monde' should have approved and sought that distinctly civilised creation, luxury.

The attitude to luxury in eighteenth-century thought is complex. Its supporters often defended it on the grounds that it stimulated commerce, brought a great deal of money into circulation, and fostered employment for countless workers. Voltaire was one of its leading champions in the early part of the century.[27] However for those who mistrusted the increasing urbanisation, it was an eloquent sign of national decline. Mirabeau denounces luxury as a cancer in the heart of metropolitan society: 'Si donc la jeunesse prime aujourd'hui dans le monde, c'est qu'elle convient mieux que tout autre à l'agencement général des mœurs, et au papillotage qui a pris en tout la place du solide. D'autre part, la prééminence du colifichet n'a pas été de choix, mais forcée par le luxe. C'est par ces liaisons indispensables que le luxe a énervé le corps.'[28] It is above all this enervating effect which draws forth his ire, how can the new generation of

Frenchmen acquire sufficient moral fibre amidst such emasculating ease?: 'La mollesse, la sottise et l'enfance perpétuelle des hommes nés au milieu de l'aisance et de l'oisiveté des villes forment une mauvaise école pour réussir aux différents travaux auxquels notre subsistance est attachée.'[29] Moreover, luxury as a conspicuous part of industry is another cause of the drift from the land.

Quesnay launches a vehement attack on commerce for creating this situation. In accordance with his physiocratic thinking, he proclaims:

Les manufactures et le commerce entretenus par les désordres du luxe, accumulent les hommes et les richesses dans les grandes villes, s'opposent à l'amélioration des biens, dévastent les campagnes, inspirent du mépris pour l'agriculture, augmentent excessive-ment les dépenses des particuliers, nuisent au soutien des familles, s'opposent à la propagation des hommes et affaiblissent l'Etat.[30]

Commerce as actively furthering luxury is also the target of criticism with Ange Goudar. Manufacturing industries have deprived the countryside of many useful labourers: 'Tous ces arts ont nécessairement enlevé une infinité de bras à l'agriculture.'[31]

In our opinion the repercussions of physiocratic thought may be found in Louvet de Couvray. The *Amours du Chevalier de Faublas* contains a passage which echoes the words of Goudar quoted above decrying the effect of commerce on agriculture and the ravenous appetite of the capital (p.907):

le commerce enlève tous les jours des bras à l'agriculture. Un fléau destructeur qu'il amène avec lui, le luxe, vient encore dans nos campagnes décimer les plus beaux hommes qu'il précipite à jamais dans le vaste abîme des capitales où s'engloutissent les générations. Que reste-t-il pour cultiver nos champs déserts? Quelques tristes esclaves, condamnés à l'oppression des heureux de la terre, qui par la plus inique des répartitions, ayant gardé pour eux l'oisiveté avec la considération, l'exemption avec les richesses, laissent à leurs vassaux la misère et le mépris, le travail et les impôts.

Agriculture, the most noble of occupations and the primary source of wealth, is equally abused by tax-immune landlords and the pernicious growth of manu-facture and luxury. Luxury is denounced here not just in traditional, moral terms but also in economic terms.[32] Commerce and luxury in displacing peasants from the land have upset the time-honoured social structures and, incidentally, widened the gap between the rich and the poor.

A Breton hero of Marmontel is also in the camp which despises luxury. During his stay in the capital, M. Plémer is disgusted by this ostentation and the people who parade it and utters: 'quelques propos d'humeur sur la sottise et la vanité du luxe à Paris, et sur le misérable orgueil de l'opulence'.[33] Parisians not only live extravagantly but have the effrontery to scorn the under-privileged. More-over, luxury was deemed to create unnecessary demands which could impoverish the unwary: 'le faste ouvre la porte aux besoins, et [...] la misère s'établit imperceptiblement chez les gens les plus riches'.[34] Luxury is an urban develop-ment, and Paris as the principal city of France is vilified as the chief consumer and propagator of an industry resulting in the moral and financial decay of the nation.

The sheer density of population in the capital favours the expansion of luxury as the Comte de Meilzuns underlines: 'Voyez dans les villes l'espèce humaine entassée, et de là ce choc éternel de tant de petites passions, mais qui enfantent de grands crimes; voyez-y surtout et méprisez ce luxe qui déploie tant de hauteur, et se soutient, par des moyens si bas, ses maximes frivoles, impertinen-tes, et songez qu'elles n'entrent jamais que dans de très petites têtes.'[35] Meilzuns has abandoned Paris for a rural existence and speaks very much in the tones of a sage. Where there is a love of superfluity, a large volume of people, vice finds an easy access.

Restif de La Bretonne recognises the importance of the immensity and anonymity of Paris as a factor in the breakdown of the provincial's virtue. When Ursule alights from the 'coche d'eau' in the capital she experiences an unease. Her apprehension is augmented by a man who first speaks to her and then follows her, causing her to reflect on the difference between her new environnent and her native village:

Cela est drôle ici comme on ne se connaît pas, chacun y dit ce qu'il pense, et on n'est pas retenu comme chez nous et à Au** par une sorte de respect humain, dans la crainte que ces petits écarts ne soient sus. Il me semble, sans être philosophe, que c'est pourquoi le vice va plus tête-levée ici qu'ailleurs; il n'a que le moment présent de la honte à craindre; la chose passée, la rue quittée, on est un être tout neuf, et absolument intact où l'on arrive. Cela est commode pour les malhonnêtes gens et tant de filles perdues qu'il y a ici.[36]

In the village, in the small town, everyone knows something about everyone, no-one is a complete stranger. On the other hand, in Paris, an individual, just like the provincial fugitives we have mentioned, can lose himself in the crowd, unknown and answerable to nobody.

This impunity was also recognised by Louis Charpentier who accords it a long disquisition in *L'Elu et son président* (i.3-5):

Environnez un homme de témoins qu'il ne puisse éviter, il fera sûrement une bonne action: laissez-lui entrevoir au contraire ou l'espérance de n'être point observé ou celle de se perdre dans la foule, il va peut-être commettre un crime. Et pour le dire en passant, voilà quelle est, ou je suis bien trompé, la source d'où se répandent tous les abus et toutes les injustices qui inondent ordinairement les capitales. Sûr de s'y dérober à l'œil trop distrait du public, on y sacrifie tout sans pudeur à ses seuls intérêts. S'il en rejaillit quelque honte, la tache qu'elle imprime ne dure qu'un jour, et le tourbillon du lendemain l'efface. Au lieu qu'il n'en saurait être de même dans les petites villes, où la moindre démarche de chaque particulier est sue le moment même, et commentée à loisir par tous les habitants.

So many atoms in a gigantic body do not form a harmonious whole. The inhabitants of a capital like Paris do not have the feeling of identification that their provincial compatriots experience in small communities. Since individual conduct is unchecked, corruptive forces are given free rein.

In post-1760 fiction one is constantly confronted by suggestions that the very atmosphere and climate of opinion are conducive to undermining virtue in the capital. The orphaned Mlle de Vasy receives fearful advice from her grand-mother before her departure for Paris:

L'air de Paris a quelque chose de particulier: il communique une certaine aisance qui n'est guère connue que dans cette ville de liberté et de luxe: dès qu'on l'a respiré un certain temps, on prend, malgré soi, les mœurs du pays, qui sont d'ailleurs trop extravagantes pour n'être pas fidèlement suivies. La société y donne mille chaînes imperceptibles; mais on les porte de si bonne grâce, qu'on appelle encore liberté ce criant esclavage.[37]

The ease and attraction of Parisian society are insidious because they take on a normative aspect for the newcomer which hides their inherent dangers. What is superficially regarded as freedom is in fact constraint, for one has to renounce one's 'selfness' to conform to a despotic pattern of social manners.

Manon is immediately affected by the ambiance of the capital: 'Je crois que l'air de Paris est contagieux, et il m'y arrive mille choses qui me surprennent: par exemple, je me suis regardée avec complaisance aujourd'hui; je m'accoutume à cet attirail d'ajustements qui me paraissait si ridicule, il relève ma beauté. Ma beauté! j'ignorais il y a deux jours que je fusse belle.'[38] Clearly Paris is presented as possessing the capacity to incite desires and realise potentialities which would have remained dormant elsewhere.[39] It is noteworthy that most writers insist on the almost invincible impact of Parisian corruption. However strong the virtue of a provincial he would seem to have little hope of overcoming such a potent force. Entrusted with the surveillance of a friend's son, the Vicomte de L*** informs a marquise: 'Je vois avec la dernière douleur que ce jeune homme va se perdre dans une ville telle que Paris, où le libertinage et les mauvais exemples peuvent corrompre les cœurs les plus honnêtes.'[40] Moreover it is difficult not to accept immoral practices when vice is so obviously the instigator of worldly success.

Provincials were shocked at the prestige accorded to the mistresses of men of social standing. Let us take Baculard's Julie as an example (p.207):

Allait-elle aux Tuileries, au Palais-Royal, ses yeux cherchaient quelque personne de son sexe, élégamment ajustée; l'avaient-ils rencontrée: qui est-elle, se demandait Julie avec empressement? C'est sans doute une femme du premier rang, elle entendait dire que c'est Mademoiselle ***, fille d'une naissance obscure: mais sa figure, ses grâces l'ont vengée des caprices du sort; elle jouit d'un état brillant, tient une très bonne maison; [...] elle est même considérée. Considérée, se disait Julie, que cette façon de penser étonnait! j'avais imaginé, jusqu'à présent, que c'était à la vertu seule qu'on accordait de la considération. [...] Les propos qu'on tenait autour d'elle établissaient des principes bien différents!

What she had been taught of morality in the provinces jars with what she sees in Paris. She had believed vice never prospered.

The preceding pages show that Paris was subjected to enormous critical scrutiny in the last decades before the Revolution. Has the rise and supremacy of the capital contributed more on the credit than on the debit side to the life of France? Baculard answers unhesitatingly no (*Germeuil*, pp.3-4):

La Province a été, de tout temps, l'objet du dédain et des froides plaisanteries de ces êtres frivoles et corrompus dont abonde la capitale. On ne disconviendra point que dans les grandes villes, la société n'ait des formes plus élégantes, un langage plus poli et plus cultivé, qu'elle ne connaisse mieux les finesses de l'usage et de la mode, toutes les propriétés du luxe, qu'elle ne soit enfin plus éclairée sur ce qu'on peut appeler la *science du monde*, qu'un petit troupeau de citoyens resserré dans une étroite enceinte, et bornés aux seuls besoins de leur famille, et d'une fortune souvent médiocre, qui ne s'étend guère au delà de ce qu'on nomme l'honnête aisance: mais ces prétendus avantages, dont Paris semble s'enorgueillir, sont-ils bien des privations réelles pour la Province? [...] Je n'imagine point que l'espèce humaine ait beaucoup gagné à se rapprocher: elle a fait, sans contredit, des acquisitions relatives aux agréments, à l'étendue des connaissances, à la jouissance des faux plaisirs: mais à quel prix? aux dépens de la vérité et de la nature.

The capital has provided opportunities for the increase of knowledge, but what is the value of this increment if it has resulted in the gradual suffocation of 'vérité' and 'nature'.

There is nothing mysterious about Paris which made it the target of so much animadversion in the fiction of this period. It is attacked as the supreme representative of civilisation. It is therefore necessary to examine the general assault on urbanisation, and particularly large towns, the better to understand the growing condemnation of the French capital in the second half of the century.

In his short story, *Rosalie*, Imbert suggests that the heights of iniquity are ever the dominant feature of big towns. Love has always been in some circumstances a prelude to crime but has never been debased to such a low level as at present: 'En tous lieux et dans tous les temps l'amour malheureux a été voisin du crime: partout on a cherché à séduire l'objet qu'on avait désiré; mais tramer la séduction avant d'avoir connu le désir, c'est un raffinement qui ne peut être connu que dans nos grandes villes.'[41] Desire might not be the most praiseworthy of individual passions, yet at least it is a natural manifestation. On the other hand, desire motivated by vanity is repugnant in the extreme, an unnatural creation of an unnatural milieu.

If natural virtue goes unrecognised town-dwellers are also intent on appearances which render individual integrity a mere plaything. Saint-Preux deplores the social habits of Parisian women: 'C'est le premier inconvénient des grandes villes que les hommes deviennent autres que ce qu'ils sont, et que la société leur donne pour ainsi dire un état différent du leur. Cela est vrai, surtout à Paris, et surtout à l'égard des femmes, qui tirent des regards d'autrui la seule existence dont elles se soucient.'[42] Those who live in large cities are not concerned with their identity as individuals but merely see themselves in relation to their fellows; indeed it is the general opinion of society which is the basis of their morality and their guideline. Ethics are not a question of personal integrity, but adherence to a collective code.[43]

The pernicious impact of urbanisation is a recurrent theme in the works of Restif de La Bretonne, an author who had himself moved from the village through the town to the city. He uses Edmond as his spokesman:

Détestable urbanité, qui multiplies nos besoins et raffines nos plaisirs, ah! que tu fais de malheureux! Prétendue barbarie, précieuse grossièreté, reviens, ah reviens! ramène-nous les glands et les forêts! les Hommes (car ce n'est plus moi) y trouveront le bonheur, plutôt que dans ces gouffres de fange, de fumée, de vices et d'horreurs, qu'on nomme villes, et qui ne sont que les cachots et le malaise du genre humain.[44]

The city is a 'gouffre' where outsiders lose their innocence and are goaded into searching for vain pleasures, for superfluous experiences. Superfluous is undoubtedly a keyword in the detractor's vocabulary. To live a virtuous existence one has no need of the refined demands of the modern Babylons. Urban sophistication has imposed a morally corrosive veneer which transforms the personalities of those it attacks: 'Dès que l'homme est policé, il a des goûts factices; aussitôt qu'il est dans l'abondance, ses goûts s'exaltent et il devient ce que nous exprimons par le mot *libertin*.'[45] The individual should be concerned with what is necessary for his subsistence and not strive for objects devoid of any consequence for his moral integrity.

Loaisel de Tréogate is another zealot in Rousseau's camp who views contemporary society with hostility. He protests there is a lack of human dignity and the advance of civilisation is largely to be blamed (*Dolbreuse*, i.131):

La cause de cette sorte de dégradation est sans doute dans l'état actuel de l'esprit humain. Sans admettre le paradoxe qu'il est dangereux d'éclairer sa raison, on ne peut disconvenir que les sciences et les arts, à force de polir la société, n'établissent le premier degré de la corruption dans un empire, et ne lui fassent faire un pas vers sa décadence. Des goûts frivoles, des inclinations molles que produisent les talents agréables, de l'abus des arts et des richesses, ont résulté, parmi nous, à l'affaiblissement de ce grand ressort de l'âme, qui lui donne une tendance irrésistible vers les grandes choses.

It is society which must be arraigned, for man is fundamentally good and capable of redemption through his own efforts (i.121-22):

Nous apprendre que nos faiblesses et nos vices sont moins l'ouvrage de nos penchants que celui de la société, c'est réveiller et flatter en même temps notre bonté naturelle; c'est faire naître le désir de lui rendre son instinct primitif; c'est provoquer le courage et les efforts de notre âme: car il est peut-être dans l'homme de chercher quelquefois à s'attester ses moyens et ses forces. Quand on lui a démontré que ses vices sont le résultat d'une impulsion générale, et que ses vices sont la source du malheur public ainsi que du malheur particulier, il veut faire voir aussi qu'il est capable de résister à cette impulsion; qu'il peut de lui-même, et par la seule puissance de sa volonté, s'arracher à la dépravation commune, et remonter courageusement la pente qui l'entraînait si loin de sa première destination.

Man has been depraved by civilisation, but he is endowed with sufficient will to counteract this evil influence and return to his original 'destination', for he realises that virtue is the true goal of his condition, one which will assure his longed-for happiness.

As is intimated in the above extract, man is always in danger if he yields to the 'impulsion générale'. Baculard d'Arnaud exemplifies the same views in his tale, *Sélicourt* (1769). Sinville is a retired soldier who embodies the qualities of a right-thinking 'philosophe'. He refuses to reside in the capital and sums up most of the arguments against the effects of populous communities:

Il prétendait que le séjour de Paris corrompait le sentiment et dénaturait l'esprit: (c'est son expression) qu'on y respirait, en quelque sorte, avec l'air, la frivolité, et une dépravation de mœurs qui entraîne presque toujours celle des idées. Il ajoutait que, pour être vertueux, il faut trouver le temps de s'entretenir avec soi-même, et qu'il n'y a que la solitude qui puisse agrandir l'âme, et étendre nos lumières. Il pensait que la société fait éclore infiniment plus de maux qu'elle ne produit de biens et d'avantages. Combien d'hommes, observait-il, sont confondus avec la multitude uniforme de la capitale, et ont à peine une existence, qui auraient conservé leurs traits particuliers, et joui de la dignité attachée à notre être, des privilèges de l'homme, s'ils avaient eu le courage de ne pas abandonner la province![46]

Here again we are presented with the idea that the inhabitants of the capital lose their 'selfness' in their adherence to collective uniformity. However the aspect of the passage, that we wish to stress in this instance, is the role given to reflection as a prerequisite for the maintenance of virtue. One remembers that Dolbreuse and his like were carried out of themselves by the speed of Parisian life and found no time to ponder on their actions. It is necessary to 's'entretenir avec soi-même' to sustain good conduct and retain one's integrity. To achieve this end one must live in an environment which allows the opportunities for meditation alien to large cities.

It would nonetheless be a mistake to suppose that Baculard is advocating a total retreat from social existence. Notwithstanding his use of the term 'solitude', he is employing it in the sense of tranquillity for self-knowledge, and therefore, proposes a life spent in a more limited and selected community: 'c'est d'elle [la société] que nous viennent la plupart de nos vices, de nos chagrins, de nos malheurs. Je n'entends pas par l'éloignement de la société, une retraite absolue, un détachement entier de tout ce qui nous environne: je veux du choix, de l'économie, de la sobriété dans nos liaisons.'[47] To foresake social intercourse would be self-destructive, man must inhabit some form of community, though to live in a densely populated environment invites corruption. Such would seem to be the 'message' of Baculard and most like-minded authors.

Paris was therefore depicted and condemned as depriving the provinces of resources and influential men. Once in the maw of the capital, provincial money was devoured by degrading pastimes and the pursuit of luxury. Parallel with the misuse of finances was the abuse of virtue. The advance of civilisation has stifled the natural, and therefore good, sentiments of the provincial with the superficial and vicious veneer of the Parisian. Moreover the Parisian has so depraved human nature that he enjoys nothing better than destroying provincial integrity. As the ultimate in perversity, the Parisian savours a campaign against virtue as an escape from general ennui. To counterbalance this bleak picture, the critical realism of post-1760 fiction began to paint a far more sympathetic portrait of provincial life than would have been conceivable in earlier years.

7. The superiority of the provinces

To see this radical change of perspective in the attitude to the provinces it is at first useful to examine the views of those who have experienced both modes of life, the returning provincials. In the works of the early century provincials return anxious to exhibit the superior gloss acquired in the capital. When the Comte de Courmont arrives in his Burgundian home: 'Il étala tout cet esprit de jargon qu'un provincial apporte mystérieusement de Paris pour le répandre avec éclat dans le sein de sa petite ville.'[1] This capacity confers on him an advantage over his competitors for the hand of the heroine who loves the less fashionable Chevalier de Nalbour in vain. Chevrier maintains here the traditional mockery of the provincial, a satirical intent he relishes elsewhere. In *Les Ridicules du siècle* of 1752 he jeers at people who spend a fruitless period in the capital only to boast of non-existent experiences back home:

Ici, c'est un jeune homme, l'idole d'une famille imbécile, qui, échappé de sa petite ville par le coche, vient dépenser mille écus à Paris pour aller exactement tous les jours d'une chambre garnie au café, du café à une table d'hôte, de là au parterre de la comédie, qu'il ne quitte que pour retourner au café; trop heureux, à la fin, de revoir sa triste patrie et d'y rapporter les noms des comédiens et une liste exacte de toutes les auberges.

Là, c'est un autre provincial, timide par sottise, qui, ne voulant pas courir les risques de la bonne compagnie, vient sans frais étudier le grand monde dans un cercle bourgeois, et ne retourne en province que pour aller dire chez madame la sénéchale, 'Que l'on vit à Paris, et qu'on végète ailleurs.'[2]

Indeed how could these prodigal sons go home and admit Paris had worked no magical transformations.

Magny's Justine indulges in the life of Paris without the author ever pointing out the vicious nature of her conduct. Nevertheless, in this novel of 1754, she finally gives up her stormy life: 'Enfin j'ai su profiter de ces leçons de l'adversité. L'inconstance du sort n'a servi qu'à m'ouvrir les yeux; j'abjure pour toujours un genre de vie qui n'est jamais sans amertume, et dont les suites sont toujours dangereuses.'[3] Now the barometer reads fair for the courtesan's retirement to her mother's home in the provinces, away from the uncertainties of the capital.

The post-1760 heroes and heroines will be glad to leave Paris and its pitfalls behind them. On a less serious plane, Mitouflet and Nicette are pleased to return to Basse Normandie in Nougaret's *Les Astuces de Paris*. The 'filous' had played outrageous tricks on them and their stay had been a continual round of dupery. They have acquired a certain lustre from their trip, but their most enriching experience is one of hard-earned wisdom! Their fellow Norman, Eraste, travels home in comparable mood in Charpentier's *L'Elu et son président*. He has failed to discover the exciting life he had dreamed of, and is now content to exercise his charges, seek a local bride, and recognise the virtues of his own province.

Some have drunk excessively at the fount of Parisian pleasures and have become sated with them. Since his arrival from Lyons, Saint-Gory has seduced Sophie, squandered large sums of money on actresses, and followed an empty routine:

Le tumulte du monde auquel je me livrai acheva bientôt de l'effacer [Sophie] de mon cœur. Mon âme rétrécie dans des cercles de coquettes mettait tout son bonheur à captiver ces fades intriguantes; mais le vide que je ressentais même au sein des plaisirs me fit abandonner Paris pour chercher un bonheur dont tout ce que je voyais n'était que l'image.[4]

Thereupon he visits other European countries and is involved in several romanesque adventures. Later he thinks about going back to Paris but realises: 'J'étais si dégoûté du monde et de ses vains plaisirs que je ne voulus point retourner à Paris. Je fus droit à Lyon pour me retirer dans mes terres' (p.147). The cavalcade of amusements in the capital has brought him no inner contentment, he regrets his behaviour and looks forward to the tranquillity of his estate.

Others recognise that Paris is not the abode of virtue and they desire to leave before they are infected. On the completion of his business transactions, Plémer offers Montalde a post in Nantes. The Breton wishes to dally no longer than is necessary and proclaims: 'L'air de Paris ne nous convient ni à l'un ni à l'autre; mes affaires y sont finies; mes adieux y sont faits; ma chaise est à deux places; partons demain pour Nantes.'[5] For Plémer, the capital is inimical to the retention of worthwhile qualities whilst Brittany offers a safe residence for solid values.

Alexis is a stout upholder of probity and yearns to wed Sophie despite her poverty. After initial reservations, Lysimon consents to the match and is honoured to welcome Alexis as a son-in-law. The marriage solemnised, there is only one suitable course of action, removal to the provinces; Sophie instigates this decision: 'Sophie avait les goûts trop naturels et trop vertueux pour se plaire dans un séjour aussi dispendieux que la capitale. Son humeur bienfaisante ne pouvait s'accomoder de ce faste aussi ridicule qu'inhumain, qui absorbait dans cette grande ville cette portion de nos revenus destinée au soulagement des malheureux.'[6] Paris is too costly both in moral and financial terms. It is better to employ their wealth in relieving the indigents of the countryside than dissipate it in exorbitant living in the city. Moreover, the frivolous Mme Bertrand is reformed by their example and alters her views: 'Cette vanité ridicule qui lui avait fait dédaigner la ville de ... comme un théâtre trop resséré pour tout l'éclat de ses charmes, n'était plus en elle qu'un objet de confusion et de repentir' (p.109). Their expectations of a superior life in the provinces are fulfilled, their change of surroundings brings true happiness.

Some provincials have of course suffered considerably in the capital. In Sade's *Le Président mystifié*, a magistrate from Aix has journeyed to Paris to obtain a bride. In time the wedding ceremony is performed but the marriage is never consummated. The bridegroom is subjected to manifold indignities as numerous tricks are played on him. Eventually he acquiesces in the dissolution of the marriage, bemoans his mishaps, and asks himself: 'ne pourras-tu pas trouver dans ta province une fille qui eût mieux valu que celle-ci et qui ne t'eût pas donné tant de peines? Tu l'as voulu, pauvre président, tu l'as voulu, mon ami, t'y voilà; un mariage de Paris t'a tenté, tu vois ce qu'il en résulte.'[7] Chastened, Fontanis sets off for Provence vowing never to contemplate matrimony in Paris again.

Bazile has learnt his lesson too. Baculard's hero has been coaxed away from his village by Rémi, Mme de Menneval's tutor. However he had only forsaken his home on the understanding that care would be taken of his widowed mother, Nicole, who had begged him to stay: 'Va, toutes ces riches dames de Paris ne savent pas, comme moi, ce que c'est que d'aimer son cher enfant' (*Bazile*, p.25). Once in the capital, Rémi had persuaded Mme de Menneval to pass Bazile off as her own son, a stratagem designed to ensure that her husband's inheritance did not revert to his family. Consequently Bazile was kept in seclusion to be tutored into the new role required of him. The method of instruction was typical of Paris: 'On attaque d'abord notre jeune villageois par tous les endroits faibles de l'humanité: on excite son orgueil; on lui insinue le fol amour de soi-même, la stupide vanité, le goût frivole de la parure' (p.39). Nevertheless Bazile still longed for the presence of his mother which forced Rémi to produce his trump card, Mlle d'Amérville. In yet another 'chance' encounter, the peasant met her strolling in a garden and was immediately smitten with her charms. Carried away by the prospect of marrying such a beauty, a rich 'parti' into the bargain, he finally agreed to do his utmost to counterfeit the Marquise's son.

Despite this resolution, he insisted on seeing his mother again. Nicole came to Paris wanting her son and not the worldly goods with which Rémi tries to suborn her. Conflict was renewed in Bazile's heart, this time between his devotion to his mother and his passion for Mlle d'Amérville. After a succession of tearful scenes Nicole consents to leave Paris and forget her last born. The nuptial proposals come to fruition and a decision is taken to celebrate the wedding a few miles from the capital. Among a crowd of peasants who had gathered to witness the ceremony was Nicole. Upon catching a glimpse of her, Bazile realised that he could no longer stifle 'la voix de la nature' and revealed before the assembly his true status and origins. Subsequently he is able to announce: 'Je renonce pour toujours à ce détestable Paris, à tout ce qui l'habite; je vais reprendre mes premiers habits, mon premier état et mon innocence avec eux' (p.113). The unveiling of his identity had relieved him of the burden of unnatural deception. Ever since his arrival in the capital he had been importuned and cajoled into assuming more and more false pretences and ideas. His rustic sincerity had been submerged under a welter of artificial niceties, he had exchanged his upright personality for an empty mask. Henceforward he will have no truck with the capital, for the provinces are the realm of virtue and the true expansion of sentiments.

Whilst in his debtors' prison, Dolbreuse receives a letter from the husband of the Comtesse he had so cowardly seduced. As the result of her adultery, she had fallen into a lethargy, Dolbreuse had even supposed her dead. However the note contains information indicating the Comtesse's recovery and the couple's imminent departure for the provinces: 'Nous partons pour nos terres, nous fuyons pour jamais cette ville maudite qui te rendit le prosélyte et l'égal du méchant' (*Dolbreuse*, ii.43). Paris had corrupted Dolbreuse who in turn had corrupted the Comtesse. She, after her recuperation, is about to leave the city, but what of her seducer? Loaisel's hero is experiencing the pangs of remorse and is disturbed at his wife's possible attitude. Ermance, as we have already shown, is compassionate and obtains his release. His first resolution is to quit this hotbed of iniquity as soon as possible (ii.63-64):

Nous partons enfin de la capitale, bien résolus de n'y rentrer de nos jours. Quand je vis un intervalle de plusieurs lieues entre moi et cette ville immense, je devins comme un homme qu'on vient d'arracher d'une mine, après un séjour de quelques années dans l'un de ces gouffres de l'espèce humaine. Le passage du chaos de Paris à la paix des campagnes, du tumulte des passions orageuses au calme des passions douces ... tout m'émeut, tout m'intéresse. Un air dégagé d'exhalaisons malfaisantes, un air salubre et rempli de matière éthérée vient agacer légèrement mes fibres détendues, leur donner de la tension et du ressort; il pénètre mes poumons, passe dans mon sang, et lui communique un mouvement uniforme et doux; il ranime en moi la flamme vitale, donne de l'expansion à mon âme, et répand un baume universel dans tout mon être.

Dolbreuse is delighted to pass through the city gates and experiences a feeling of liberty as he reaches the countryside. The air he breathes is pure, both literally and morally. One recognises an almost physical euphoria, a sensuous contemplation and imbibing of the surroundings where he will regain his former dignity and individuality.

To aid his reintegration into the calm of provincial life he retreats to a monastery for three months. There he enjoys long conversations on human frailty and divine beneficence with a sympathetic monk. He is now in a fit state to return to his wife, and their reunion is completed by the birth of a daughter – a symbol of his own renaissance. Dolbreuse goes on to extol his happy relationship with Ermance and compares it with the boredom experienced with the 'femmes du monde'.

At a later date they learn of Rousseau's death and propose a pilgrimage to his grave in Ermenonville. They are anxious to pay their respects to the memory of the great writer, yet do not plan the shortest itinerary for, as Dolbreuse explains:

Paris était sur notre route; mais nous nous détournâmes, pour ne point rencontrer cette ville funeste. En voyant de loin les brouillards qui s'élèvent au-dessus de ses tours et de ses édifices, je ne pus m'empêcher d'ouvrir mon cœur à de tristes souvenirs et de m'écrier: O Paris, ville de crimes et de misères! les vapeurs qui sortent de ton sein sont plus contagieuses que tous les levains de la peste, exerçant ses ravages, sont plus mortelles que tous ses poisons, troublant et infectant l'atmosphère dans ces temps de calamité.[8]

It is almost as if an aversion therapy has cured him. The sight of the physical exhalations of the capital incites a loathing of all connected with the city. He has truly recovered his provincial integrity and 'selfness'. Loaisel is emphasising that the rebirth of virtue can only be maintained by eschewing the capital. In the service of critical realism, Dolbreuse has suffered in Paris the better to praise the provinces.

A significant character presented as returning to the provinces in late eighteenth-century fiction is the landowner. Absenteeism, as we have shown, was much censured in some quarters and the novelist is reflecting current ideas when he depicts a landowner acknowledging the importance of agriculture to the nation. M. de Montalban has partaken of the pleasures that Parisian society offers yet has decided to retire to his estates. His so-called retirement is by no means synonymous with inactivity for he has been converted to the new doctrines concerning agriculture.[9] His visitors from the capital are stunned to see the transformation in his character. Whereas the ladies had expected to find Parisian entertainments continued in the usual manner of 'maisons de campagne', they discover their host exalting the laborious processes of cultivation. Montalban has realised the futility of his former life and is now engaged in a useful industry for the nation. The stimulation of rural pursuits has contributed something of both personal and public benefit to his life. Barbé-Marbois is using his novel as a vehicle for the critical presentation of contemporary society and ideas, Montalban's agricultural activities are inserted for a prescriptive purpose.

Similarly in the 'contes moraux' of Marmontel, we are offered portraits of beneficent landlords. Through vanity Bélise has ruined a liaison with Lindor and decides to retire to the country: 'Bélise fut anéantie, et prit dès ce moment le parti de renoncer au monde et de s'ensevelir à la campagne. Allons végéter, disait-elle, je ne suis bonne qu'à cela.'[10] She has the traditional forebodings of a dreary existence outside the capital but Marmontel has other plans for her. Near Bélise's estates are those of the Comte de Pruli: 'Dans le voisinage de cette campagne, était une espèce de philosophe dans la vigueur de l'âge, qui, après avoir joui pendant six mois de l'année à la ville, venait jouir six mois de lui-même dans une solitude voluptueuse.' Pruli is not a man to neglect his duties towards his land and peasants and enjoys the countryside. He describes his mode of life to his neighbour: 'Je vois quelquefois notre pasteur, à qui j'enseigne la morale; je cause avec des laboureurs plus instruits que tous nos savants: je donne le bal à de petites villageoises les plus jolies du monde; je fais pour elles des loteries de dentelles et de rubans; et je marie les plus amoureuses' (p.139). Bélise is surprised to learn of the contentment of the peasants when they are reputed to be so notoriously abused.

Now the moment is ripe for Marmontel to elucidate the actions of a true 'seigneur'. Being informed that the peasants' condition has improved considerably in comparison with previous years, Bélise asks for the secret behind this changed state of affairs and is told (pp.140-42):

J'ai quarante mille livres de rente; j'en dépense dix ou douze à Paris dans les deux saisons que j'y passe; huit ou dix dans ma maison de campagne; et pour cette économie, j'ai vingt mille livres à perdre sur les échanges que je fais. – Et quels échanges faites-vous? J'ai des champs bien cultivés, des prairies bien arrosées, des vergers clos et plantés avec soin. – Eh bien? – Eh bien! Lucas, Blaise, Nicolas, mes voisins et mes bons amis, ont des terrains en friche ou appauvris; ils n'ont pas de quoi les cultiver: je leur cède les miens troc pour troc; et la même étendue de terrain qui les nourrissait à peine, les enrichit dans deux moissons. La terre ingrate sous leurs mains devient fertile dans les miennes. Je lui choisis la semence, le plant, l'engrais, la culture qui lui convient, et dès qu'elle est en bon état, je pense à un nouvel échange: ce sont là mes amusements. Cela est charmant, s'écria Bélise: vous savez donc l'agriculture? – Un peu, madame; je m'en instruis; je confronte la théorie des savants avec l'expérience des laboureurs; je tâche de corriger ce que je vois de défectueux dans les spéculations des uns et des autres: c'est une étude amusante. – Oh! je le crois, et je veux m'y livrer aussi. Comment donc! Mais vous devez être adoré dans tous ces cantons; ces pauvres laboureurs doivent vous regarder comme leur père. – Oui, madame, nous nous aimons beaucoup.

Pruli does not pursue farming in traditional, out-dated ways but applies modern methods to cultivation and rearing.[11] True to an eighteenth-century empirical approach, he sets out to experiment with new ideas in practical ventures, modifies them through trial and error, and never forgets to consult the age-old expertise of the peasants.

The above extract illustrates that Marmontel is not portraying the land-owner/vassal relationship exclusively in an idyllic manner but in social and economic terms. The peasants are not created in a pastoral mould but are shown to need means of encouragement and subsistence. To further their well-being, Pruli has introduced other technical advances as his blossoming friendship with Bélise brings out (pp.144-45):

Leurs entretiens ne roulaient que sur l'étude de la nature, sur les moyens de rajeunir cette terre, notre vieille nourrice, qui s'épuise pour ses enfants. La botanique leur indiquait les plantes salutaires aux troupeaux, et celles qui leur étaient pernicieuses; la mécanique leur donnait des forces pour élever les eaux à peu de frais sur les collines altérées, et pour soulager le travail des animaux destinés au labourage; l'histoire naturelle leur apprenait à calculer les inconvénients et les avantages économiques, dans le choix de ces animaux laborieux. La pratique confirmait ou corrigeait les observations, et on faisait les expériences en petit, afin de les rendre moins coûteuses.

Bélise is impressed by the Comte's initiatives and his standing in the community: 'Mon amant, disait-elle en elle-même, est le dieu qui les encourage; son humanité, sa bienfaisance, sont comme des ruisseaux qui fertilisent ces champs. Elle aimait à s'entretenir avec les laboureurs, des bienfaits que répandait sur eux ce mortel qu'ils appelaient leur père' (pp.154-55). Pruli is indeed depicted in a paternalistic role, yet is in reality a combination of the old and the new. On the one hand he exemplifies the re-establishment of the traditional social structure of the countryside, on the other, he embodies the new ideas of agronomy, economics, and 'bienfaisance'. Marmontel does not suggest that the landowner remain the whole year on his estates but merely that he devote sufficient time and money to ensure that the land is well tilled and the peasant well fed.

The overtly paternalistic role of Pruli will receive amplification in *Le Misanthrope corrigé* of 1765. We remember that Molière's play ends with Alceste fleeing society. Marmontel's tale begins with him arriving in the provinces where he encounters happy peasants and learns that they no longer fear iniquitous taxation: 'Nous avions peur autrefois; mais, dieu merci, le seigneur du lieu nous a ôté cette inquiétude. Il fait l'office de notre bon roi: il impose, il reçoit lui-même; et au besoin il fait les avances. Il nous ménage comme ses enfants' (*Contes moraux*, v.99). Before long Alceste sees labourers toiling on the roads and is taken aback to discover they are paid and not exploited by the 'corvée'. This reform was also the feat of the local 'seigneur', the Vicomte de Laval: 'Alceste redoubla d'estime pour l'homme sage et bienfaisant qui gouvernait ce petit peuple. Qu'un roi serait puissant, disait-il, et qu'un état serait heureux, si tous les grands propriétaires suivaient l'exemple de celui-ci! Mais Paris absorbe et les biens et les hommes; il dépouille, il envahit tout' (v.101-102). Laval, however, has not limited his endeavours to lightening the burden of taxation and abolishing the hated 'corvée', he has also provided work for the unemployed. When labour is not required on the land, Alceste is informed, the peasants work in an 'atelier' established by their benefactor (v.103):

Notre bon seigneur, lui dit-on, en a fait les avances. C'était peu de chose d'abord, et tout se faisait à ses risques, à ses frais et à son profit; mais après s'être bien assuré qu'il y avait de l'avantage, il nous a cédé l'entreprise; il ne se mêle plus que de la protéger; et tous les ans, il donne au village les instruments de quelqu'un de nos arts; c'est le présent qu'il fait à la première noce qui se célèbre dans l'année.

Just like Pruli, Laval has been willing to experiment and defray the costs whatever the outcome of the enterprises.

Alceste is anxious to meet Laval who more than lives up to his expectations. This encounter affords Marmontel an opportunity to underline the evils of contemporary taxation and to suggest remedies through the good offices of a diligent landowner. Laval tells Alceste of the predicament of the people when he came to their aid (v.113-14):

Ce peuple, nouvellement conquis, se croyait perdu sans ressource; et dès que je lui ai tendu les bras, son désespoir l'y a précipité. A la merci d'une imposition arbitraire, il en avait conçu tant d'effroi, qu'il aimait mieux souffrir les vexations que d'annoncer un peu d'aisance. Les frais de la levée aggravaient l'impôt; ces bonnes gens en étaient excédés; et la misère était l'asile où les jetait le découragement. En arrivant ici, j'y trouvai établie cette maxime désolante et destructive des campagnes: Plus nous travaillerons, plus nous serons foulés. Les hommes n'osaient être laborieux, les femmes tremblaient de devenir fécondes. Je remontai à la source du mal.

At first Laval saw a 'préposé' without success but later tackled an 'intendant' who agreed to his requests. As a result, Laval himself paid the 'taille' and was reimbursed through the work of the peasants who could now produce greater profits without incurring extra taxation.[12]

The founding of the 'atelier' was designed to supplement the income of the peasant community but never to distract it from its primary endeavour, agriculture; Laval informs his visitor (v.117):

Enfin, comme il y avait ici bien du temps superflu et des mains inutiles, j'ai établi l'atelier que vous avez pu voir. C'est le bien de la communauté: elle l'administre sous mes yeux; chacun y travaille à la tâche; mais ce travail n'est pas assez payé pour détourner de celui des campagnes. Le cultivateur n'y emploie que le temps qui serait perdu. Le profit qu'on en tire est un fonds qui s'emploie à contribuer à la milice et aux frais des travaux publics. Mais un avantage plus précieux de cet établissement, c'est d'avoir fait naître des hommes. Lorsque les hommes sont à charge, on n'en fait qu'autant qu'on en peut nourrir; mais dès qu'au sortir du berceau ils peuvent se nourrir eux-mêmes, la nature se livre à son attrait sans réserve et sans inquiétude. On cherche des moyens de population, il n'en est qu'un, c'est la subsistance, l'emploi des hommes. Comme ils ne naissent que pour vivre, il faut leur assurer de quoi vivre en naissant.

The ideas expressed in the extracts from the 'contes moraux' are not of Marmontel's making but reflect the influence of the society he frequented. He is fictionalising ideas he had assimilated in conversing with fellow 'encyclopédistes' and reading works of agronomic and physiocratic inspiration. During his editorship in the late 1750s the *Mercure de France* devoted a great deal of space to articles on economic and technical matters.[13] Marmontel himself reviewed Mirabeau's *L'Ami des hommes* and Pattullo's influential *Essai sur l'amélioration des terres*.[14] In short Marmontel utilises these tales to show what could and should be done in the society of his day. If the depiction of happy peasants and their benevolent masters is idealised, it is because it contrasts sharply with the reality of contemporary life. Showing a landowner returning to benefit his estates and people, Marmontel points out the inadequacies of absenteeism and the attractive results of his own proposals.

The Marquise d'Herfilie has likewise settled on her provincial properties and refuses the overtures of friends begging her to come back to the capital. The Baronne de Cotyto chides her correspondent on her prolonged absence in a tone typical of the traditional attitude to the provinces: 'Je vous conseille fort de quitter votre antique château, et de revenir bien vite orner la capitale.'[15] The letter produces no effect on the Marquise who later writes to the Comtesse de Fionie: 'Je suis devenue absolument philosophe; j'aurais maintenant beaucoup de peine à me faire à la vie dissipée que l'on mène à Paris. Je fais travailler considérablement dans mon jardin.'[16] No more does she long for the frenzied socialising of Paris for she has discovered contentment in country pursuits in the confines of her provincial estates.

The esteem attached to agriculture gathered enormous momentum in the final years before the Revolution. Baculard's Gourville, who has lost his fortune in Paris, holds an exalted opinion of it: 'l'agriculture est la première et la plus noble d'occupations' (*Julie*, p.194). An illuminating observation is contained in Boufflers's *Aline, reine de Golconde*. Romanesque adventures have led the hero to the Utopian realm of Golconde. Here he discovers that the government is not bent on abusing its citizens and, more especially in this context: 'les gens de campagne y étaient retenus par l'abondance et la liberté qui y régnaient, et par les honneurs que le Gouvernement rendait à l'Agriculture' (p.13). The allusion to the contemporary situation and attitude in France is transparent. The enlightened administration of Golconde values its peasants by providing them with sufficient work and wages to meet their needs, and they, in turn, feel no impulsion driving them from their homes to seek subsistence in the towns – a pointed lesson for the French régime.

The soldier who has retired after an active career in the service of his country can do no better than return to his lands rather than dissipate his last years in Paris.[17] Emilie puts forward this suggestion in a letter to Laure: 'L'agriculture est, sans doute, une chose très estimable. Je la crois même une occupation digne d'un gentilhomme qui a payé son tribut à celle des armées.'[18] In youth the nobleman has brought glory to his homeland on the battlefield, in old age he can bring succour to its economy by ensuring that his fields are ploughed and his crops harvested.

The Marquis de Joinville has witnessed an inordinate number of deaths and considerable degradation during his lifetime. Age brings wisdom and he decides to retire to his family estates where his wife's name is revered. In the final letter of the work Mme Dosbrun relates to her daughter that the Marquis has left the court and town 'pour aller faire le bonheur de ses vassaux, à l'exemple de feu son épouse, dont la mémoire sera longtemps en vénération parmi les villageois de ses terres; réputation bien au-dessus de celle qu'on acquiert dans les villes où l'on vous oublie dès qu'on ne vous voit plus'.[19] People in a restricted community are in a position to appreciate the benevolence of their local landowner, and the latter will no doubt be touched by the gratitude they express in return.[20] In a far less exalted rank of the social hierarchy comes the hero of Ussieux's *Alexis* whose frankness costs him post after post before he succeeds in amassing a moderate fortune. Despite the conventional tenor of the tale until this point, the author then turns to the theme of agriculture. Alexis goes back to his village in the role of an 'homme bienfaisant' bent on aiding the indigent peasantry and stimulating the cultivation of its lands.

It will be manifest from the foregoing pages that not only was agriculture to be encouraged but its labourers to be respected. Doubtless the peasants and small farmers were incapable of sustaining high-brow conversations with their masters, but they possessed a fund of wisdom drawn from centuries of hard work and practical application.[21] These countrymen were not the ignorant, prattling characters so frequently portrayed in French comedies, but subjects endowed with valuable qualities such as a contentment with the necessary and a disinterest in superfluities. An idealised example of the behaviour of peasants towards their mistress is contained in *La Fin des amours de Faublas*. Mme de Lignolle and Faublas leave the capital for her estates where the Comtesse wishes to show her concern for those who live and toil on her land. News of their arrival brings many people to the château but the Comtesse refuses to receive the upstart nouveaux riches and an inept country squire boasting of his ancestry. Instead as Faublas recounts:

sa nombreuse cour se composa tout entière de ces hommes presque partout dédaignés et partout respectables, à qui la plupart des gens prétendus comme il faut ont persuadé que le premier des arts était un vil métier. Moins crédule et plus fortuné, chacun des honnêtes laboureurs que je voyais paraissait avoir la conscience de ses talents en particulier et, en général, le noble orgueil de son état. Tous montraient devant Mme de Lignolle une modeste assurance; tous étaient redevenus des hommes, depuis qu'une femme les avait protégés [...] Pressés autour de ma charmante maîtresse, les femmes l'accablaient de remerciements et d'éloges, les filles la couvraient de fleurs, les enfants se disputaient sa robe pour la baiser. Digne de l'amour qu'elle inspirait, Madame de Lignolle avait retenu tous les noms, elle adressait au vieux Thibaut un remerciement affectueux, à la bonne Nicole une obligeante question, un compliment flatteur à la jeune Adèle, une douce caresse au petit Lucas. Elle s'inquiétait avec intérêt des affaires communes: en vérité, vous eussiez dit une tendre mère tout à l'heure revenue au sein de son heureuse famille.[22]

Here indeed is a scene fit for the brush of Greuze, as Louvet illustrates both the 'bienfaisance' of the landowner and the dignity of the peasants.

Rousseau is a dedicated champion of the land and the peasants who work it. In a letter to Milord Edouard, Saint-Preux outlines the desires of Julie and Wolmar to keep the peasants in their native region; they are eager to:

contribuer autant qu'on peut à rendre aux paysans leur condition douce, sans jamais leur aider à en sortir. Les plus aisés et les plus pauvres ont également la fureur d'envoyer leurs enfants dans les villes, les uns pour étudier et devenir un jour des messieurs, les autres pour entrer en condition et décharger leurs parents de leur entretien. Les jeunes gens, de leur côté, aiment souvent à courir: les filles aspirent à la parure bourgeoise: les garçons s'engagent dans un service étranger; ils croient valoir mieux en rapportant dans leur village, au lieu de l'amour de la patrie et de la liberté, l'air à la fois rogue et rampant des soldats mercenaires, et le ridicule mépris de leur état; [...] on leur apprend à honorer leur condition naturelle en l'honorant soi-même; on n'a point avec les paysans les façons des villes; mais on use avec eux d'une honnête et grave familiarité, qui, maintenant chacun dans son état, leur apprend pourtant à faire cas du leur. Il n'y a point de bon paysan qu'on ne porte à se considérer lui-même, en lui montrant la différence qu'on fait de lui à ces petits parvenus qui viennent briller un moment dans leur village et ternir leurs parents de leur état.[23]

The peasant is encouraged to stay on the land since it is his *natural* environment. There he can live and maintain his family in well ordered circumstances and derive contentment from a worthy occupation.

Marmontel voices the same view in his representation of the peasants, Annette and Lubin, who live together in blissful harmony. To earn a living, they sell their wares in the city and are able to see their existence in perspective: 'Ils comparaient leur sort à celui des citoyens les plus opulents, et se trouvaient plus heureux et plus sages.'[24] They appreciate that the necessities of their daily routine are more conducive to happiness than the extravagances demanded by the urban inhabitant.

Happiness was of course a topic under widespread discussion in the eighteenth century,[25] and prose fiction in the later part of the era associated it increasingly with the country. The author of *Le Cultivateur* has the Comte de Meilzuns inform the Parisian Lindor (pp.69-70):

c'est dans nos champs qu'habite le bonheur, ou du moins cette paix de l'âme, qui seule peut tenir lieu aux faibles mortels de la chimère qu'ils nomment et qu'ils n'attraperont jamais. Suis l'habitant des villes dans ces prisons où il resserre son être; tu le trouveras flétri par l'ennui, s'il est oisif; et s'il ne l'est pas, accablé de travaux sédentaires, malsains; tremblant à toutes ces petites révolutions des états qui peuvent l'écraser, puisque tous ses biens sont dans la main des hommes. D'un autre côté, regarde le cultivateur ayant ses richesses dans le sein de la terre, ne craignant que ces grands événements qu'amène à peine une longue suite de siècles, et qui souvent ne change rien à son sort.

The juxtaposition of the security and continuity of country life with the uncertainty and vicissitudes of the large town brings into relief the importance of stability in the psychological make-up of most people. The provinces are thus the best environment for a contented outlook on life. Lindor is proselytised by this argument of Meilzuns and weds the Comte's daughter as if to underline his conversion. Even his cynical companion, the Marquis de S., ends up admiring the advantages of the provinces for: 'le plaisir peut naître quelquefois dans le tumulte des villes; mais le bonheur ne se trouve jamais que dans la paix de la campagne'.[26] The Marquis acknowledges that pleasure and happiness are not synonymous; his former delight in the amusements brought him temporary diversion but not true happiness.

La Nouvelle Héloïse contains a letter from Saint-Preux to Bomston which is full of informative comments (pp.534-35):

La condition naturelle à l'homme est de cultiver la terre et de vivre de ses fruits. Le paisible habitant des champs n'a besoin pour sentir son bonheur que de le connaître. Tous les vrais plaisirs de l'homme sont à sa portée [...] Quand il est question d'estimer la puissance publique, le bel esprit visite les palais du prince, ses ports, ses troupes, ses arsenaux, ses villes: le vrai politique parcourt les terres et va dans la chaumière du laboureur.

Disregarding the second part of the extract where Rousseau claims that the people in their simple chores are more indicative of the state of a nation than its ostentation of power and finery, let us analyse the first. In Rousseau's view the rural inhabitant has no need to reflect on a formula for happiness, he knows it as a natural element of his own existence. Town-dwellers fail to achieve any real happiness if they are obliged to ponder on the means to attain it. It must indeed be an unhappy people which is so preoccupied by happiness.

The superiority of the provinces flourishes as a theme in a host of minor works published after 1760. Musset's Marquis enthuses over his discovery of nature at Clerfontaine. Were it not for his mother, he would no longer think of the capital:

Si vous n'habitiez pas Paris, je n'y penserais jamais. J'ai ici tout ce qu'il peut m'offrir de séduisant. A ses spectacles, j'oppose le paysage qui m'environne; à ses concerts, celui des rossignols qui semblent avoir affectionné l'allée sombre où je vais rêver; au lieu de ses ballets, j'ai les danses de nos jeunes paysannes; au lieu de ses festins somptueux, j'ai les productions simples, mais saines, de la nature. J'y trouve un cœur et des sens nouveaux.[27]

The simple pastimes of the Berry easily surpass those of the sophisticated capital. The Marquis much prefers to dance in the genuinely gay company of village maidens than in the elaborate surroundings of a ball.[28] He is astonished at the joy he experiences: 'Tout contribue à mon bonheur; je ne croyais pas le plaisir si facile à trouver. On le paye si cher à Paris, et on le goûte si rarement! A la campagne, on l'a sous la main et il ne coûte rien' (p.42). The countryside imbues its inhabitants with immediate satisfactions which are either impossible or at best rare in Paris.

The Marquise d'Herfilie has comparable sentiments and her provincial sojourn is an acquaintanceship with what is of real value in life. Gacon-Dufour strives to wax lyrical to convey his heroine's emotions: 'De grandes prairies toujours nouvelles et rafraîchies par les eaux qui descendent des collines voisines, une quantité prodigieuse de hameaux et de villages, un passage continuel de bateaux, offrent sans cesse à mes yeux un tableau bien plus riant que vos fêtes de Paris, où le luxe et la magnificence éblouissent les yeux sans toucher le cœur.'[29] Mme d'Herfilie enjoys exercising her 'sensibilité' and knows that Parisian society cannot afford her such multiple opportunities. The prodigality of the capital pales beside the natural wealth of the countryside.

Yet another marquise echoes these feelings. The Marquise de Ben** is attempting to dissipate her sadness in Paris as the result of a friend's counsel. She discovers, however, that it is by no means a suitable place:

Tous ces plaisirs que Paris nous offre et que vous m'ordonnez de chercher, ce tourbillon du monde, cette vie dissipée, ces bals, ces spectacles, ces assemblées brillantes, en un mot, ces soupers que vous me peignez si charmants, tout cela ne remplit point mon cœur [...] Une matinée passée dans les charmantes prairies de votre habitation est mille fois plus agréable pour moi que dix heures de Paris.[30]

Residence in a rural ambience would be a more satisfactory remedy as the marquise would have time to sort out her problems without being bothered by the pressures of society.[31]

The freedom in the provinces to have time to oneself constitutes a major argument in their favour. Without periods of reflection, it is impossible to be 'oneself', to enjoy one's individuality, and not to be enmeshed as a cog in the machine of society. Rousseau censures the depersonalising experience of mass groups with their mass identification labels. Wolmar expresses the author's views: 'Le judicieux Wolmar trouve dans la naïveté villageoise des caractères plus marqués, plus d'hommes pensant par eux-mêmes, que sous le masque uniforme des habitants des villes où chacun se montre comme sont les autres plutôt que comme il est lui-même.'[32] The uniformity of manners, ideas, judgements which are characteristic of the citizens of the capital is alien as a concept and in practice to a true provincial.

After his invigorating return to Brittany, Dolbreuse appreciates the calm of his childhood surroundings and its salubrious atmosphere (*Dolbreuse*, ii.100):

On n'y est ni sage par nécessité, ni fou par complaisance; jamais fatigué par les ennuyeux à prétension, affadi par les flatteurs, excédé par des sots et surtout par cette foule d'ignorants présomptueux qui abondent dans les grandes villes, et particulièrement dans la capitale; l'on n'y est pas choqué de l'insolence du vice, révolté de ses excès, si effrayé de sa punition.

Away from the importunates of Parisian society one can develop one's personality in tune with the regular tempo of provincial life. Loaisel de Tréogate is advocating the provinces as a wholesome alternative to over-sophisticated cities.

Miss de Tobers is another who cherishes country existence as the sole location appropriate for the cultivation of one's 'selfness'. From Béziers she writes to Célidor of her home-coming: 'Me voilà enfin de retour chez moi, mon ami; j'ai revu mon habitation avec un plaisir que je ne puis vous exprimer. Mon séjour à Paris m'a fait doublement sentir le bonheur d'être rendu à soi-même.'[33] It is as if during her stay in the capital she had had to dissemble her real character only to set it free anew in the provinces.

Outside Paris, in the small towns and countryside, people are able to enjoy a frankness which indicates the true expression of sentiment. It is no wonder, then, that friendship is a bond of inestimable value between provincials, untainted by the malice so common in Parisian relationships. Voltaire's Colin shows his quality when he rescues Jeannot and his family after their ruin in the capital: 'toutes les grandeurs de ce monde ne valent pas un bon ami [...] nous vivrons gaiement dans le coin de terre où nous sommes nés' (*Jeannot et Colin*, p.136). Notwithstanding Jeannot's disdain for his provincial friend while he was revelling in Paris, Colin is generous enough to forgive him and reveal the continuing strength of friendship.

A quality which is part and parcel of friendship is gratitude. Whereas the city dweller resents help and advice as an insult to his capacities, his country cousin is always ready for aid and, moreover, remembers it gratefully. The Doyen Bridel asserts: 'A la campagne, où les mœurs sont moins corrompues, où la soif de l'or, l'avidité, l'intérêt ne règnent pas avec tant de fureur; on oublie rarement les faveurs qu'on a reçues: mais à la ville, à la ville, on s'en moque, on en rit.'[34] Gratitude and mutual service are a normal feature of small groups where community spirit forms an integral part of daily life.

The provinces allow the full development of one's 'sensibilité',[35] natural instincts are more acute and can be enjoyed extensively. Paternal devotion is an example which Baculard underlines: 'L'amour paternel a des douceurs qui sont encore plus senties dans la retraite que dans le fracas des villes' (*Julie*, p.195).

Julie's father delights in an even closer relationship with his daughter after their removal from the capital.

Virtue is an essential feature of a provincial's character which may not be exclusively the gift of nature but can be aided by an excellent upbringing. Girls are not encouraged to acquire a lack-lustre personality like their Parisian counterparts:

A Paris, comme la prétension de former à son gré le caractère d'une jeune femme est la chimère de tous les maris, l'attention de toutes les mères est d'élever leurs filles dans un état de réserve et de dissimulation qui ne laisse rien voir de décidé en elles [...] En province on n'a pas le même soin de tenir caché le naturel d'une jeune personne; et ce n'est pas pour elle une règle de bienséance de garder le secret de son âme et de son esprit.[36]

Here again one notes the attack on uniformity as a Parisian characteristic. The girl in the provinces, it seems, would be granted far greater liberty to mature her own 'selfness'. Moreover let no-one think that Parisian 'demoiselles' enjoy a superiority over their provincial sisters: 'Il y a des familles très anciennes qui ne sont jamais sorties de leur province, et qui sont heureuses. Leur éducation n'en a pas été plus négligée. Vous connaissez madame de Brie [...] elle a quatre filles, qui feraient honte à bien des habitantes de la capitale: elles n'y ont pourtant jamais été, ni leur mère non plus.'[37] The provincial 'demoiselle' is in fact a composite of traditional virtue and the better qualities of the capital.

If the moral climate of the country was superior, so indeed was the level of health. A sane mind was paralleled by a robust constitution. A Parisian marquise is horrified at the lack of refinement in the country, yet is dismayed to discover the health of the local population. An innkeeper's wife reveals their recipe: 'Nous ne nous écoutons pas; nous travaillons, et pardi si vous en faisiez autant, vous vous porteriez bien, mais dame aussi: vous seriez plus heureuses que nous, ce qui ne serait pas juste.'[38] In addition they enjoy their tasks. The same lady is informed by Jeannot: 'notre travail est rude, nous en convenons; mais nous le faisons de bon cœur: nous ne connaissons pas la trahison, l'ingratitude'.[39] Their manners may be boorish, their clothes inelegant, but they are engaged in furthering the natural processes of life, they would have no time for the back-biting of Parisian society. The peasant obtains dignity from his work; Lucile understands Micholle's predilection for finery but prefers her own situation: 'Je respecte votre goût, lui répondait Lucile; mais les habits du travail, un teint sillonné à la sueur et les fatigues sont plus du mien qu'une livrée fastueuse, qu'un air bouffi de paresse et de luxe.'[40] Again we are told that the country dweller is satisfied by the necessary and has no interest in the superfluous.

A provincial upbringing is most healthy for children, and their abundance is a sign of their parents' contentment with their lot. Faublas points out to Mme de Lignolle: 'Mais voyez donc, madame la comtesse, comme ces paysannes sont jolies. – Et comme ces jeunes gens ont bonne mine, me répondit-elle. Vraiment je suis tentée de croire qu'il se fait ici beaucoup d'enfants, et de beaux enfants, parce que les pères sont contents de leur sort.'[41] Faublas is in no doubt about his mistress's conjecture since the peasants are under her benign régime and feel free to procreate without worrying about finding sufficient subsistence.

The growing appeal of the provinces in fiction brought portrayals of Parisians leaving the city to sample the benefits. The Baron d'Olban is bored with his old routine: 'J'ai quitté Paris, mon cher Lurset, et je passerai quelques mois au château de M. de Théville. Je retrouve enfin la nature: tout offre ici cette heureuse innocence, et cette naïve simplicité qu'on s'efforce d'écarter à la ville; ici l'on fait aimer, à Paris l'on ne fait que peindre l'amour.'[42] D'Olban's theories are proved correct for it is not long before he is smitten with the charms of his host's daughter and a story of true love commences. Taking into account the moral and physical superiority of the provinces anyone who leaves them would indeed be very foolish. It is therefore the express aim of the post-1760 writers to urge provincials to stay in their homes. Dolbreuse apostrophises (pp.125-26):

Nobles qui vivez dans des châteaux: honnêtes gens qui, loin des villes, habitez des maisons commodes et riantes! craignez qu'un vain espoir de fortune ne vous arrache de vos tranquilles demeures, et ne vous fasse aller chercher au loin un bonheur que vous ne trouverez que chez vous. Fuyez le concours des peuples pervertis par le luxe et l'ambition; fuyez, comme un repaire de serpents, le séjour des cités, d'où l'on ne rapporte jamais que des malheurs et des habitudes dépravées, et persuadez-vous bien qu'il est plus avantageux pour le repos et la vertu d'habiter une cabane que de vivre dans le palais des Rois.

These noblemen are exhorted to remain in the ancestral homes and to leave only to fight for king and country.

Delacroix proffers similar advice in his *Lettres d'un philosophe sensible*. Montendre deprecates Paris and pleads: 'Habitants des campagnes, qui vivez heureux et tranquilles, restez à jamais dans vos foyers. Préférez le repos, l'aisance, la liberté à l'inquiétude, à la gêne, aux tourments: n'approchez point de cette ville où les humiliations, et peut-être bientôt la misère empoisonneraient vos moments' (p.200). The capital has nothing, in Montendre's eyes, to offer someone at liberty to enjoy the reality of the countryside.

Throughout his *Epreuves du sentiment* Baculard is at pains to warn against the dangers of the city. He is particularly fond of placing counsel in the mouths of wise parents. Bazile receives such caution from the lips of his dying father: 'Surtout, je te recommende expressément, ne vas point quitter le village pour aller demeurer à la ville; on dit qu'il y a là ni probité, ni religion.'[43] The village and small town provide all that is necessary for a good life, so why should anyone desire more? All things considered, in the estimation of these authors, man is judged happiest in his natural element. Julie de Wolmar makes sure that her workers are contented, for transplantation will wreak disastrous results: 'La grande maxime de Mme de Wolmar est donc de ne point favoriser les changements de condition, mais de contribuer à rendre heureux chacun dans la sienne, et surtout d'empêcher que la plus heureuse de toutes, qui est celle du villageois dans un état libre, ne se dépeuple en faveur des autres' (*La Nouvelle Héloïse*, p.536). Restif puts forward this point of view in the most succinct manner when he declares that our true Eden: 'est partout où l'homme est né: c'est le sol natal qui est notre paradis terrestre'.[44] Those who are raised in a community are more likely to be happily integrated than those who uproot themselves. Furthermore if this community is dominated by a virtuous code of conduct, as is the case of the provinces, it is the ideal environment.

The post-1760 novelists can thus be seen to have transformed the literary presentation of the provinces. Their predecessors had either mocked them or accorded them no attention at all. The provinces were now portrayed as possessing all the worthwhile human qualities, health, happiness, and virtue. Moreover the later writers wished their readership to be practically influenced by their works and therefore depicted the consequences of a move or return to the country. The appeal to landowners is not to disinterest but to an enjoyment of 'bienfaisance' and traditional relationships. As critics of society, these authors are proposing constructive remedies to contemporary ills.

Conclusion

THE relationship between Paris and the provinces is clearly an important theme in eighteenth-century prose fiction. How, then, can we sum up the presentation of this relationship both in its historical context and relate it to the development of the novel? Inheriting the disdain for the provinces from the literature of the preceding era, Paris continued frequently to be portrayed in a favourable light. However from around 1760 we find a changing attitude to the capital which gathered momentum until the Revolution.

To illustrate this contention, let us look at the work of Marivaux and Restif. In Marivaux's major novels we are presented with the experiences of a stranger in Paris. The city is a backcloth utilised to bring out the dawning of Marianne's and Jacob's self-awareness. Their trials and tribulations are depicted to develop their characters and *not* to convey a comprehensive picture of the influence of the capital. Marivaux's young hero and heroine are in the process of forming their own personalities and their creator is above all interested in exploring this subtle maturation. With Restif the newcomer is imbued with a set of virtuous principles, he has nothing to learn of personal value in life. Marianne will pierce Climal's evil designs, overcome them and, at the same time, give evidence of her native vanity. Climal is a hypocrite who represents, no doubt, a Parisian type, but who is not an incarnation of the city's values. Ursule, in Marianne's position, would have taken the bait and succumbed to Climal's overtures. Her fall would not have been solely the triumph of her seducer, but the result of the corruption of Paris. Similarly, Jacob's affairs with the society ladies cause him no anguish, no real soul-searching, but are merely stepping-stones to success. Edmond would have been gradually demoralised by this procedure, he would have compromised his provincial virtue and would, in his earlier days, have felt remorse.

Why is there this difference? To claim that Marivaux was interested in characterisation and Restif was not is a travesty of the truth. On the other hand, to assert that Restif was interested in social pressures and Marivaux was not is likewise untrue. The real reason lies somewhere in between the two propositions. For Marivaux Paris was first and foremost a suitable milieu for literary invention, while for Restif it was a vehicle for social comment.

If in Magny's *Mémoires de Justine* (1754) the heroine is corrupted by Paris, it is to introduce a series of stories, it is merely to entertain the reader. When Restif's Ursule is depraved by Paris, it is to present the reader with social instruction. A good moral with critical intent has replaced a good tale aimed at diversion. Paris is no longer portrayed as the zenith of civilisation, but as the nadir of nature. If the virtuous provincial is perverted by the Parisian, it is because the latter has moved too far away from natural surroundings, it is because he has acquired an artificial 'nature'. Man is no more considered the victim of original sin, but the victim of civilised vice.

If man has been undermined by the march of civilisation, and therefore urbanisation, his intellectual arrogance must be apportioned blame, hence the attack on 'philosophie'.[1] All man needs to know is in the natural appreciation of simple values, his goodness or at least his potentiality for the good is an immanent trait of each individual. The post-1760 novel is consequently directed in its evaluation of our theme into a social instrument of vulgarisation, its justification is less its authenticity than its intent. Whereas there is already a certain social criticism in Crébillon fils, even in Marivaux, this malaise is implicit, but in Restif and his contemporaries it is of an overt and explicit order. Jacques Rustin writes of the libertine novelists of the early part of the century:

Ils se sentent portés à être d'abord des moralistes, non pas tant parce que la morale leur importe, que parce qu'ils ne veulent rien perdre d'un spectacle qui les amuse. Ils ne dénoncent pas vraiment la corruption; ils la montrent, ils l'étalent, la répandent, s'en font les complices, et leurs indignations sont suspectes, ou, à tout le moins, sans importance.[2]

The post-1760 novelists will convey far more conviction in their moral commentaries on the society of their day.

This shift of emphasis did not arise in a vacuum. On the contrary, it stems from the controversies of the day. The eighteenth century, possibly more than most ages, questioned its values, its morality, its 'sacred cows'. In an era which saw the undermining of Cartesianism by sensationalism, often exchanged Christianity and anthropormorphic conceptions of God for deism and atheism, there was evidently an atmosphere of turbulent debate. Moreover such radical alterations created an epoch of uncertainty where even profound thinkers such as Diderot and Rousseau were frequently unable to distinguish between private and public good, making synonymous contradictory interests. This ambience of uncertainty questioned the very foundations of civilisation, the origin of society, and increasingly the place of the individual in society.

It is neither our task nor in our competence to chart these thorny questions but to point out their relevance to our own topic.[3] If society was not created in accordance with divine law, the meliorists argued that it could be refashioned into a more favourable structure. For some the increasing pace of urbanisation was manifestly disadvantageous to the commonweal. Leading this group in economic terms were the physiocrats who, as we have indicated, saw agriculture as the primary source of wealth. Understandably, they viewed absentee landlords and poverty-stricken peasants abandoning the soil as a disaster for the nation. In addition, the multitude of fallow fields constituted a threat to any hope of reviving France's sagging economy.

To mention agriculture and the countryside leads us to a brief consideration of Rousseau. In his attacks on large towns he used Paris as his prinicipal target. People confined in crowded communities lost their 'selfness' and natural characteristics to exchange them for artificial, uniform appearances. His works contain an indictment of civilisation without seriously positing the 'bon sauvage' as a viable alternative. What he advocated was a return to a simpler mode of existence based on the necessities and not the superfluities of life. Since his influence was widespread, it is no wonder that many minor writers we have discussed either interpreted or misinterpreted his ideas as the case may be. Understood or not, the outline of Rousseau's theories was propounded to the advantage of the countryside and to the detriment of Paris.[4]

In what measure were the works we have read and cited reflecting a real provincial migration to the capital? Historically speaking, this is a vexed question. In fiction the provincials are usually young noblemen, sons and daughters of rich bourgeois, and occasionally peasants. Their motivation for travelling to Paris is frequently to search for pleasure but also to 'faire fortune'.[5] But did the provinces send droves of its inhabitants to the capital? The majority of contemporary observers certainly thought so. Let Ange Goudar be their spokesman: 'Il y a près de cent mille étrangers qui font leur résidence dans cette capitale; c'est-à-dire cent mille Français qui ont quitté d'autres villes, villages, bourgs, hameaux de différentes parties du royaume, pour établir leur domicile dans cette ville.'[6] This exodus was deemed a pernicious influence over the rest of the nation, particularly in relation to agriculture and rural depopulation:

Ce tas prodigieux d'hommes assemblés dans un même lieu, affaiblit l'activité de la culture générale des terres.

Il n'y a que les environs de nos principales villes qui s'en ressentent; la plupart des autres cantons de l'Etat demeurent en friche.

Ces cent mille sujets, répandus géométriquement dans les différents districts du royaume, en feraient vivre, par l'Agriculture, cent mille autres.[7]

If only this enormous number of immigrants could be induced to go back to their provinces, they would provide either as workers or consumers a stimulus of inestimable value to agriculture.

Goudar's attack is uncompromising and he goes on to denounce the parasitical appetite of Paris: 'Une ville immense s'est élevée; elle a englouti le royaume. Paris est aujourd'hui le lieu de l'Assemblée générale de la nation, le congrès universel de ses peuples, une seconde Rome, qui avait tous ses citoyens dans ces murailles. Bientôt il n'y aura plus d'Etat; Paris sera le royaume' (p.36). This is a sweeping condemnation of the effect of Paris and conveys an anxiety about the future of the nation unless something is done to stem the tide.

Nevertheless, however eloquent these passages of Goudar may be, we believe his claims may be exaggerated. It was common among many thinkers in the eighteenth century to suppose that France was suffering from depopulation; this assumption has proved to be a fallacy. Could it be that those who worried about a large provincial emigration were likewise deluded?[8] In any case, the important point is that these authors believed in this shift of population and wrote accordingly, wishing to accomplish their public duty by underlining a social evil.

The theme of Paris and the provinces was not confined to prose fiction in eighteenth-century France. If one looks for similar developments in the theatre and poetry, one can certainly adduce affinities. The tradition of mocking the provincial survived well into the century and is evidenced in Voltaire's *Le Comte de Boursoufle ou mademoiselle de la Cochonnière* (1734). The Baron greets a chevalier by exclaiming: 'Par Henri IV: voilà un gentilhomme tout à fait de mise. Tête-bleu! monsieur le comte, Thérèse sera heureuse. Corbleu! touchez là; je suis votre beau-père et votre ami' (act I, sc. 3). His daughter, Thérèse, dreams of marriage and removal to the capital: 'Me voilà mariée, me voilà comtesse, me voilà à Paris! [...] Premièrement, une grande maison magnifique, et des diamants, et des perles comme s'il en pleuvait, et six grands laquais, et l'Opéra tous les jours, et toute la nuit à jouer, et tous les jeunes gens amoureux de moi, et toutes les femmes jalouses! La tête me tourne, la tête me tourne de plaisir' (act II, sc. 4). Mlle de La Cochonnière will marry anyone who will take her to Paris; her obsessional desires make her utterly ridiculous.

The usual jibes are still found in Gresset's *Le Méchant* (1747). Valère propounds the supremacy of Paris to Géronte (act III, sc. 9):

> On peut vous rendre un homme aimable,
> Mettre votre maison sur un ton convenable,
> Vous donner l'air du monde au lieu des vieilles mœurs,
> On ne vit qu'à Paris, et l'on végète ailleurs.

Nonetheless there is a certain shift of emphasis already emerging in this play, Parisian manners are criticised and the provincial does not lose by it.

Marivaux's *La Provinciale* (1761) is a rather conventional piece. Mme Riquet has arrived in Paris and, through vanity, changed her name to the Marquise La Thibaudière. She is ashamed of her country cousin, M. Lormeau, who gives no sign of culture or refinement. Her disdain is augmented by the glib tongue of Mme Lépine (sc. 8):

MME LÉPINE   Ha! que ce gentilhomme est grossier, marquise! que monsieur votre cousin est campagnard!

MME LA THIBAUDIÈRE   Ha! d'un campagnard, d'un rustique!

As usual the provincial does not wish to show her ignorance of good manners, but she does find herself in a quandary when she receives a 'billet doux' from a casual acquaintance (sc. 8):

MME LA THIBAUDIÈRE   C'est-à-dire que ma difficulté est encore un reste de barbarie. Ah! maudite éducation de province, qu'on a peine à se défaire de toi! Sachez donc que parmi nous on ne peut recevoir un billet doux du premier venu sans blesser les bonnes mœurs.

CATHOS   Dame! oui, voilà ce que la vertu de chez nous en pense.

MME LÉPINE   La plaisante superstition! Quel rapport y a-t-il d'une demi-feuille de papier à de la vertu?

CATHOS   Quand ce serait une feuille tout entière?

MME LA THIBAUDIÈRE   Que voulez-vous? j'arrive, à peine suis-je débarquée, et je sors du pays de l'ignorance crasse.

MME LÉPINE   Renvoyez un billet! vous seriez perdue; il n'y aurait plus de réputation à espérer pour vous. A Paris, manquez-vous de mœurs? on en rit, et on vous le pardonne. Manquez-vous d'usage? vous n'en revenez point, vous êtes noyée.

A plot is afoot to filch money from Mme La Thibaudière, to purchase a fictitious regiment for the Chevalier de La Trigaudière. In the nick of time M. Lormeau arrives in the company of M. Derval, his cousin's suitor. The latter unmasks the false Chevalier and La Thibaudière, realising she has been duped, ends the play by affirming: 'Adieu, je vais me cacher dans le fond de ma province' (sc. 23). This one-act piece centres on the traditional misfortune and gullibility of a stranger at the hands of Paris, though, in Lormeau, we are presented with an upright man.

If the novels and short stories of the last decades before the Revolution show a growing trend to praise the provinces over the capital, the new genre, the 'drame', will do likewise. Instead of the preoccupation with the aristocracy and the noble passions of tragedy, or the mocking of the bourgeoisie in comedy, the 'drame' will portray the virtues of the less privileged classes. Having talked of the natural goodness of man in one context, Félix Gaiffe proceeds to illustrate it in another:

La même conception philosophique fera sans cesse opposer les vertus de la campagne aux vices de la ville, les qualités solides des classes laborieuses à la malsaine frivolité des heureux de ce monde. Voilà pourquoi le drame offre à notre admiration tant de bergers candides, de bergères innocentes, d'ouvriers vertueux, d'indigents héroïques: laboureurs saluant, les yeux mouillés de larmes, le lever de l'astre du jour par un hymne reconnaissant à l'Etre suprême, villageoises accortes et décentes, respectueuses de l'autorité paternelle et fidèles au jeune pasteur que leur cœur a choisi.[9]

The provinces are no longer treated with derision, since their inhabitants contribute far more to the commonweal than the luxury-loving citizens of the capital.

If Diderot was the pre-eminent theorist of the 'drame', and Sedaine's *Le Philosophe sans le savoir* (1765) its masterpiece, Mercier was certainly its most prolific exponent. He attacks the corrupt values of his day and in *Le Campagnard ou le riche désabusé* (1779) he sets out to prove the advantages of country existence over that of the capital: 'On a voulu peindre le nouvel état de l'homme raisonnable et détrompé, qui, ayant su préférer les beautés de la campagne aux décorations artificielles de la ville, a oublié, en présence du spectacle majestueux de la nature, les misères pompeuses dont brillent les cités' (p.iii). In the provinces, the new, right-thinking man can survey the panorama of nature which 'lui inspire sans doute des idées plus graves et plus saines que n'en font naître les chimères mouvantes, dont se repaît l'avide oisiveté du prisonnier des villes, plus distrait qu'amusé, plus fatigué dans ses plaisirs que satisfait' (pp.iii-iv). Urbanisation has created artificial problems and anxieties for the human race; man is disorientated in a complex society and yearns for simplicity. Outside the city, man is content to *be* and harbours no desires to *become*: 'Débarassé du poids importun des affaires, loin de la gêne et de la sollicitude des sociétés, il [l'homme] n'a plus cette inquiétude secrète qui ronge l'ambitieux, poursuivant le fantôme de la fortune dans l'air empoisonné des villes' (p.v). Mercier goes on, in his foreword, to complain at the lack of respect paid to farmers who till the soil and are the mainstay of the nation.

The play itself centres on the reactions to, and of, two Parisian ladies in the provinces. Jeannot is asked by one of them if he would like to serve in Paris (act I, sc. 3):

s'il faut vous le dire, un sarreau de toile nous habille tout aussi bien qu'un habit rouge et vert; Dieu ne nous a pas donné des bras pour jouer incessamment aux cartes dans une antichambre, ou bien des membres pour nous tenir debout derrière un carrosse, et sautiller là sur la pointe du pied devant tous les passants qui se mettent à rire [...] Nous ne voulons pas du nom de domestique; nous pensons que celui de laboureur ou de vigneron vaut beaucoup mieux.

We are presented with a criticism of servants suggesting it is more dignified to toil in the fields than to accomplish petty tasks and be at the beck and call of Parisian whims. Toinette is delighted at Jeannot's resolution and protests at the continual rape of the provincial population: 'Mais, voyez donc ces gens de Paris qui viennent comme ça vous enlever tous les garçons du village, tantôt pour le Roi et la guerre, tantôt pour le service de ces grandes dames parées ... Dis-moi, est-ce que le monde entier est fait pour ce maudit Paris?' (act 1, sc. 9). The tentacles of the capital are sucking the very life-blood from the provinces without offering any compensatory benefits.

The Parisian visitors hope to find some metropolitan sense in the company of the local landowner. Bourval, however, has foresaken his Parisian pastimes, is a convert to physiocratic theory, and treats the ladies to an exposition on his agrarian interests. They inform him of their eventual destination, Pau, where they expect to enjoy themselves by flaunting their Parisian superiority. These expectations provoke a sarcastic observation from their host: 'Mais vous serez en province; il n'est pas possible de s'y amuser; il n'y a là ni goût, ni esprit, ni lumière, ni sentiment; il n'y a de tout cela qu'à Paris; les provinciaux ne sont plus des hommes [...] Cela, n'est-il pas reçu dans quelques assemblées de beaux esprits de la capitale?'[10] Finally convinced that they will discover no amusement at this turncoat's home, the ladies depart, much to everyone's undisguised relief.

We have chosen to cite this text since we have discovered it has similarities with, indeed borrowings from, two novels we have discussed which are dissimilar in other respects, namely Barbé-Marbois's *La Parisienne en province* and Barthe's *La Jolie femme*. In common with Mercier's play the novels record the visit of two ladies to an old Parisian friend. In Barbé-Marbois's work, Mme de Migneville and Mme de Mélicourt visit M. de Montalban and expect to enjoy the normal Parisian pleasures associated with a 'maison de campagne'. Yet they are disabused for Montalban has been converted to the new agrarian doctrines and comments on them at length.[11] They had inquired of a 'portier' as to the whereabouts of his master and obtained the following reply: 'il est actuellement avec son fermier, ou bien il se promène avec son vicaire' (p.143). The ladies were aghast at the idea of Montalban walking with a 'vicaire'! In Barthe's novel, the Marquise and Mme de Lorevel travel to the estates of M. Sainval anticipating comparable amusements. They too are shocked to learn that Sainval has mended his ways and is devoting his time to farming efficiency and the well-being of his tenants. To locate him they asked a peasant woman who informed them: 'il se promène là-bas dans le jardin avec son ami Monsieur le Vicaire' (p.146). The Marquise de *** and Mme Delatesse in Mercier's play are told by Toinette of the agricultural improvements M. Bourval has made and so are slightly better prepared for their meeting. They find him through the directions of Toinette's mother, Mathurine, who declares: 'Notre bon maître se promène là-bas dans le jardin, avec son bon ami M. le Vicaire' (act 1, sc. 3). On meeting Bourval the ladies are stunned when he sings the praises of agriculture and the 'économistes' as we mentioned above.

In Mercier's play, the visitors had already left the capital, but in the novels they express misgivings at their provincial exile. Mme de Migneville cannot refrain from exclaiming: 'car, comment peut-on vivre en Province?'[12] The same cry of apprehension passes the lips of Barthe's Marquise: 'Comment peut-on vivre en Province!'[13]

In Barthe's novel the Marquise asks an innkeeper's wife the reason for their healthy constitutions to which the woman retorts: 'Nous ne nous écoutons pas, nous travaillons, et pardi si vous en faisiez autant, vous vous porteriez bien, mais dame aussi! vous seriez plus heureuse que nous, ce qui ne serait pas juste' (p.121). Mercier's Mathurine is questioned by Mme Delatesse in search of the same formula. This is her reply: 'Nous ne nous écoutons pas; nous travaillons, et pardi, mesdames, si vous en faisiez autant, vous vous porteriez bien: mais, aussi vous seriez alors plus heureuses que nous; ce qui ne serait pas juste' (act I, sc. 3). Mme de Migneville is greatly taken by the sight of the sun rising: 'Ce spectacle était absolument nouveau pour la marquise, qui n'avait jamais vu lever le soleil qu'à l'Opéra.'[14] Barbé-Marbois may have inspired Mercier's M. Bourval who praises not a sunrise but a sunset while comparing it to the artificial mock-ups of the Opera in act II, sc. I.

Furthermore, in all three works, one of the ladies is attracted to a village lad. The Marquise in Barthe's tale goes as far as to flirt with Jeannot, but achieves nothing with her promises of taking him to Paris.[15] She flatters him: 'Sais-tu, Monsieur Jeannot, qu'à Paris on fait fortune avec une taille comme la tienne' (p.125). Mme Delatesse tries similar tactics with Jeannot in *Le Campagnard*: 'Sais-tu qu'on fait fortune à Paris avec une taille comme la tienne' (act I, sc. 3). Mme de Migneville exercises her charms in a different style but for the same purpose with Colin: 'Tu n'es pas fait pour la campagne, [...] viens à la ville; je serai ta maîtresse et tu seras mon serviteur; j'aurai de l'amitié pour toi, mon cher Colin.'[16] In each case the peasant rejects the offer since he regards domestic service as beneath his dignity.

Our last comparison is limited to Mercier and Barthe. In the novelist's work, the Marquise asks an innkeeper's daughter if she would like to wear a fine gown; the girl refuses; here is the ensuing conversation:

c'est que je ne suis pas une belle dame comme vous; je ne suis qu'une paysanne, mais j'ai un beau corset que je mets le dimanche, lorsque nous dansons. – Ah, ah! vous dansez donc, et Monsieur le Curé le permet? – Il ne le défend pas certains jours de fête; s'il ne le voulait pas aussi, nous irions danser au village prochain, et itou à confesse. – Et avec qui dansez-vous, petite? – Avec tous ceux qui me prient. – Et vous prie-t-on souvent? – Autant de fois qu'il se trouve de la place. – Et aimez-vous bien à danser? – Oh! oui. – Mais je crois que c'est un petit péché. – Petit ou gros, je n'en ai jamais de regrets.[17]

In the play, Toinette tells the Marquise that she does not envy the ladies' elegant dresses since they would not suit her station in life (act I, sc. 5):

TOINETTE   [...] je ne suis pas une belle dame comme vous; je ne suis qu'une paysanne, mais nous avons dans l'armoire un beau corset que nous mettons le dimanche, lorsque nous dansons.

LA MARQUISE   Ah, ah, vous dansez le dimanche! et M. le Curé le permet? [...]

TOINETTE   Il ne le défend pas, s'il ne voulait pas aussi, nous irions danser au village prochain, et itou à confesse.

LA MARQUISE   Et avec qui dansez-vous, petite?

TOINETTE   Avec tous les garçons qui me prient.

LA MARQUISE   Et vous prie-t-on souvent?

TOINETTE   Autant de fois qu'il se trouve de la place.

LA MARQUISE   Aimez-vous bien à danser?

TOINETTE   Oh! c'est un grand plaisir parce que cela arrive tous les dimanches, et une fois la semaine tout seulement […]

LA MARQUISE   Mais, je crois que c'est là un petit péché.

TOINETTE   Point, point; car nous n'en avons jamais senti de remords […] Ainsi, il n'y a point de mal à ça.

Since both novels were first published in 1769 Mercier is evidently guilty of plagiarism though it is the choice of theme which is of importance for our purpose.

To sum up our glance at the theatre's depiction of the relationship between Paris and the provinces, we can assert that similar objectives and opinions emerge at comparable periods. Though many traditional thrusts at provincials survive into the mid-century there is already an undercurrent of criticism of the capital. With the advent of the 'drame', we witness a marked change of attitude. The stereotyped and laughable peasants of a Dancourt are no more. Peasants are now presented with a dignity and a common sense unknown to their literary forebears. Furthermore we suggest that there is a link between the rise of the 'drame' and that of the novel. The 'drame' was a hybrid genre, composed of both comedy and tragedy, while the novel had little historical pedigree, and was therefore open to abuse as a genre not consecrated by antiquity. They were consequently both fighting for survival and searching for means to establish their 'droit de cité'. By concerning themselves with the type of material analysed in this study, namely themes derived from contemporary society, they proved their own utility and responsibility. By crusading for the virtue and dignity of the provinces, they were simultanteously proclaiming the virtue and dignity of their own genres.

French poetry also shows affinities with our theme. Voltaire writes on the problem of the village lad leaving his home to seek his fortune in the capital:

> Plutus est dans Paris, et c'est là qu'il appelle
> Les voisins de l'Adour, et du Rhône, et du Var!
> Tous viennent à genoux environner son char;
> Les uns montent dessus, les autres dans la boue
> Baisent en soupirant, les rayons de sa roue.
> Le fils de mon manœuvre, en ma ferme élevé,
> A d'utiles travaux à quinze ans enlevé,
> Des laquais de Paris s'en va grossir l'armée.
> Il sert d'un vieux traitant la maîtresse affamée;
> De sergent des impôts il obtient un emploi:
> Il vient dans son hameau, tout fier; *De par le roi,*
> Fait des procès-verbaux, tyrannies, emprisonne,
> Ravit aux citoyens le pain que je leur donne,
> Et traîne en des cachots le père et les enfants.[18]

So even Voltaire voices the familiar complaints about able-bodied peasants joining the ranks of the Parisian 'valetaille'. It would be erroneous to enrol Voltaire in the anti-civilisation movement, but his choice of the subject either suggests he was following contemporary trends or was writing from personal experience as a 'gentilhomme de campagne'.[19]

The disillusionment with Paris is summarised in F. B. Hoffman's *Stances d'un provincial* (*Almanach des muses*, 1787):

> Enfin j'ai vu la ville immense
> Où les provinciaux vont chercher le bonheur;
> J'ai dit en la voyant: quelle magnificence!
> La France est un grand corps dont Paris est le cœur.
>
> J'ai vu ces tours où l'art insulte à la nature,
>   Temples saints que l'orgueil bâtit:
> J'ai vu ces longs bosquets, colosses de verdure,
> Et ces palais si grands où l'homme est si petit [...]
>
> Enfin dans ce Paris chacun veut aller vivre;
>   C'est le rendez-vous des souhaits.
>   Cependant je n'y vis jamais
> Un seul homme content, à moins qu'il ne fût ivre.[20]

We find in Hoffman's words the change of attitude which finds happiness alien to the finery and the artificial splendours of the capital. Walter Moser, commenting on the poetry as the century progresses, claims: 'La ville, lieu de divertissements innombrables mais artificiels, se trouve souvent opposée aux charmes de la campagne où réside la variété naturelle. Il faut donc en sortir et s'en éloigner pour se procurer des jouissances authentiques.'[21] The country offers a variety of genuine experiences and Delille invites people to leave 'ce Paris, séjour de l'uniformité'.[22] Edouard Guitton writes: 'La poésie descriptive a surgi dans le champ des beaux-arts aux alentours de 1758, exactement comme le drame bourgeois sur la scène du théâtre, comme le conte moral et l'héroïde.'[23] Therefore we see poetry extolling the countryside and decrying Paris at the same time as the novel.

Across the English Channel we find literature preoccupied by similar problems, urbanisation and the exaggerated status of London. Max Byrd asserts that there is: 'a general trend of London malediction prominent in the literature of the mid-century'.[24] London like Paris is depicted as possessing considerable drawing-power over the provinces[25] and subjecting its new arrivals to comparable hazards, for example young girls being unwittingly housed in brothels.[26] The English novel also conveys pro-agrarian views censuring luxury and the exodus to London as factors in the corruption of man.[27]

Although literature can be an untrustworthy mirror of its age, it is our belief that the development of the eighteenth-century novel paralleled and was influenced by the contemporary climate of ideas. Whereas Paris is presented as the proper place for characters seeking happiness and fulfilment in the early novels of our period, the countryside assumes this role in works published after 1760. The extreme 'glorification' of Paris is transformed into an equally extreme eulogy of the provinces.[28]

To see in this idealisation of country life merely nostalgia and preoccupation with the 'bon sauvage' is to distort the intentions of our authors and to divorce their works from other contemporary ideas. Writers such as Louvet and Restif attack the disdain for agriculture and the transformation of peasants into metropolitan servants, through the impact of 'philosophical' ideas. Similarly, in exhorting absentee landlords to return to their estates and sow their fallow fields, Marmontel is advocating reforms under discussion in his own day.[29] Urbanisation has fostered the spread of luxury and debauchery and destroyed the traditional life-pattern of the nation. In supporting the renewal of the old master/man relationships, Rousseau and Baculard were grafting a revamped feudalism onto a modern economic programme, the 'bon seigneur' was not rewarded in the Christian's hereafter but in the humanitarian's here and now. These authors were employing prose fiction as a means to an end and *not* an end in itself.

We noted that a salient feature of pre-1760 fiction was the growth of social realism. The origin of this growth has been analysed by Georges May:

Dès qu'on essaie donc de gratter un peu la surface des problèmes posés par le réalisme social, on s'aperçoit de la nécessité qu'il y a à résister à la tentation de les étudier en historien des mœurs et en sociologue. Les racines de ces problèmes sont presque toujours esthétiques et littéraires. Si l'on veut donc examiner des problèmes à la lumière de l'histoire, c'est à l'histoire littéraire qu'il est sage de recourir, et non pas à celle des idées sociales.[30]

Further on he insists that the moralising prefaces of the early novels were usually sham convention (pp.248-49):

Dans le fond, on peut dire qu'entre 1725 et 1761 les bons romanciers qui n'entonnent pas le refrain moral sont rarissimes, mais ceux qui le firent sans mauvaise foi aucune furent au moins aussi rares. Tandis qu'après 1761, le même refrain est repris de la meilleure foi du monde par Marmontel, par Restif, par Baculard d'Arnaud, par Bernardin de Saint-Pierre.

It is indeed true that the prefaces of later works may carry more conviction, for, if their origins are literary and aesthetic, they have now been fortified by the influence of current ideas. These works were not composed in a vague, moralising aim, but, increasingly, for definite social purposes. In the pursuit of critical realism, Paris must be painted black, the provinces white. Compromises and nuances are alien to the concept and practice of this new realism, exaggeration is the order of the day, artistry is subordinated to social ends. Criticism of French society was no longer to be conveyed by Montesquieu's Persians or mme de Graffigny's Peruvian, but to be conveyed openly by Frenchmen, by provincials. Moreover Restif, Baculard, Loaisel were no longer mocking particular foibles but censuring general abuses. In their hands, the novel would cease to be an escapist palliative to become an incitement to thought and action, indeed, in terms of propaganda, being more effective than the more subtle 'conte philosophique'.

The championing of the provinces in the novel should not, however, blind us to the ambivalent attitudes of many of our authors. Despite their theoretical disapproval, Rousseau, Restif, Baculard all found that Paris exercised a particular magnetism. Mercier may denounce the strangle-hold of the capital but is forced to concede: 'C'est dans les grandes villes que le philosophe lui-même se plaît, tout en les condamnant; parce qu'il y vit plus libre'.[31] The freedom which becomes licence for immorality is also the freedom which stimulates writers and thinkers. Just as for Balzac, the capital inspires fascination and horror.

The paradoxes and inconsistencies of the more important writers of the later period would seem to indicate an inner tension.[32] The polarity of Paris and the provinces is perhaps the exteriorisation of a malaise afflicting authors in a society in the process of decomposition. One senses a clash between the growing demands of individualism and the needs of social stability. In fiction this tension is translated into a reassuring mirage of absolutes. But underneath the superficial certainty of the novelists' message lurk the doubts which will find expression in the personal and confessional novel of subsequent years.

This concern with individual and national identity provided the eighteenth-century novel with one of its most fertile discoveries. Its endeavour to define the nature of man led it to a consideration of the true Frenchman. In pre-1760 fiction, Duclos depicted him in both novels and commentaries as a Parisian: 'C'est dans Paris qu'il faut considérer le Français, parce qu'il est plus Français qu'ailleurs'.[33] To be a Frenchman one must cultivate the refinement and polished manners associated with the capital. Rousseau, however, will take the opposite view and employs Saint-Preux as his spokesman:

Je n'ignore pas que les capitales diffèrent moins entre elles que les peuples, et que les caractères nationaux s'y effacent et confondent en grande partie, tant à cause de l'influence commune des cours qui se ressemblent toutes, que par l'effet commun d'une société nombreuse et resserrée, qui est le même à peu près sur tous les hommes et l'emporte à la fin sur le caractère original.

Si je voulais étudier un peuple, c'est dans les provinces reculées, où les habitants ont encore leurs inclinations naturelles, que j'irais les observer.[34]

and: 'Ce ne sont pas les Parisiens que j'étudie, mais les habitants d'une grande ville; et je ne sais si ce que j'en vois ne convient pas à Rome et à Londres, tout aussi bien qu'à Paris' (p.243). Rousseau realises that Paris possesses an almost supernatural life in which a cosmopolitan population can never truly represent the genius of a separate nation. To understand the real nature of a Frenchman, one must therefore have recourse to the provinces.

Subsequent generations of writers have surely sided with Rousseau. In search of subject-matter, they have turned increasingly to the provincial, albeit to portray him in the capital. When one thinks of the famous heroes and heroines of French literature, one is struck by the preponderance of provincials: Rastignac, Rubempré, Dominique, Germinie Lacerteux, Emma Bovary, Thérèse Desquey-roux, Frédéric Moreau, Julien Sorel, and others. The eighteenth-century novelist had already pioneered this rich source of characters: Marianne, Jacob, Ursule, Edmond, Dolbreuse, Manon, Des Grieux, Julie, Saint-Preux, etc. In addition, the novelists of our period created a mode of fiction which no longer sought for the extraordinary or the comic, but drew its material from contemporary society, and, in so doing, secured for itself an honourable place in the history of the novel in France.

Notes

Notes to the preface

[1] See Angus Martin, Vivienne Mylne and Richard Frautschi, *Bibliographie du genre romanesque français 1751-1800* (London 1977), pp.73, 151.

[2] Georges Gusdorf notes the affinity between the town-countryside and the capital-provinces polarity in his *Naissance de la conscience romantique au Siècle des Lumières* (Paris 1976), p.371.

[3] With the exception of the 'poissard' passages, spellings in eighteenth-century texts have been modernised throughout.

Notes to the introduction

[1] Orest Ranum, *Paris in the age of absolutism* (New York 1968), pp.259-82. Cf. Leon Bernard, *The Emerging city: Paris in the age of Louis XIV* (Durham, North Carolina 1970), p.284.

[2] *The Ancien Régime* (London 1967), p.13.

[3] P. Gaxotte, *Paris au XVIIIe siècle* (Paris 1968), p.55.

[4] *Classes laborieuses et classes dangereuses à Paris dans la première moitié du dix-neuvième siècle* (Paris 1958), *passim.* Cf. the same author's *Les Parisiens* (Paris 1967), p.174: 'Tout au long de l'Ancien Régime, la population parisienne se renouvelle essentiellement par sa propre fécondité, sans grandes différences entre les époques, sans contraste entre les quartiers. Si l'aristocratie, fondamentalement étrangère à la ville, s'alimente aux diverses provinces, bourgeois et gens du peuple restent pétris de la même pâte.'

[5] 'Dix-neuf millions et demi sur vingt demeuraient attachés à la terre, au lopin, à la cabane, à la chaumière, au quartier où ils étaient nés. Ce ne sont pas les agitations, les brassages, les migrations d'hommes qui caractérisent l'ancienne France, mais bien la sédentarité. Sauf les aventuriers de toujours, on ne migrait que sous la poussée de la nécessité, qui était souvent la misère' (Pierre Goubert, *L'Ancien Régime*, t.i, *La Société*, Paris 1969, p.46).

[6] *Le Rayonnement de Paris au XVIIIe siècle* (Paris 1946), p.9.

[7] *Letters of a Russian traveller, 1789-90*, trans. F. Jones (New York 1957), p.179.

[8] *Les Mœurs de Paris* (Amsterdam 1747), préface, p.iii.

[9] *Mémoires du comte de Tilly*, ed. C. Melchior Bonnet (Paris 1965), p.150.

[10] *Lettres d'un Français* (La Haye 1745), i.2.

[11] *Colloques, Cahiers de Civilisation, Paris, Croissance d'une capitale* (Paris 1961), p.118.

[12] F. Fosca, *Histoire des cafés de Paris* (Paris 1934), *passim.*

[13] *Œuvres romanesques*, ed. H. Bénac (Paris 1962), p.395.

[14] R. Poisson, *Le Baron de la Crasse* (1662), sc.2.

[15] P. Quinault, *L'Amant indiscret* (1654) act IV, sc.9.

[16] La Bruyère is scathing in *Les Caractères*, ed. R. Garapon (Paris 1962): 'Le noble de province inutile à sa patrie, à sa famille, et à lui-même, souvent sans toit, sans habits, et sans aucun mérite, répète dix fois le jour qu'il est gentilhomme, traite les fourrures et les mortiers de bourgeoisie, occupé toute sa vie de ses parchemins et de ses titres, qu'il ne changerait pas contre les masses d'un chancelier' ('De l'homme', pp.339-40). Cf. 'Il suffit

de n'être pas né dans une ville, mais sous une chaumière répandue dans la campagne, ou sous une ruine qui trempe dans un marécage, et qu'on appelle château, pour être cru noble sur sa parole' (*De quelques usages*, p.415).

[17] Ed. H. Weber (Paris 1969), p.741.

[18] Ed. A. Adam (Paris 1958), pp.550-51.

[19] *La Prétieuse ou le mystère des ruelles*, ed. E. Magne (Paris 1938-1939), i.226 (1st ed. 1656-1658).

Notes to chapter 1

[1] *Considérations sur les mœurs de ce siècle*, ed. F. C. Green (Cambridge 1946), p.13.

[2] Ed. M. de Cheyrou in *Romanciers du XVIIIe siècle*, vol.ii (Paris 1965), p.217.

[3] *Thémidore* (Londres 1781), p.129 (1st ed. 1745).

[4] *Les Surprises*, in *Les Femmes de mérite* (n. p. 1759), pp.47-48. Cf. Bastide, *Le Tombeau philosophique* (Amsterdam 1751), p.13; Marivaux, *Journal et œuvres diverses*, ed. F. Deloffre and M. Gilot (Paris 1969), p.20.

[5] *Journal et œuvres diverses*, p.26.

[6] *Œuvres complètes* (Paris 1806), viii.252.

[7] *Lettres de Thérèse ou mémoires d'une demoiselle de province pendant son séjour à Paris* (La Haye 1740-1742), p.11.

[8] The article 'Provincial' in Diderot's *Encyclopédie* states (xiii.523): 'La politesse ne dit pas une provinciale, mais une dame de province.'

[9] In his commentary on the capital La Peyre claims: 'Les Parisiens ont une façon brillante de s'énoncer, leur accent est des plus beaux; les femmes en ont une haute idée; aussi rient-elles de ceux qui ne l'ont pas. Un de leurs grands défauts est de s'estimer infiniment plus que les dames de province: il leur semble qu'elles soient stupides, grossières' (*Les Mœurs de Paris*, p.23). The author admits the superiority of the Parisian lady but chides her with flaunting it.

[10] Gimat de Bonneval, *Fanfiche ou les mémoires de mademoiselle de **** in *Bibliotheque choisie et amusante* (Amsterdam 1749), iv.91.

[11] *Les Lettres de Thérèse*, pp.110-11.

[12] *La Nouvelle Héloïse*, in *Œuvres complètes*, ed. H. Coulet (Paris 1961), ii.602. A comparable critical attitude is expressed by mme Riccoboni's English lord in a letter to Cardigan: 'J'arrive de la campagne. L'ennui m'en a chassé. Loin de jouir dans le plus beau lieu du monde des agréments que je m'y promettais, j'y ai trouvé le faste de la ville, sa contrainte gênante, ses frivoles amusements, tout ce qui détourne de l'intéressante contemplation de la nature, d'un exercice utile et de la douceur de se recueillir en soi-même. Les Français, fort amoureux de l'Agriculture, en parlent beaucoup à Paris et ne s'en occupent guères à la campagne. Rien de simple, rien de champêtre ne m'a fait apercevoir d'un changement de séjour. Donner des spectacles, des feux d'artifice, soutenir un gros jèu, faire servir sa table avec une abondance capable d'étonner le plus avide parasite; rassembler chez soi vingt ou trente maîtres, souvent davantage; voilà ce qu'une partie des Français riches ou distingués appellent éviter la foule et goûter les douceurs de la retraite' (*Lettres de mylord Rivers à sir Charles Cardigan*, Paris 1777, pp.148-49).

[13] See chapter 7, 'The indictment of Paris and civilisation'.

[14] *Contes moraux* (Paris 1801-1808), iv.2. In the anonymous *Le Cultivateur* (Amsterdam 1770), a provincial 'baronne' is derided in the traditional style: 'La Baronne de B..., jeune veuve très riche, était une de ces personnes pour qui il est malheureux d'avoir vu la capitale; sans cela n'ayant rien à dire, elles se tairaient peut-être, et comme tant

d'autres, ne seraient sottes qu'*incognito*. Ces femmes si instruites décident de tout: *cela se fait à Paris* est toujours un mot sans réplique' (pp.59-60). Despite the superficial appearance to the contrary, this is an indirect attack on Paris as later extracts from the novel will show.

[15] Lyon, Paris 1770, p.117.

[16] Amsterdam, Paris 1770, pp.46-47. A hero of Nougaret is likewise ridiculed: 'Qu'aurait-on pensé de moi si l'on m'eût vu abandonner le séjour de Paris, le centre des plaisirs, de l'aimable folie, où non seulement ce qu'il y a de mieux en France s'empresse de se ruiner, mais encore l'élite des Seigneurs Allemands et Anglais? Je me serais à jamais déshonoré si j'eusse abandonné une ville où il est du bon ton de paraître avec tout l'éclat possible, pour aller m'enterrer dans le fond de la Province, jouer le triste rôle de gentilhomme campagnard' (*Les Travers d'un homme de qualité*, Bruxelles 1788, ii.254).

[17] *La Jolie femme*, i.117; cf. ii.20: ' toute Parisienne transplantée en province a toujours un succès passager'. Mercier is equally critical of the pretensions of the Parisian: 'Quand un Parisien a quitté Paris, alors il ne cesse en province de parler de la capitale. Il rapporte tout ce qu'il voit à ses usages et à ses coutumes; il affecte de trouver ridicule ce qui s'en écarte; il veut que tout le monde réforme ses idées pour lui plaire et l'amuser ... Il y jouit d'un crédit considérable; son nom est cité. Il n'y a enfin de savoir, de génie, de politesse qu'à Paris' (*Tableau de Paris*, i.87). Also Nougaret, *Les Travers d'un homme de qualité*, i.5-6.

[18] Paris 1788, p.9.

[19] Nougaret, *Le Danger des circonstances* (Paris, Bruxelles 1789), i.110.

[20] pp.110-11. The same set-piece is found in Elie de Beaumont's *Lettres du marquis de Rozelle* (Londres, Paris 1764). Valville mocks the Marquis's esteem for Mlle de Ferval: 'Quelque éloge que l'enjouement te fasse faire de cette beauté, c'est une provinciale, peu riche, et nous savons ce que c'est qu'une provinciale. Je ne m'efforcerai point de rabaisser les grâces que tu lui prêtes, ce serait te fâcher inutilement. Mais ce qui me passe, c'est qu'après avoir bravé les traits de Madame d'Asterre, la femme de Paris la plus aimable, et dont le choix ne pouvait te faire honneur en dépit de tes pieuses maximes, tu ailles tomber dans les liens d'une petite personne de campagne' (ii.68-69). Worldly renown, the highest good, is not enhanced by dallying with a provincial. It is enlightening to compare these passages and attitudes with an extract from Bastide's *Les Ressources de l'amour* (Amsterdam 1752). A Parisian thinks he has discovered a suitable partner but is soon disabused: 'C'était une femme de province qui arrivait à Paris pour recueillir un héritage. Elle était jeune et jolie. Un certain air d'inexpérience qui régnait sur son visage la rendait presque intéressante. Enfin il me fallait une femme, j'optai pour celle-là. Mais une chose assez importante eut bientôt dérangé mes idées, c'est qu'elle était bête comme un pot. Que faire d'une bête? Mon courage m'eut bientôt abandonné; je me mis à chercher sur nouveaux frais' (i.122-23). The provincial at this date is still a target of derision.

[21] *Monsieur Nicolas ou le cœur humain dévoilé*, ed. J. J. Pauvert (Paris 1959), Première époque, p.38n.

Notes to chapter 2

[1] Baculard d'Arnaud, *Bazile* (1st ed. 1773), in *Les Epreuves du sentiment* (Maestricht 1779), iv.22.

[2] *La Paysanne parvenue* (Amsterdam 1746), i.20.

[3] *La Paysanne pervertie* (La Haye 1784), i.87.

[4] In *Le Temple de la piété* (Avignon 1765), p.178.

[5] Compan adds the ironic comment: 'En effet la province offre une perspective bien triste, et c'est être mort que de ne pas vivre à Paris' (pp.178-79).

[6] Sainte-Croix, *La Comédienne fille et femme de qualité* (Bruxelles 1756), i.5. The Comte de Kermalec experiences a similar joy at the prospect of moving to the capital with his father: 'L'éclat de cette capitale du royaume me charma: je sentis un plaisir secret de devenir un de ses heureux habitants' (Gaillard de La Bataille, *Mémoires et aventures de M. le Comte de Kermalec*, La Haye 1749, i.7; 1st edition, 1740-1741).

[7] Bastide, *Les Aventures de Victoire Ponty* (Amsterdam, Paris 1758).

[8] Ussieux, *Alexis*, in *Nouvelles françaises* (Paris 1779), ii.10.

[9] Restif de La Bretonne, *La Fille du savetier du coin*, in *Les Contemporaines du commun* (Paris 1962), p.47.

[10] Rutlidge, *Premier et second voyages de mylord à Paris* (Yverdon 1777), p.277. For a study of this Franco-Irish writer, see R. Las Vergnas, *Le Chevalier Rutlidge, gentilhomme anglais 1742-1794* (Paris 1932).

[11] *Le Monde moral ou mémoires pour servir à l'histoire du cœur humain*, in *Œuvres* (Amsterdam, Paris 1783-85), xxix.4-5.

[12] In *Les Contemporaines*, ed. Assézat (Paris 1876), iii.133.

[13] J. A. R. Perrin, *Henriette de Marconne ou les mémoires du chevalier de Présac* (Amsterdam 1763).

[14] In the *Journal et œuvres diverses, Quatrième feuille*, p.128.

[15] *Œuvres romanesques*, ed. H. Bénac (Paris 1962), p.614.

[16] Marquis de Sade, *La Marquise de Télème*, in *Œuvres complètes*, ed. J. J. Pauvert (Paris 1966-1967), xiv.230.

[17] Mme de Violaine, *Mémoires de monsieur de Saint-Gory* (Londres, Paris 1776), p.28.

[18] *Le Paysan perverti* (La Haye 1776), i.220.

[19] Coteneuve, *La Confiance trahie ou lettres du Chevalier de Murcy* (Amsterdam 1777), pp.4-5.

[20] Nougaret, *Les Faiblesses d'une jolie femme* (Amsterdam 1779), p.102.

[21] *Œuvres complètes*, ed. J. J. Pauvert, xiv.242. Cf. Mailhol, *Le Cabriolet* (Amsterdam 1755), p.53.

[22] Campan, *Le Mot et la chose* (n. p. 1752), p.139.

[23] Longchamps, *Les Aventures d'un jeune homme* (Londres, Paris 1765), ii.2-3. Cf. Coteneuve, *La Confiance trahie*, p.15.

[24] Amsterdam 1744, p.3.

[25] Just like her namesake, Jeannette loathes her rural apparel: 'Deux choses cependant révoltaient mon orgueil et ma vanité. La bassesse de mon extraction, et l'habit villageois qui, quoique propre, ne donnait point à ma beauté tout l'éclat qu'elle aurait emprunté d'une autre parure' (pp.4-5).

[26] Amsterdam 1751, p.62. Cf. *Le Cultivateur*, p.37, where the Marquis tries to curry favour with Hortense: 'Parée d'une figure noble, intéressante, continua-t-il, embellie de toute la fraîcheur de la Jeunesse; quel rôle éclatant vous joueriez dans cette ville heureuse où la beauté commande en souveraine!'

[27] *Laurette* (1765), in *Contes moraux*, iii.197

[28] *Correspondance d'Eulalie ou tableau du libertinage de Paris* (Londres 1785), ii.160.

[29] *Aline, reine de Golconde*, ed. S. Davies (Exeter 1977), p.10 (1st edition, 1761).

[30] J.-A.-R. Perrin, *Les Egarements de Julie* (Paris 1806), i.20 (1st edition, 1755). Cf. *Le Cabriolet*, passim.

[31] Bret, *La Belle Allemande ou les galanteries de Thérèse* (Strasbourg 1764), p.27 (1st edition, 1745).

[32] pp.31-32. Cf. the anonymous *Les Trois voluptés* (n. p. 1746), p.10.

[33] This prostitution of girls by relatives does not seem to be a figment of the literary imagination. Fougeret de Monbron complains: 'Une autre espèce de malheureuses dont Paris regorge aujourd'hui, ce sont les mères qui corrumpent l'innocence de leurs filles, et ne les élèvent que dans la vue de les vendre' (*La Capitale des Gaules ou la nouvelle Babylone*, Londres 1760, p.111).

[34] Restif de La Bretonne, *Monsieur Nicolas*, Reprise de la huitième époque, p.407.

[35] *Jacques le fataliste*, pp.614-15.

[36] Du Castre d'Auvigny, *Mémoires du Comte de Comminville* (Amsterdam 1735), pp.7-8.

[37] *Le Vicomte de Barjac* (Dublin 1784), p.39.

[38] Thomas Laffichard, *L'Amour chez les philosophes* (La Haye 1748), p.3.

[39] Gimat de Bonneval, *Fanfiche*, p.118.

[40] Gorgy, *Victorine* (Paris 1789), p.97.

[41] Marquis d'Argens, *Mémoires du chevalier de* *** (Paris 1747), p.7.

[42] Desbiefs, *Nine* (Amsterdam, Paris 1756), p.35. Cf. Luchet, *Une seule faute ou les mémoires d'une demoiselle de qualité* (Bruxelles 1788), p.43.

[43] *Les Ridicules du siècle*, in *Œuvres complètes* (Londres 1774), iii.58-68.

[44] J.-B.-M. Magny, *Mémoires de Justine ou les confessions d'une fille du monde qui s'est retirée en province* (Londres 1754), p.59.

[45] Cinquième époque, p.225. Cf. Troisième époque, p.316, where Marguerite confides: 'dès que je ne pourrai plus cacher mon état, j'irai à Paris'. Also Perrin, *Les Egarements de Julie*, ii.130; Sophie tells her tale to Julie: 'Prévoyant ne pouvoir plus longtemps cacher ma grossesse, je pris le parti de disparaître sans rien dire, et de me rendre à Paris chez une sage-femme, où je fis mes couches.' See also Rutlidge, *Le Vice et la faiblesse ou mémoires de deux provinciales* (Lausanne, Paris 1785), i.66.

[46] *Le Paysan perverti*, iii.47.

[47] Campan, *Le Mot et la chose*, pp.172-73.

[48] This anecdote is to be found in Jullien, *dit* Des Boulmiers, *Honny soit qui mal y pense, ou histoires des filles célèbres du XVIIIe siècle* (Londres 1761).

[49] Cinquième époque, p.300. These escapes were not merely novelistic sensationalism. F. Cognel describes meeting an 'échappée femelle de couvent' on his return to Paris from Rouen: 'elle nous raconta qu'on l'avait fait entrer au couvent contre son gré; elle en était sortie en grimpant le long d'un espalier jusqu'au sommet d'un mur d'où elle s'était laissée glisser sur le chemin, et tout porte à croire qu'elle glissera plus d'une fois sur sa route: cette malheureuse, qui a grand peur d'être poursuivie, désire évidemment trouver un protecteur' (*La Vie parisienne sous Louis XVI*, Paris 1882, p.137). Cognel, a provincial, visited Paris towards the end of the ancien régime and the work is a journal of his great adventure.

Notes to chapter 3

[1] Gaillard de La Bataille, *Jeannette seconde*, pp.193-94. Cf. p.194.

[2] *Le Paysan perverti*, ii.29. Cf. J.-H. Marchand, *Les Délassements champêtres ou mélanges d'un philosophe sérieux à Paris, et badin à la campagne* (La Haye 1767), ii.30. One recalls Rousseau's comments in his *Confessions*: 'Combien l'abord de Paris démentit l'idée que j'en avais! La décoration extérieure que j'avais vue à Turin, la beauté des rues, la symétrie et les alignements des maisons, me faisaient chercher à Paris autre chose encore. Je m'étais figuré une ville aussi belle que grande, de l'aspect le plus imposant, où l'on ne voyait que de superbes rues, des palais de marbre et d'or. En entrant par le faubourg Saint-Marceau, je ne vis que de petites rues sales et puantes, de vilaines maisons noires, l'air de la

malpropreté, de la pauvreté, des mendiants, des charretiers, des ravaudeuses, des crieuses de tisane et de vieux chapeaux. Tout cela me frappa d'abord à tel point, que tout ce que j'ai vu depuis de magnificence réelle n'a pu détruire cette première impression, et qu'il m'en est resté toujours un secret dégoût pour l'habitation de cette capitale' (ed. J. Voisine, Paris 1964, book IV, p.179). Voltaire also noted the wretched entrance to Paris in chapter 22 of *Candide* (1759) and *Le Monde comme il va* (1748): 'Il arriva dans cette ville immense par l'ancienne entrée, qui était toute barbare, et dont la rusticité dégoutante offensait les yeux. Toute cette partie de la ville se ressentait du temps où elle avait été bâtie: car, malgré l'opiniâtreté des hommes à louer l'antique aux dépens du moderne, il faut avouer qu'en tout genre les premiers essais sont toujours grossiers' (*Romans et contes*, ed. H. Bénac, Paris 1960, p.68). For a discussion of Voltaire's attitude to Paris see Roger Mercier, 'Voltaire et Paris, des rêves d'urbanisme aux "pleurs sur Jérusalem"' in *La Ville au XVIIIe siècle* (Aix-en-Provence 1975), pp.33-47.

[3] *Sophie* (Amsterdam, Paris 1779), pp.217-18.

[4] *Les Amours du chevalier de Faublas*, ed. Marguerite du Cheyron, in *Romanciers du XVIIIe siècle* (Paris 1965), ii.419.

[5] pp.419-20. Karamzin confirms these contrasts in his journal: 'Never have I approached a city with such curiosity, such impatience! ... Soon we entered the Faubourg Saint-Antoine, but what did we see? Narrow, filthy, muddy streets, miserable houses, and ragged people. "Can this be Paris," I thought, "the city which from afar appeared so splendid?" The scene changed completely, however, when we reached the banks of the Seine. Here, there appeared before us beautiful buildings, houses six stories high, rich shops. What throngs! What colour, what noise! Carriage racing after carriage, continuous shouts of "Gare! Gare!" and the people surging like the sea' (*Letters of a Russian traveller 1789-90*, pp.179-80).

[6] *Le Véridique ou les mémoires de M. de Fillerville* (Amsterdam 1769), p.83. Cf. Karamzin, p.185.

[7] Rousseau, *La Nouvelle Héloïse*, p.232.

[8] It would of course be erroneous to suggest that all post-1760 novels brought out this contrast. In Charpentier's *L'Elu et son président* (Paris 1769), pp.26-27, Eraste states: 'Il en faut convenir, le premier coup d'œil de Paris est séduisant. Si le jeune homme qui ne l'a point vu commence à sentir, il en doit être enchanté. Sa grandeur prodigieuse qui lui donne un air majestueux, les édifices magnifiques qui le décorent, les superbes jardins qui l'embellissent, les spectacles qui s'y multiplient de jour en jour, et qui en font le charme; l'esprit, les talents, les sciences, les arts s'y rassemblent en foule des quatre coins du Royaume, tout contribue à en faire concevoir la plus haute idée.' For an interesting study of this writer see Angus Martin, 'Argent, commerce et autres thèmes bourgeois vers 1770: les romans et contes de Louis Charpentier', *Zeitschrift für französische Sprache und Literatur* 84 (1974), pp.307-24.

[9] Loaisel de Tréogate, *Dolbreuse ou l'homme du siècle ramené à la vérité par le sentiment et la raison* (Amsterdam, Paris 1783), i.118-20. For Loaisel, see the articles collected in Loaisel de Saulnays, *Un méconnu, Loaisel de Tréogate* (Algiers 1930) and Michel Delon 'Vision du monde "préromantique" dans *Dolbreuse* de Loaisel', *Annales de Bretagne* 83 (1976), pp.829-38.

[10] Restif de La Bretonne, *Le Paysan perverti*, ii.160.

[11] La Solle, *Mémoires de Versorand* (Amsterdam 1751), p.23.

[12] Londres 1750, p.8. Cf. Restif de La Bretonne, *Le Paysan perverti*, ii.161 and Claude-François Lambert, *La Nouvelle Marianne* (La Haye 1740), iv.21-22.

[13] Perrin, *Les Egarements de Julie*, i.28.

[14] Nougaret, *La Paysanne pervertie ou les mœurs des grandes villes* (Londres, Paris 1777), p.250. Cf. the marquis d'Argens, *Lettres chinoises* (La Haye 1751), pp.6-7; Bridard de La

Garde, *Les Lettres de Thérèse*, pp.43-48; Montesquieu, *Lettres persanes*, ed. P. Vernière (Paris 1960), Letter xxiv, p.52; L. S. Mercier, *Tableau de Paris*, vol.i, chapter entitled 'Gare! Gare!'; Karamzin, p.185; Muralt, *Lettres sur les Anglais et les Français et sur les voyages*, ed. C. Gould (Paris 1933), sixth letter, p.270.

[15] Chasles, *Les Illustres Françaises*, ed. F. Deloffre (Paris 1959), i.1-2. Traffic jams were used as a means to further plots as Laurent Versini has noted in *Laclos et la tradition* (Paris 1968), p.149.

[16] *Le Danger des spectacles ou les mémoires de M. le duc de Champigny* (Paris 1780), i.454.

[17] Yon, *Les Surprises*, in *Les Femmes de mérite*, p.79. Cf. mme Robert, *La Voix de la nature* (Amsterdam 1770), i.14.

[18] Sainte-Colombe, *Les Plaisirs d'un jour ou la journée d'une provinciale à Paris* (Bruxelles 1764), p.154. Cf. Sainte-Croix, *La Comédienne fille et femme de qualité*, p.217.

[19] Bridard de La Garde, *Lettres de Thérèse*, iii.32-33.

[20] *La Paysanne pervertie*, ii.7-8.

[21] *Les Dangers d'un premier choix* (La Haye, Paris 1785), pp.41-42. Cf. Mercier's description in *Le Tableau de Paris*, v.8.

[22] *La Voix de la nature*, i.22.

[23] *Lettres de Thérèse*, ii.4. Cf. Mouhy, *Paris ou le mentor à la mode*, p.141; mme de Graffigny, *Lettres d'une Péruvienne*, ed. Nicoletti (Bari 1967), p.217; Gaillard de La Bataille, *Jeannette seconde*, pp.227-28; *La Nouvelle Héloïse*, 3rd pt., letter xiii, where Saint-Preux shows himself a more discerning critic of the Opera.

[24] Cubières-Palmézeaux, *L'Ecole des filles* (Cassel 1784), p.26. Rousseau knew full well the narcissistic nature of much theatre-going and Saint-Preux declares on his behalf: 'Personne ne va au spectacle pour le plaisir du spectacle, mais pour voir l'assemblée, pour en être vu, pour ramasser de quoi fournir au caquet après la pièce; et l'on ne songe à ce qu'on voit que pour savoir ce qu'on en dira' (*La Nouvelle Héloïse*, p.254). Cf. Bridard de La Garde, *Lettres de Thérèse*, p.127; Louvet, *La Fin des amours de Faublas*, p.906; Desforges, *Mémoires, anecdotes pour servir à l'histoire de M. Duliz* (Londres 1739), p.109.

[25] *Histoire de Gogo* (La Haye 1739), p.201.

[26] Lesage, *La Valise trouvée* (Paris 1740), 1st pt., letter 2, p.15.

[27] *La Vie de Marianne*, ed. F. Deloffre (Paris 1963), p.17.

[28] *Les Egarements de Julie*, i.30.

[29] Ed. F. Deloffre (Paris 1959), p.9.

[30] Jacob does however feel a sudden desire to return to rural security when threatened with a dungeon or a 'pre-cuckolded' marriage: 'Enfin je me trouvai dans le jardin, le cœur palpitant, regrettant les choux de mon village, et maudissant les filles de Paris' (p.31).

[31] Perrin, *Henriette de Marconne*, pp.7-8.

[32] *Les Dangers d'un premier choix*, p.2. One observes again a reference to the contrast between 'palais' and 'masures'.

[33] Desbiefs, *Nine*, p.37.

[34] Yon, *Les Surprises*, p.75

[35] *Œuvres choisies* (Amsterdam 1784; 1st ed. 1745), xxxiii.24.

[36] Carmontelle, *Le Triomphe de l'amour sur les mœurs de ce siècle* (Amsterdam 1773), p.38.

[37] *La Paysanne pervertie*, ii.4.

Notes to chapter 4

[1] Marchand, *Le Véridique*, pp.56-57.

[2] *Journaux et œuvres diverses*, p.16.

[3] *Lettres de Thérèse*, pp.53-54.

[4] Carmontelle, *Le Triomphe de l'amour*, p.4.

[5] 'On se lève de bonne heure dans les provinces. On n'y a point encore contracté l'habitude, si familière aux habitants de la capitale, de dormir le jour et veiller la nuit' (Charpentier, *L'Elu et son président*, p.78). Cf. Voltaire, *L'Ingénu*, p.228.

[6] *Mémoires du comte de Vaxère ou le faux rabbin* (Amsterdam 1737), p.10.

[7] *Les Astuces de Paris*, p.11.

[8] Jean Bardou, *Histoire de Laurent Marcel* (Lille 1779), ii.2-10.

[9] Mouhy, *Paris ou le mentor à la mode*, p.4.

[10] *Les Filoux*, ed. J.-J. Pauvert, xiv.275.

[11] *Lettres de Montmartre*, p.75. Cf. *Candide*, pp.188-189. Actual confirmation of the provincials' gullibility can be found in Cognel, p.91: 'Nous y fîmes connaissance de deux demoiselles qui nous prirent fort habilement dans nos poches, d'abord nos mouchoirs, puis à Jacquinot un couteau en nacre de perle, et, à moi, une fort jolie bonbonnière [...]; nous ne portâmes pas plainte contre ces filles pour éviter de faire rire à nos dépens pensant que ces sortes de choses n'arrivent qu'aux gens de province.'

[12] Marivaux, *Le Spectateur français*, pp.128-29.

[13] Mouhy, *Le Financier* (Amsterdam 1755), pp.37-38.

[14] *Lettres sur les Anglais et les Français*, lettre troisième, p.204. In a section entitled 'Du jeu' the German Neimitz claims that anyone who hopes to appreciate the life of high society must first acquaint himself with the games in fashion: 'Un homme de qualité qui veut profiter de son séjour à Paris doit aller dans le monde. Or, comme on ne trouve guère à Paris des sociétés où l'on ne joue, il ne sera bien reçu que s'il sait jouer. Les Français et surtout les dames aiment fort cette distraction. Aussi trouve-t-on certaines maisons où tout le monde peut aller jouer sans avoir été présenté. Ces maisons retirent chaque année un grand bénéfice du jeu, et même quelques gens de condition n'ont pas honte de donner ainsi de jouer chez elles' (Alfred Franklin, *La Vie privée d'autrefois*, vol. xxi, Paris 1897, *La Vie de Paris sous la Régence*, p.120). Cf. Fougeret de Monbron, *La Capitale des Gaules*, p.14.

[15] *Le Mot et la chose*, p.83. Cf. Montesquieu, *Lettres persanes*, p.118: 'Le jeu est très en usage en Europe: c'est un état que d'être joueur. Ce seul titre tient lieu de naissance, de bien, de probité: il met tout homme qui le porte au rang des honnêtes gens, sans examen, quoiqu'il n'y ait personne qui ne sache qu'en jugeant ainsi il s'est trompé très souvent; mais on est convenu d'être incorrigible. Les femmes y sont surtout très adonnées. Il est vrai qu'elles ne se livrent pas guère dans leur jeunesse que pour favoriser une passion plus chère; mais, à mesure qu'elles vieillissent, leur passion pour le jeu semble rajeunir, et cette passion remplit tout le vide des autres.' Diderot likewise illustrates the prevalence of gaming and its female devotees; in *Les Bijoux indiscrets* he writes: 'La plupart des femmes qui faisaient la partie de la Manimonbanda jouait avec acharnement; et il ne fallait point avoir la sagacité de Mangogul pour s'en apercevoir. La passion du jeu est une des moins dissimulées; elle se manifeste soit dans le gain, soit dans la perte, par des symptômes frappants. Mais d'où vient leur fureur? se disait-il en lui-même; comment peuvent-ils se résoudre à passer les nuits autour d'une table de pharaon, à trembler dans l'attente d'un as ou d'un sept? cette frénésie altère leur santé et leur beauté, quand elles en ont, sans compter les désordres où je suis sûr qu'elle les précipite' (*Œuvres romanesques*, pp.29-30).

[16] pp.59-60. Descriptions of the social acceptability of gambling abound in fiction in the first half of the century: see Godard d'Aucour, *Thémidore*, p.192 (1st edition, 1745) and La Morlière, *Angola*, ed. Octave Uzanne (Paris 1879), pp.48-49 (1st edition, 1746).

[17] Lesage in his veiled survey of Parisian society mentions a nobleman who has sunk to this commerce: 'C'est un hidalgo des plus pauvres, qui, pour subsister, donne à jouer sous la protection d'un grand' (*Le Diable boiteux*, in *Romanciers du XVIIIe siècle*, Paris 1960,

i.464). We recall that Mme and Mlle d'Aisnon run a gaming establishment to eke out a living in *Jacques le fataliste*, p.614.

[18] *Alphonsine ou les dangers du grand monde* (Londres 1789), p.32.

[19] Fougeret de Monbron attacks these dens and estimates their number: 'Il y a dans Paris, à la honte du bon ordre, deux cents maisons de jeu, ou plutôt deux cents coupe-gorge, qui sont le rendez-vous des filoux et des dupes' (*La Capitale des Gaules*, p.14).

[20] *Le Début ou les premières aventures du Chevalier de* *** (Paris 1770), pp.109-10. Cf. *Candide*, p.193. The gambling dens also provide another variety of diversion; Thémidore speaks of a certain Mlle de l'Ecluse: 'c'est la femme soi-disant d'un Officier, qui donne à jouer pour l'amusement des autres et pour son profit. Il s'y rencontre assez bonne compagnie en hommes et assez libertines en femmes. Il ne se passe rien dans cette maison; mais il est bien commode d'avoir quelques endroits dans Paris où on puisse voir aisément de jolies personnes sans scandale, et en choisir à son gré sans avoir la réputation et l'air d'en chercher par besoin. [...] J'étais instruit qu'il s'y trouvait depuis peu une jeune provinciale qui venait solliciter un procès à Paris' (*Thémidore*, p.175).

[21] *Les Astuces de Paris*, ii.23-24.

[22] *La Paysanne pervertie*, iii.296.

[23] Bardou, *Histoire de Laurent Marcel*, ii.78. Cf. the fate of the hero of the anonymous *Les Aventures d'un provincial ou l'histoire du Chevalier de Jordans* (Paris 1782), p.122.

[24] Marmontel, *La Mauvaise mère*, pp.17-18.

[25] For a discussion of this topic, see R. Mauzi, 'Ecrivains et moralistes du xviiie siècle devant les jeux du hasard', *Revue des sciences humaines* 90 (1958), pp.219-56.

[26] pp.9-10. Soldiers would seem susceptible to this vice as it is illustrated again in the tale of M. de La Clamières in Mouhy's *Le Financier*, pp.76-100.

[27] *Dolbreuse*, ii.11. Cf. Mérard de Saint-Just, *Histoire de la baronne d'Alvigny* (Londres, Paris 1788), pp.157-58.

[28] Considerable sums of money were lost in a short space of time. Edmond confesses: 'j'ai perdu l'autre jour avec des Officiers, mille louis en une séance...' (*Le Paysan perverti*, iii.21). Cf. Andréa de Nerciat, *Le Diable au corps*, ed. Apollinaire (Paris 1910), p.216, and Sade, *Faxelange*, ed. J.-J. Pauvert, x.194.

[29] *Dolbreuse*, ii.12-13.

[30] ii.16. Cf. *Histoire de la baronne d'Alviguy*, p.15: 'Le jeu [...] est une passion aveugle, sinistre, sordide, frénétique, et à laquelle on peut donner toutes les qualifications dégradantes. Cette passion fait braver l'opinion publique qu'on affecte de mépriser. L'usage, la loi impérieuse des gens du monde, des besoins chimériques nés d'un luxe scandaleux, d'absurdes conventions ne cessent d'augmenter cette passion effrénée; elle influe sur toutes les circonstances de la vie privée.'

[31] Jean-Robert Armogathe notes that the eighteenth century came to condemn gaming on moral rather than theological grounds. Numerous laws were passed against it but: 'les jeux sont l'objet d'interdictions passionnées à partir des années 1760-1770', *Le Jeu au XVIIIe siècle* (Aix-en-Provence 1976), p.29.

[32] We do not contend that gambling did not have its critics in pre-1760 fiction but it did not arouse the opprobrium evidenced in the later period. For early criticism of gambling see Lesage, *Le Diable boiteux* (1st edition, 1707), pp.284-85; also Duclos, *Les Confessions du Comte de* *** (1st edition, 1741), p.248. Duclos makes similar observations in his *Considérations sur les mœurs de ce siècle*, pp.108-109.

[33] *Les Nuits de Paris* (Londres 1788), 2nd pt., xlixe nuit, p.470.

[34] Fougeret de Monbron, *Margot la ravaudeuse*, postface by M. Saillet (Paris 1965), p.96. Cognel noted in his record of his stay in Paris, pp.15-16: 'à l'issue des spectacles, [...] les filles, en costumes de gala, viennent exercer le pouvoir de leurs charmes [...] elles s'offrent

comme un marchand offre sa marchandise, et, dès que le but de leur promenade est atteint, elles emmènent chez elles leur proie, ou se font conduire dans l'enceinte du Palais-Royal, dans des lieux qui ont le nom de grottes.'

[35] *Le Paysan et la paysanne pervertis* (La Haye 1784-87), iii.486.

[36] Mme Violaine, *Les Mémoires de Saint-Gory*, p.31. Cf. Nougaret, *Les Travers d'un homme de qualité*, ii.4.

[37] pp.31-32. Foreigners apart, Chevrier claims that the usual prey of the 'filles d'Opéra' are: 'Des Français de Province et quantité d'autres automates que les ressorts de la tendresse lyrique font mouvoir pour la circulation de l'argent et le bien-être des prêtresses de la bonne Vénus' (*Paris, histoire véridique anecdotique morale et critique*, La Haye 1767, p.81).

[38] *Correspondance d'Eulalie*, i.8.

[39] Baculard d'Arnaud, *Germeuil*, pp.64-65.

[40] C.F.Lambert, *Les Aventures de trois coquettes ou les promenades des Tuileries* (Paris 1779; 1st edition, 1740), p.67.

[41] *Thérèse philosophe*, ed. R. Dugéry (Paris 1966), p.136 (1st edition, 1748).

[42] Jullien, *dit* Des Boulmiers, *Histoire d'une comédienne qui a quitté le spectacle*, p.47, in *Honny soit qui mal y pense*.

[43] *Les Ridicules du siècle*, p.48.

[44] Sainte-Croix, *La Comédienne, fille et femme de qualité*, pp.154-55.

[45] *La Marmotte parvenue*, p.76, in *Honny soit qui mal y pense*.

[46] *Les Aventures de trois coquettes*, p.149.

[47] Is this a scene borrowed from *La Vie de Marianne* or is it a stock situation in the contemporary novel? Another unfortunate is picked up in ecclesiastical surroundings by Mme Fanel who sells her to a minister, M. de Carmeline. The wretch suspected nothing; Ninette avows: 'En vérité [...] j'étais encore si peu au fait de l'usage de Paris, ou pour mieux dire, si imbécile qu'au lieu de ne douter de quoi il s'agissait, la vanité si naturelle aux jeunes personnes de mon âge, me fit désirer une préférence, cependant si contraire à la vertu que je chérissais' (Mouhy, *Le Danger des spectacles*, iii.161).

[48] Jeannette in Nougaret's *La Paysanne pervertie* has unwittingly been escorted to a brothel too. One also remembers Saint-Preux's seduction after being tricked into supping in a 'lieu suspect'.

[49] *Les Egarements de Julie*, iii.73.

[50] *Les Ridicules du siècle*, p.66.

[51] *Lucile ou les progrès de la vertu* (Paris 1768), p.23. Cf. Fougeret de Monbron, *Margot la ravaudeuse*, p.11.

[52] Sainte-Colombe, *Les Plaisirs d'un jour*, pp.257-58.

[53] pp.142-43. Criticism of society and pity for the wretched state of the whore are commonplace opinions in the works of the more liberal writers in the last few decades before the Revolution. See for example, Mercier, *Le Tableau de Paris*, passim; Restif, *Les Nuits de Paris*, 1st. pt., VIIIe nuit, p.59; Mme Benoist, *Les Erreurs d'une jolie femme ou l'Aspasie française* (Bruxelles 1781), pp.218-19.

[54] Louvet suggests that the capital gains many of its whores from the provinces (*Les Amours de Faublas*, p.474). Olwen Hufton writes: 'The prostitutes of Paris were Alsatians and Lorraines from the Ile de France, Burgundy, and the Bourbonnais' (*The Poor of eighteenth-century France 1750-1789*, Oxford 1974, p.311).

Notes to chapter 5

[1] For a discussion of Marivaux's treatment of Paris and the provinces in his journals see W. Pierre Jacobée, *La Persuasion de la charité* (Amsterdam 1976), pp.135-40.

[2] Damiens de Gomicourt, *Dorval ou mémoires pour servir à l'histoire des mœurs du dix-huitième siècle* (Amsterdam 1769), pp.117-18.

[3] The treacherous nature of Parisian friends is a topic exploited by Marmontel. The visitor is deceived by the welcoming nature of the capital's inhabitants. L'Etang is most pleased with his reception: 'L'Etang fut surpris du nombre d'amis qu'il trouva dans la bonne ville. Ces amis ne l'avaient jamais vu; mais son mérite les attirait en foule' (*La Mauvaise mère*, p.15). His merit was exclusively in his purse of which his companions made a communal kitty. Mélidor is another who is prepared to share out his means and earns the comment: 'Personne à Paris n'a autant d'amis qu'un homme opulent et prodige. Ceux de Mélidor, à son souper, ne manquaient pas de le louer en face; et ils avaient l'honnêteté d'attendre qu'on fût hors de table pour se moquer de lui' (*La Femme comme il y en a peu* (1765) in *Contes moraux*, iv.199). La Solle states in like vein: 'Les donneurs d'avis sont en plus grand nombre à Paris que les amis' (*Mémoires de Versorand*, ii.46).

[4] Leroy de Lozembrune, *Tableau des mœurs* (Mannheim 1786), p.50.

[5] The corruption of the large city and the evil influence of a mentor are a familiar theme in Baculard's *Epreuves du sentiment*, for example, *Fanny* (1764) i.

[6] Lesuire, *Le Crime* (Bruxelles 1789), i.44-45.

[7] i.57. On the same page César sneers at the provinces: 'Tu me trouverais déjà très changé. Quand je me représente tous nos provinciaux, à commencer par toi-même, je sens une certaine commisération qui marque bien l'intérêt que vous m'inspirez encore, tous tant que vous êtes.'

[8] Rutlidge, *Alphonsine*, pp.82-83.

[9] Barthe, *La Jolie femme*, pp.15-16.

[10] p.18. For a sympathetic treatment of this novel see Eileen Thompsett, 'The theme of seduction in the eighteenth-century French novel: Barthe's *La Jolie femme*', *Forum for modern language studies* 12 (1976), pp.206-16.

[11] In *Les Epreuves du sentiment*, i.198.

[12] p.212. Cf. Sainte-Colombe, *Les Plaisirs d'un jour*, p.50.

[13] *La Paysanne pervertie*, i.131.

[14] i.12. Cf. i.334 (note): 'Comme le vice entre peu à peu dans les cœurs à la ville! car Ursule était bonne et franche, ainsi qu'Edmond; ils étaient sortis bons tous deux des mains de Dieu et de nos parents.'

[15] In his article, 'Restif de La Bretonne und Pierre-Jean-Baptiste Nougaret', *Germanisch-Romanische Monatschrift* 17 (1967), Dietmar Rieger analyses the relationships between these two writers. He suggests Restif was inspired to write on the theme of the peasant corrupted by Paris through acquaintanceship with Nougaret's *Lucette, ou les progrès du libertinage* (1765), an earlier version of the latter's *La Paysane pervertie*. We would reject this suggestion on the grounds that Restif was above all recreating his own life cycle in a literary form. If one looks for sources, one could equally put forward claims for Marivaux's *Le Paysan parvenu* or even Mouhy's *La Paysanne parvenue*.

Notes to chapter 6

[1] Marquis de Mirabeau, *L'Ami des hommes* (La Haye 1758), pp.88-89.

[2] *Le Tableau de Paris*, vol. i, *Grandeur démesurée de la capitale*, p.15. Cf. i.14.

[3] *Le Tableau de Paris*, vol. iv, ch. 354, *De l'influence de la capitale sur les provinces*, pp.296-97.

[4] *Emile*, ed. F. and P. Richard (Paris 1961), Livre cinquième, pp.599-600. Cf. Rousseau's *Lettre à m. d'Alembert* (Genève, Lille 1948), p.125: '[Paris est] la capitale de la France et le gouffre des richesses de ce grand Royaume.'

⁵ *Lettres d'un philosophe sensible* (La Haye 1769), p.188.

⁶ The influx of provincial capital and the habit of the nobility in residing in the city substantially increased rents according to d'Argenson: 'Les loyers des maisons deviennent partout d'un prix excessif, preuve de la fréquence et de l'attrait de demeurer à Paris et de quitter les provinces, tandis qu'on devait renvoyer tous les gens riches dans les campagnes pour y mettre l'aisance au lieu de la misère' (quoted in Ducros, *La Société française au XVIIIe siècle*, Paris 1922, p.110).

⁷ *L'Ami des hommes*, p.190. Cf. Arthur Young: 'It is thus that banishment alone will force the French nobility to execute what the English do for pleasure – reside upon and adorn their country estates' (*Travels in France*, ed. M. Betham Edwards, London 1924, p.66).

⁸ pp.192-93. Cf. p.305. A. Allem cites the marquis d'Argenson's *Gouvernement de la France*, published in 1764 but previously circulated in manuscript: 'Les grands terrains deviennent bon marché, étant cultivés par peu de monde; les campagnes sont désertes; les seigneurs n'habitent plus leurs terres, s'en désintéressent' (*Le Marquis d'Argenson et l'économie politique au début du XVIIIe siècle*, Paris 1900, p.54).

⁹ *La Nouvelle Héloïse, préface de Julie ou entretien sur les romans*, p.20. He continues his attack: 'Les auteurs, les gens de lettres, les philosophes ne cessent de crier que, pour remplir ses devoirs de citoyen, pour servir ses semblables, il faut habiter les grandes villes. Selon eux, fuir Paris, c'est haïr le genre humain, le peuple de la campagne est nul à leurs yeux ... les contes, les romans, les pièces de théâtre, tout tire sur les provinciaux; tout tourne en dérision la simplicité des mœurs rustiques; tout prêche les manières et les plaisirs du grand monde; c'est une honte de ne les pas connaître; c'est un malheur de ne les pas goûter. Qui sait de combien de filous et de filles publiques l'attrait de ces plaisirs imaginaires peuple Paris de jour en jour. Ainsi les préjugés et l'opinion, renforçant l'effet des systèmes politiques, amoncellent, entassent, les habitants de chaque pays sur quelques points de territoire, laissant tout le reste en friche et désert; ainsi, pour faire briller les capitales, se dépeuplent les nations; et ce frivole éclat, qui frappe les yeux des sots, fait courir l'Europe à grands pas à sa ruine.' Mirabeau had already condemned seventeenth-century comedies for the lasting damage they had caused by their presentation of provincials: 'en ridiculisant les gentilshommes campagnards, les Barons de la Crasse, les Sottenville etc., ils n'ont cru attaquer que la sotte vanité et la plate ignorance des seigneurs châtelains; mais les mots de campagnard et de provincial sont devenus ridicules. La crainte du ridicule ferait passer un Français par le gouleau d'une bouteille; tout le monde a voulu devenir homme de cour ou de ville, et adieu les champs' (*L'Ami des hommes*, p.133).

¹⁰ For example: 'On envoya le jeune baron à Paris, où il devait demeurer pendant plusieurs années pour s'y perfectionner dans les différents exercices propres à former un jeune gentilhomme de sa naissance et de son rang' (abbé Lambert, *Mémoires et aventures d'une dame de qualité qui s'est retirée du monde*, La Haye 1741, ii.5). Cf. *Histoire de monsieur de Terny et de mademoiselle de Barnay*, in Chasles, *Les Illustres Françaises*, i.128; d'Argens, *Le Mentor cavalier ou les illustres de notre siècle* (Londres 1736), p.2; Desbiefs, *Sophie* (La Haye 1756), p.6.

¹¹ For example Villaret, *Le Cocq ou mémoires du Chevalier de V**** (Amsterdam 1742), p.61; d'Argens, *Mémoires du Comte de Vaxère*; F. Marchant, *Le Roman sans titre* (Paris 1788); Laffichard, *Histoire du curé de ****, in *L'Amour chez les philosophes*; Charpentier, *L'Elu et son président*, pp.20-21. Ange Goudar attacks this centralisation of instruction as another nail in the coffin of the provinces: 'les Académies, les Universités, les Ecoles Publiques, ... attirent à elles un grand nombre de provinciaux à Paris, et ... les y fixent à la fin ... S'il y a un homme de génie dans nos provinces, ces Académies l'attirent d'abord à Paris, et presque toujours il s'y établit' (*Les Intérêts de la France mal entendus*, Amsterdam 1756, i.182-83). He goes on to complain that they deprive the provinces of their most capable sons and suggests removing these institutions to less populous areas to stimulate growth.

The present situation: 'prive leurs provinces des secours qu'elles étaient naturellement en droit d'en attendre. Pourquoi ne pas destiner, au contraire, certaines villes du Royaume les plus dépeuplées pour ces Universités et Ecoles Royales? Cela remettrait en partie l'équilibre de notre population, et rendrait florissante l'Agriculture dans plusieurs provinces où elle est languissante, faute de consommateurs' (p.184).

[12] For example Gimat de Bonneval, *Le Voyage de Mantes* (Amsterdam 1753), p.4.

[13] vi.127. The Chevalier de La Morlière makes a comment on the superabundance of servants in *Angola*, p.148, when the Princesse Luzéide comes to court preceded by: 'une foule de domestiques, *un tas d'inutiles* qui suivent ou précédent les grands seigneurs, qui ne leur sont d'aucune utilité, qu'ils ne connaissent seulement pas, qui ne servent qu'à désoler tout le monde dans les endroits où ils passent, et à crever *les chevaux de poste.*' Here, however, is an early jibe aimed at no real critical end.

[14] Diderot puts forward similar proposals in the article 'Homme' in the *Encyclopédie*, viii.278. Ange Goudar also reflects the excessive numbers of servants in the capital: 'On ne saurait nier qu'il y ait trop de domestiques dans cette capitale' (*L'Anti-Babylone*, Londres 1760, p.176). Pierre Gaxotte estimates that there were between forty and fifty thousand domestics in the capital in the middle of the eighteenth century. These were divided amongst over seventeen thousand families, the majority possessing just one employee. It is evident that the richer echelons of society employed innumerable servants in what could have been little more than a decorative function. See *Paris au XVIIIe siècle*, pp.57-58.

[15] Avignon 1763, p.208. In *Le Paysan parvenu*, in addition to Jacob, the other servants are of provincial origin, pp.71, 102.

[16] La Haye 1769, pp.58-59. Servants are often criticised as a manifestation of the corrupt society that employs them, indeed Saint-Preux used them as a yardstick: 'Les valets imitent les maîtres; et, en les imitant grossièrement, ils rendent sensibles dans leur conduite les défauts que le vernis de l'éducation cache mieux dans les autres. A Paris, je jugeais des mœurs des femmes de ma connaissance par l'air et le ton de leurs femmes de chambre; et cette règle ne m'a jamais trompé' (*La Nouvelle Héloïse*, p.445). Cf. the anonymous *Les Deux amis* (Amsterdam 1767), p.10.

[17] *Jacques le fataliste*, p.760.

[18] See our article 'Diderot and the problem of the servant', *Quinquereme* 2 (1979), pp.180-90.

[19] The tale appears in *Le Médecin de l'amour* (Paris 1787), p.239.

[20] *Les Amours du chevalier de Faublas*, p.761.

[21] *Les Confessions d'un fat* (Frankfurt 1750), p.7.

[22] La Salle d'Offement, *Le Maladroit*, pp.43-44.

[23] Charpentier, *L'Elu et son président*, p.71.

[24] Mme Le Prince de Beaumont, *Œuvres mêlées* (Maestricht 1775), ii.46.

[25] Bricaire de La Dixmerie, *Les Dangers d'un premier choix*, p.14.

[26] Marchand, *Le Véridique*, p.42.

[27] For an analysis of this question, see A. Morize, *L'Apologie du luxe au XVIIIe siècle et 'Le Mondain' de Voltaire* (Paris 1909) and H. T. Mason, 'Voltaire's poems on luxury' in *Studies in the French eighteenth century*, presented to John Lough (University of Durham 1978), pp.108-22. With his experience as a landowner actively working his estates, Voltaire's attitude may have modified in later years as John Pappas suggests in 'Voltaire et le luxe: une mise au point', in *Enlightenment studies in honour of Lester G. Crocker*, ed. A. J. Bingham and V. W. Topazio (Oxford 1979), pp.221-30.

[28] *L'Ami des hommes*, p.196.

[29] p.207. Further on Mirabeau claims the desire and effects of luxury are spreading:

'Le luxe gagne également tous les ordres de la société, du premier au dernier, chacun dans sa proportion, et en conséquence il s'établit la paresse et le désir de consommer beaucoup et de travailler peu' (p.199).

[30] *Œuvres économiques et philosophiques*, ed. A. Oncken (Frankfurt, Paris 1888), p.189.

[31] *Les Intérêts de la France mal entendus*, i.96.

[32] M. R. de Labriolle-Rutherford notes that the eighteenth century increasingly replaced the moral attitude to luxury by an economic one ('L'évolution de la notion du luxe depuis Mandeville à la Révolution', *Studies on Voltaire* 26 (1963), pp.1025-36).

[33] *Le Franc Breton, Nouveaux contes moraux*, ii.209.

[34] C.-P.-B. Wouters, *L'Art de corriger* (Londres 1783), p.60.

[35] *Le Cultivateur*, p.30. Cf. Loaisel de Tréogate, *Ainsi finissent les grandes passions; ou les dernières amours du Chevalier de* ... (Paris 1788), p.119.

[36] *La Paysanne pervertie*, pp.129-30. Ursule finds herself free to meet the disgraced Laure as she tells her sister: 'Vois pourtant, ma chère sœur, ce que c'est qu'une grande ville! Nous voilà que nous nous parlons et que personne ne le trouve mauvais! Suppose notre village, que de discours! Il aurait fallu passer notre vie à nous regarder noir, ou nous exposer à mille désagréments' (p.136).

[37] Barthe, *La Jolie femme*, p.14. The old lady has already warned: 'Vous allez dans une ville aimable et séduisante pour la jeunesse! Là, des pièges enchanteurs vous seront offerts de toutes parts: on n'y voit que des spectacles, des bals, des divertissements de toute espèce; on y tient table le jour, on y joue la nuit. Tout cela me fait frémir: votre salut va être en grand danger. Paris est une nouvelle Babylone, de grâce ne vous y damnez point' (p.12).

[38] Le Prince de Beaumont, *Œuvres mêlées*, ii.83. Cf. Baculard d'Arnaud, *Pauline et Suzette*, in *Les Epreuves du sentiment*, iv.238: 'En effet, Mademoiselle de Monticourt ne fut pas longtemps à Paris sans se ressentir de cet air contagieux de légèreté qu'on semble y respirer.'

[39] When the Comte learns that Nougaret's Jeannette is to come to the capital, he is overjoyed: 'elle sera bientôt dans Paris ... disons simplement qu'elle n'a plus que quelques jours à s'enorgueillir de sa haute sagesse: j'ai lieu de tout attendre de l'air contagieux de la ville, que cette vertu sauvage va respirer' (*La Paysanne pervertie*, p.240). The same terms are employed in the early novel but are only used to develop plot and character. Sainte-Croix's heroine confesses: 'Il faut que l'air de Paris soit contagieux. Je sentis en moi le germe de la coquetterie se développer tout à coup; je ne respirais plus que les plaisirs tumultueux, que les compliments flatteurs, que les assemblées nombreuses et brillantes, que les spectacles fréquentés, que les promenades à la mode, que la parure la plus recherchée; je ne m'étudiai plus qu'à plaire, qu'à charmer' (*La Comédienne fille* (1755), p.16). Cf. Desbiefs, *Sophie*, p.212.

[40] Nougaret, *La Paysanne pervertie*, iv.278.

[41] *Lecture du matin* (Paris 1782), pp.4-5. Cf. Mercier, *Le Tableau de Paris*, i.34-35.

[42] *La Nouvelle Héloïse*, p.273. Cf. *Lettre à m. d'Alembert*, p.115.

[43] Baculard condemns metropolitan populations in the same vein as Rousseau: 'Si un peuple sur la terre peut nous donner une idée de la simplicité grecque, ce sont, sans contredit, les Anglais; j'entends ceux qui vivent dans la contrée ou la campagne, et non les citoyens de Londres; car tous les habitants des grandes villes se rassemblent: parvenus au même degré de corruption, ils ont à peu près le même fonds de vices et de folies' (*Fanny*, préface, p.xiii).

[44] *Le Paysan perverti*, iv.83. Restif claims that citizens are sometimes oblivious of their own corruption: 'il [Monsieur Nicolas] conçut que le plus grand nombre de ceux que renferment les villes ont l'âme corrompue sans peut-être s'en douter' (*Monsieur Nicolas, reprise de la huitième époque*, p.308).

[45] *Monsieur Nicolas, cinquième époque*, p.103.

[46] In *Les Epreuves du sentiment*, ii.292-93.

[47] p.294. Cf. Nougaret, *La Paysanne pervertie*, pp.xv-xvi: 'je ne dis point qu'il faille que les villes soient dépeuplées; mais je dis qu'on devrait y voir moins le désordre, le luxe insolent, la pauvreté affligeante, et je fais des vœux ardents pour que l'innocence ne soit pas toujours exposée à la séduction, au désespoir, à l'infamie.'

Notes to chapter 7

[1] Chevrier, *Les Mémoires d'une honnête femme* (first edition, 1753) in *Œuvres complètes* (1774), ii.248.

[2] pp.49-50. Mercier makes a similar point but in a more censorious tone in *Le Tableau de Paris*, iv.298-99.

[3] *Mémoires de Justine*, p.111.

[4] Mme de Violaine, *Mémoires de Saint-Gory*, pp.42-43.

[5] Marmontel, *Le Franc Breton*, p.253.

[6] Longchamps, *Les Aventures d'un jeune homme*, pp.107-108.

[7] *Œuvres complètes*, xiv.203.

[8] p.133. The passage recalls the valedictory remarks which close book IV of Rousseau's *Emile*, p.444: 'Adieu donc, Paris, ville célèbre, ville de bruit, de fumée et de boue, où les femmes ne croient plus à l'honneur ni les hommes à la vertu. Adieu, Paris: nous cherchons l'amour, le bonheur, l'innocence, nous ne serons jamais assez loin de toi.'

[9] Barbé-Marbois, *La Parisienne en province*, pp.141-59. Throughout these pages Montalban expatiates on the virtues of agriculture. The general influence of physiocratic thought on this novel and other works we shall mention seems certain. The basic dogma of this group of political economists was that agriculture was the primary source of wealth. For a re-appraisal of the physiocrats, see Elizabeth Fox-Genovese, *The Origins of physiocracy: economic revolution and social order in eighteenth-century France* (Ithaca 1976).

[10] *Le Scrupule*, p.138. This tale first appeared in the *Mercure de France* in 1756 and is chronologically in the early period of the century we have established. We are, however, using 1760 as a guideline and not a rigid demarcation line.

[11] For the increasing interest in farming technique in the second half of the century, see A. J. Bourde, *The Influence of England on the French agronomes 1750-1789* (Cambridge 1953).

[12] Marmontel asserts that intransigent 'intendants' are often stumbling-blocks to necessary reform (p.119).

[13] Jacques Wagner, *Marmontel journaliste et le 'Mercure de France' (1725-1761)* (Grenoble 1975), pp.210, 244-45.

[14] Reviewing Pattullo's work Marmontel: 'ne recule pas devant les aspects les plus techniques de la question'; Jacques Wagner, 'Marmontel journaliste au *Mercure de France* (1758-1760)', in *De l'Encyclopédie à la Contre-Révolution, Jean-François Marmontel (1723-1799)*, ed. J. Ehrard (Clermont-Ferrand 1970), p.87.

[15] Gacon-Dufour, *Les Dangers de la coquetterie* (Paris 1788), p.6.

[16] p.148. Cf. the anonymous *Adoulzin ou les dangers d'une mauvaise éducation* (La Haye 1787), p.48.

[17] Loaisel de Tréogate claims that the life of the town is most prejudicial to the maintenance of an effective army: 'le séjour des villes [...] leur [aux soldats] soit infiniment préjudiciable [...] Ce serait dans la campagne, loin des objets du luxe, et des scènes de la débauche, qu'on pourrait plus sûrement les préparer aux fatigues de la guerre [...] Les filles de mauvaise vie, si communes dans les garnisons, les maladies, les

vices destructeurs qui résultent de leur commerce, ces causes et plusieurs autres énervent les forces du soldat' (*Dolbreuse*, pp.52-53, note).

[18] Bricaire de La Dixmerie, *Les Dangers d'un premier choix*, p.10.

[19] Nougaret, *Les Dangers des circonstances*, iv.420.

[20] The Commandeur d'Holney takes his duties very seriously, almost in a feudal manner, he aspires above all to: 'rendre justice à ses vassaux, les concilier, prévenir leurs besoins, les récompenser de leurs travaux, adoucir leurs charges' (Bette d'Ettienville, *La Marquise de Ben****, Spa, Paris 1788, i.14-15). Cf. Musset, *Correspondance d'un jeune militaire ou mémoires du marquis de Luzigni et d'Hortense de Saint-Just* (Yverdun 1778), i.179-80.

[21] Célidor is a young man keen on travelling to broaden his knowledge who believes that acquaintance with peasants is a sound guide to living: 'L'agriculture, étant, selon moi, l'art le plus utile, et malheureusement le plus avili, c'est en conversant souvent avec ces hommes simples et rustiques, dénués de tout artifice, que l'on peut s'instruire dans la connaissance du cœur humain' (Gacon-Dufour, *L'Homme errant*, Paris 1787, p.9).

[22] *Les Amours du Chevalier de Faublas*, pp.905-906.

[23] *La Nouvelle Héloïse*, 5th pt., letter 2, pp.535-36. Julie believes that those who desert their villages will be demoralised by their dealings with urban communities: 'Or, de mille sujets qui sortent du village, il n'y en a pas dix qui n'aillent se perdre à la ville, ou qui n'en portent les vices plus loin que les gens dont ils les ont appris. Ceux qui réussissent et font fortune la font presque tous par les voies déshonnêtes qui y mènent. Les malheureux qu'elle n'a point favorisés ne reprennent plus leur ancien état, et se font mendiants ou voleurs plutôt que de devenir paysans' (pp.536-37).

[24] *Annette et Lubin* (1761), *Contes moraux*, iii.131.

[25] See R. Mauzi, *L'Idée du bonheur au dix-huitième siècle* (Paris 1960).

[26] p.121. Writing to her husband, the Marquise de Joinville muses on what life must have been like in earlier epochs. Formerly lords were content to reside on their domains and she hopes to recapture this tranquillity: 'Me voilà de retour dans le château de vos pères, où ils se plaisaient à fixer leur demeure, et où je tâche de les remplacer, en imitant une partie du bien qu'ils y ont fait autrefois. Que les mœurs antiques devaient procurer un bonheur parfait! Leur simplicité, leur bonhomie assuraient des jours sans trouble et vraiment heureux. Ils bornaient leur ambition à vivre dans leurs domaines, au milieu des villageois qu'ils rendaient fortunés. Maintenant ils habitent à la cour, ou dans le sein du luxe ruineux de la capitale; ils préfèrent à la tranquillité dont ils pourraient jouir dans leurs terres, l'agitation et les soucis d'une ambition jamais satisfaite et toujours renaissante' (Nougaret, *Les Dangers des circonstances*, ii.119).

[27] *Correspondance d'un jeune militaire*, i.40-41.

[28] Cf. Nougaret, *La Paysanne pervertie*, ii.98. Louise tells her sister that the rough common sense of the country is better than town wit and adds: 'Le dimanche est consacré dans les campagnes à un amusement qui surpasse tous ceux que l'on recherche à la ville: le soir, après les vêpres, nous nous assemblons sous l'ormeau, dans le beau milieu du village, non pour nous regarder, mais pour rire, pour danser'.

[29] *Les Dangers de la coquetterie*, i.10.

[30] Bette d'Ettienville, *La Marquise de Ben****, p.7.

[31] Montendre is not impressed by what he sees in Paris: 'Je ne trouve point à Paris, dans cette ville, dont on parle avec tant d'emphase, quelque chose de comparable à ce joli Belvédère d'où je découvrais une campagne si riante, où je respirais un air si frais, si pur. Depuis cinq jours que j'ai quitté mon hermitage, je n'aperçois rien qui en approche. J'ai vu de belles maisons, de grands salons bien ornés, enrichis de tableaux; mais ces tableaux ne valent pas celui que j'avais devant les yeux' (Delacroix, *Lettres d'un philosophe sensible*, p.10).

[32] *La Nouvelle Héloïse*, 5th pt., letter 2, p.554. Cf. *Lettre à m. d'Alembert*, p.80.

[33] Gacon-Dufour, *L' Homme errant*, p.51. Cf. Musset, *Correspondance d'un jeune militaire*, p.41.

[34] *Les Infortunes du jeune Chevalier de La Lande* (Paris 1783), p.35.

[35] The Chevalier de La Lande claims urban inhabitants have only a minimum dosage of 'sensibilité' due to the life they lead: 'Je ne suis pas surpris que les habitants des villes aient si peu, mais si peu de sensibilité: la petitesse de leurs occupations, la frivolité de leurs entretiens, la vivacité de leurs plaisirs, la fureur du jeu, ont bientôt étouffé cette touche sentimentale, ce tact fin et délicat, qui ne peut s'entretenir que dans la retraite et la solitude des campagnes' (pp.19-20).

[36] Marmontel, *Le Franc Breton*, pp.265-66.

[37] Gacon-Dufour, *L'Homme errant*, p.86.

[38] Barthe, *La Jolie femme*, p.121.

[39] pp.134-35. The Parisians' susceptibility to ailments unknown in the provinces is often instanced in the fiction of the second half of the century. Lubin is asked by his sweetheart to explain the origin of the vapours afflicting a lady she had seen lying on a couch, he replies: 'je me doute que c'est quelqu'une de ces maladies que l'on gagne à la ville, et qui ôtent l'usage des jambes aux personnes de qualité' (Marmontel, *Annette et Lubin*, p.133). The Comte de Murcin is astonished on his first visit to Paris to find that all is not gay: 'Je croyais qu'à Paris où tout respirait le plaisir, tout le monde était très gai, et que l'on s'y portait à merveille; presque toutes les femmes que nous vîmes se plaignaient de leur santé; c'était des insomnies, des maux de nerfs, de mauvais estomacs, des langueurs, et des anéantissements d'une tristesse épouvantable' (Carmontelle, *Le Triomphe de l'amour*, p.36).

[40] Charpentier, *Lucile*, in *Nouveaux contes moraux* (Amsterdam 1767-1778), ii.9-10.

[41] *Les Amours du Chevalier de Faublas*, p.907.

[42] Mme de Coteneuve, *Lettres du baron d'Olban* (Amsterdam, Paris 1777), pp.1-2. Cf. Marmontel's *Le Scrupule*, pp.139-40, where Pruli tells Bélise of the superiority of country love: 'Ils s'aiment comme des tourterelles; ils me donnent appétit d'aimer. – Vous avouerez cependant que cela aime sans délicatesse. – Eh! madame, la délicatesse est un raffinement de l'art: ils ont l'instinct de la nature, et cet instinct les rend heureux. On parle d'amour à la ville; on ne le fait que dans les champs. Ils ont en sentiment ce que nous avons en esprit.'

[43] *Bazile*, p.8. Julie's mother doubts the wisdom of sending her to Paris: 'Hélas vous allez dans une ville où il est aisé de s'égarer, où tout respire la séduction; Paris est le séjour du crime' (*Julie*, p.200).

[44] *Monsieur Nicolas, neuvième époque*, p.265.

Notes to the conclusion

[1] The term 'philosophe' enjoyed an ambiguous usage in contemporary vocabulary. As we have seen in this study it is employed for a Parisian corruptor as well as a provincial sage. For a discussion of the term see John Lough,'Who were the *philosophes*', in *Studies in eighteenth-century French literature*, presented to Robert Niklaus, ed. J. H. Fox, M. A. Waddicor and D. A. Watts (Exeter 1975), pp.139-50.

[2] *Le Vice à la mode: étude sur le roman français du XVIIIe de 'Manon Lescaut' à l'apparition de 'La Nouvelle Héloïse' (1731-1761)* (Paris 1979), p.73.

[3] Two of the most useful studies in this area are L. G. Crocker, *An Age of crisis* (Baltimore 1959) and Peter Gay, *The Enlightenment: an interpretation: the rise of modern paganism* (London 1967).

[4] R. Grimsley provides a useful summary of his ideas, 'Rousseau's Paris' in *City and society in the eighteenth century*, ed. P. Fritz and D. Williams (Toronto 1973), pp.3-18.

[5] We cannot agree with Bernard Gille who claims that at this time: 'On ne monte pas à Paris pour faire fortune comme on le fera dans les romans de Balzac dans la première moitié du xixe siècle, on va à Paris fortune faite' (*Colloques. Paris. Fonctions d'une capitale*, p.141).

[6] *Les Intérêts de la France*, i.179.

[7] i.180. This section is entitled: *Il faut commencer par diminuer le nombre des provinciaux qui habitent Paris.*

[8] There is of course no doubt that the capital's population was augmented by provincial recruits: 'Paris would probably have lost population in the eighteenth century had it not been for a steady flow of immigrants from the provinces' (Jeffry Kaplow, *The Names of kings: the Parisian laboring poor in the eighteenth century*, New York 1972, p.81).

[9] *Le Drame en France au 18e siècle* (Paris 1910), p.256.

[10] Act ii, sc. 5. Mercier likewise underlines his support for agriculture and rural workers in *L'Indigent* (1772) and *Le Juge* (1774).

[11] *La Parisienne en province*, pp.141-59, *passim*.

[12] *La Parisienne en province*, p.47.

[13] *La Jolie femme*, p.117.

[14] *La Parisienne en province*, p.69.

[15] *La Jolie femme*, pp.134-35.

[16] *La Parisienne en province*, p.62.

[17] *La Jolie femme*, p.122.

[18] *Epître à Saint-Lambert* (1769), M.x.407. Saint-Lambert had great success with *Les Saisons* (1769). Margaret Cameron writes that 'Saint-Lambert, comme Thomson, appelle les riches au secours des déshérités de la terre. Mais le lieu commun du poème anglais devient une doctrine dans les *Saisons* françaises, l'auteur demandant des réformes sociales définies, destinées à améliorer le sort du paysan français' (*L'Influence des 'Saisons' de Thomson sur la poésie descriptive en France (1759-1810)*, Paris 1927, pp.145-46). Saint-Lambert overtly used his poem to champion agriculture and the country-side as a philosophic duty.

[19] Voltaire was a practical man and one should be wary of reading too much into a statement which really conveys the status quo. Similarly one could make too much of the admission of the abbé de St Yves: 'Il y a [...], je l'avoue, beaucoup d'inconstants et de fripons parmi nous; et il y en aurait autant chez les Hurons s'ils étaient rassemblés dans une grande ville' (*L'Ingénu*, p.240). One remembers that Mlle de Kerkabon worries that Hercule may be 'caché dans quelqu'une de ces vilaines maisons de joie' in Paris (p.257). Nevertheless Voltaire does have anxieties about aspects of Parisian life which we feel Roy Wolper underplays in 'The toppling of Jeannot', *Studies on Voltaire* 183 (1980), pp.69-83. Since our study was completed, J. M. Fahmy has published an extended treatment of the topic: *Voltaire et Paris*, Studies on Voltaire 195 (1981).

[20] Cited in P. Citron, *La Poésie de Paris dans la littérature française de Rousseau à Baudelaire* (Paris 1961), i.106.

[21] 'De la signification d'une poésie insignifiante: examen de la poésie fugitive au xviiie siècle et de ses rapports avec la pensée sensualiste en France', *Studies on Voltaire* 94 (1972), p.349.

[22] *Epître sur les voyages* (1765) in *Œuvres complètes de J. Delille* (Paris 1824), i.44.

[23] *Jacques Delille (1738-1813) et le poème de la nature en France de 1750 à 1820* (Paris 1974), p.25.

[24] *London transformed: images of the city in the eighteenth century* (New Haven, London 1978), p.86.

[25] For example John Cleland, *Memoirs of a woman of pleasure*, ed. P. Quennel (New York 1963), p.32.

[26] See Samuel Richardson, *Clarissa Harlowe* (Oxford 1930), vol. iii, letter LIX, p.315; William Dodd, *The Sisters or the history of Lucy and Caroline Sanson entrusted to a false friend* (London 1781), p.27; Henry Mackenzie, *The Man of feeling*, ed. B. Vickers (London 1967), p.60; Charlotte Lennox, *Henrietta* (London 1758), i.30-31.

[27] See J. R. Foster, *History of the pre-Romantic novel in England* (New York 1949), p.162. In poetry too the drift from the land to the city is denounced, for example Thomas Gray's *Elegy written in a country churchyard* (1751) and Oliver Goldsmith's *The Deserted village* (1770).

[28] The tradition of Virgil and pastoral literature in general must have contributed to this idealisation of the countryside as the locus of authenticity. One often senses that novelists depict the countryside following literary tradition rather than representing the rural life of the eighteenth century. An extended treatment of the influence of classical writers in this area would be illuminating. J. M. Blanchard has provided a useful starting point in his 'Style pastoral, style des lumières', *Studies on Voltaire* 114 (1973), pp.331-46. D. J. Fletcher also raises stimulating points for further treatment in '*Candide* and the theme of the happy husbandman', *Studies on Voltaire* 161 (1976), pp.137-47.

[29] When Marmontel was composing his first tales agronomic works were being produced in abundance. 'Aux environs de 1750, le grand public, provincial et parisien, s'engoua d'agronomie' (M. Morineau, *Les Faux-semblants d' un démarrage économique: agriculture et démographie en France au XVIIIe siècle*, Paris 1971, p.7). Turbilly earned success with his *Mémoires sur les défrichements* (1760): 'Turbilly y expose ses idées sur le soutien à apporter à l'agriculture et à la population, sur les abus fiscaux à corriger, sur les moyens de lutter contre l'absentéisme, l'exode rural, le luxe, la mendicité et divers autres abus' (A. Sauvy and J. Hecht, 'La population agricole française au XVIIIe siècle et l'expérience du marquis de Turbilly', *Population* 13 (1958), p.279). The authors go on to claim: 'Il est certain qu'après 1760, grâce en partie à la publicité physiocratique et à la diffusion d'écrits comme le *Mémoire sur les défrichements*, plusieurs nobles s'intéressèrent à l'agriculture' (p.285). Indeed Harry C. Payne claims 'After 1750 social criticism in France focused primarily on conditions in the countryside' (*The Philosophes and the people*, New Haven, London 1976, p.48).

[30] *Le Dilemme du roman au XVIIIe siècle* (New Haven 1963), pp.180-81.

[31] *Tableau de Paris*, vol. v, chapter 7, p.25. Cf. iv.27: 'Si l'on compte qu'il n' y a point eu d'homme célèbre né en province qui ne soit venu à Paris pour se former, qui n'y soit venu par choix, et qui n'y soit mort, ne pouvant quitter cette grande ville, malgré l'amour de la patrie: cette race d'hommes éclairés, tous concentrés sur le même point, tandis que les autres villes du royaume offrent des landes d'une incroyable stérilité, devient un profond objet de méditation sur les causes réelles et subsistantes qui précipitent tous les gens de lettres dans la capitale, et les y retiennent comme par enchantement.'

[32] To evaluate the sincerity of hacks is an impossible undertaking. Nevertheless, the plethora of attacks on Paris and the abundance of praise for the provinces in the minor works of the later period do, at least, underline the force of current opinion, since their authors were obviously 'cashing in' on the marketing of fashionable ideas. Baculard's attitude to Paris would seem to have evolved as in an early work he presents it as being a valuable school for youth; see Robert Dawson, *Baculard d'Arnaud: life and prose fiction*, Studies on Voltaire 141-142 (1976), i.116. A study of Grub Street writers engaged in producing fiction, plays, pamphlets, journalism, etc., might prove a fascinating piece of research in the last years before the Revolution. Robert Darnton offers interesting insights

in this field in 'The high Enlightenment and the low-life of literature in pre-Revolutionary France', in *French society and the Revolution*, ed. D. Johnson (Cambridge 1976), pp.53-87.

[33] *Considérations sur les mœurs*, p.13.

[34] *La Nouvelle Héloïse*, 2nd pt., letter XVI, p.242.

List of works consulted

Primary sources

With the exception of modern editions, first editions of eighteenth-century French fiction have been used for the most part. Where other editions have been employed the date of the first edition has been indicated in parentheses.

Adoulzin ou les dangers d'une mauvaise éducation. La Haye 1787

Amour vainqueur du vice, ou lettres du marquis de Cousanges, L'. Amsterdam 1775

André, J.-F., *La Méchante femme.* Paris 1788

Arcq, P.-A. de Sainte-Foix, chevalier d', *Le Roman du jour, pour servir à l'histoire du siècle.* Londres 1754

Argens, J.-B. de Boyer, marquis d', *La Vie de mademoiselle Carville.* Cythère 1745

— *Le Mentor cavalier ou les illustres infortunés de notre siècle.* Londres 1736

— *Lettres chinoises.* La Haye 1757 (1739)

— *Mémoires du chevalier de ***.* Paris 1747 (1745)

— *Mémoires du comte de Vaxère ou le faux rabbin.* Amsterdam 1737

— *Thérèse philosophe.* ed. R. Dugéry, Paris 1966

Arnaud, F.-T.-M. de Baculard d', *Les Epreuves du sentiment.* vols i-ii, Vienna 1787, vols iii-vi, Maestricht 1779. *Bazile* (1774), *Clary* (1767), *Fanny* (1764), *Germeuil* (1777), *Julie* (1767), *Nancy* (1767), *Pauline et Suzette* (1777), *Sélicourt* (1769)

Aubigné, Théodore-Agrippa d', *Les Avantures du baron de Faeneste.* ed. H. Weber, Paris 1969

Auvigny, J. Du Castre d', *Mémoires du comte de Comminville.* Amsterdam 1735

Aventures d'un provincial ou l'histoire du chevalier de Jordans, Les. Paris 1782

Barbé-Marbois, F., marquis de, *La Parisienne en province.* Amsterdam, Paris 1770 (1769)

Barbier, E.-J.-F., *Journal historique et anecdotique du règne de Louis XV.* Paris 1874

Bardou, J., *Histoire de Laurent Marcel.* Lille 1779

Barret, P., *Mademoiselle Javotte.* Bruxelles 1883 (1757)

Barthe, N.-T., *La Jolie Femme ou la femme du jour.* Lyon, Paris 1770 (1769)

Bastide, J.-F. de, *Contes.* Paris 1763

— *Les Aventures de Victoire Ponty.* Amsterdam, Paris 1758

— *Les Confessions d'un fat.* Frankfurt 1750 (1749)

— *Les Ressources de l'Amour.* Amsterdam 1752

— *Le Tombeau Philosophique.* Amsterdam 1751

Beauharnais, F. de, *Le Somnambule.* Paris 1786

Béliard, F., *Lettres critiques sur le luxe et sur les mœurs de ce siècle.* Amsterdam 1771

— *Rézéda.* Amsterdam 1751

Benoist, F.-A. Puzin de La Martinière, *Les Erreurs d'une jolie femme ou l'Aspasie française.* Bruxelles 1781

Bertrand (de Montpellier), *Mémoires d'un Languedocien.* Montpellier 1772

Bette d'Ettienville, J.-C.-V. de, *La Marquise de ***.* Spa, Paris 1788

Blondel, J., *Des hommes tels qu'ils sont et doivent être.* Londres 1758

— *Loisirs philosophiques.* Londres 1756

Boisgiron, madame de, *Les Suites d'un moment d'erreur.* Amsterdam, Paris 1775

Boudier de Villemart, P.-J., *L'Ami des femmes.* Paris 1758

Boufflers, S. J., marquis de, *Aline reine de Golconde,* ed. S. Davies. Exeter 1977

Bret, A., *La Belle Allemande ou les galanteries de Thérèse.* Strasbourg 1764 (1745)

Bricaire de La Dixmerie, N., *Les Dangers d'un premier choix.* La Haye, Paris 1785

Bridard de La Garde, P., *Les Lettres de Thérèse ou mémoires d'une jeune demoiselle pendant son séjour à Paris.* La Haye 1740-1742 (1737?)

Bridel, J.-L., *Les Infortunes du jeune Chevalier de La Lande.* Paris 1783

Briel, J.-H.-D., *Les Heures du loisir.* Londres

1786
Brooke, H., *The Fool of quality*. London 1872

Campan, D., *Le Mot et la chose*. n. p. 1752
Campion, C.-M., *Œuvres*, ed. E. Seeber & H. Remak. Indiana 1945
Carmontelle, L. C., dit de Pestels de Levis, comte de, *Le Triomphe de l'Amour sur les mœurs de ce siècle*. Amsterdam 1773
Caylus, A.-C.-P. de Tubières-Grimoard, *Histoire de Guillaume Cocher*. Paris 1970
Charpentier, L., *L'Elu et son président*. Paris 1769
— *Nouveaux contes moraux*. Amsterdam 1767
— *Vos loisirs*. Amsterdam, Paris 1768
Chasles, R., *Les Illustres Françaises*, ed. F. Deloffre. Paris 1959
Chevrier, F.-A., *Le Colporteur*. n. p. 1762
— *Les Mémoires d'une honnête femme*, in *Œuvres complètes*. Bruxelles 1774, vol. ii (1753)
— *Les Ridicules du siècle*, in *Œuvres complètes*. vol. ii (1753)
— *Paris, histoire véridique, anecdotique, morale et critique*. La Haye 1767
Cleland, J., *Memoirs of a woman of pleasure*, ed. P. Quennel. New York 1963
Cognel, F., *La Vie Parisienne sous Louis XVI*. Paris 1882
Collé, C., *Journal et mémoires*. Paris 1868
Compan, abbé, *Le Temple de la Piété*. Avignon 1765
Contant d'Orville, A.-G., *Sophie*. Amsterdam, Paris 1779
Corneille, P., *Le Menteur*. 1644
Corneille, T., *La Baron d'Albikrac*. 1669
Correspondance d'Eulalie ou tableau du libertinage de Paris. Londres 1785 (1784)
Coteneuve, de, *La Confiance trahie*. Amsterdam 1777
— *Lettres du Baron d'Olban*. Amsterdam, Paris 1772
Coustelier, A.-U., *Lettres de Montmartre*. Londres 1750
Crébillon (fils), C.-P. Jolyot de, *Les Egarements du cœur et de l'esprit*, ed. R. Etiemble. Paris 1961
— *Collection complète des œuvres*. Londres 1777
Cubières-Palmézeaux, M. de, *L'Ecole des filles*. Cassel 1784
Cultivateur, Le. Amsterdam, Paris 1770

Damiens de Gomicourt, A.-P., *Dorval ou mémoires pour servir à l'histoire des mœurs du dix-huitième siècle*. Amsterdam 1769

Delille, J., *Œuvres complètes*, vol. i. Paris 1824
Desbiefs, L., *Nine*. Amsterdam, Paris 1756
— *Sophie*. La Haye, Paris 1756
Desforges, *Mémoires, anecdotes pour servir à l'histoire de M. Duliz*. Londres 1739
— *Les Deux amis*. Amsterdam 1767
Diderot, D., *Œuvres romanesques*, ed. H. Bénac. Paris 1962
Diderot, D. *et al.*, *L'Encyclopédie*. (reprint) Stuttgart 1966-1967
Didot, P., *L'Ami des jeunes demoiselles*. Paris 1789
Digard de Kerguette, J., *Mémoires et aventures d'un bourgeois qui s'est avancé dans le monde*. La Haye 1750
Dodd, W., *The Sisters or the history of Lucy and Caroline Sanson entrusted to a false friend*. London 1781
Donneau de Visé, J., *Le Gentilhomme Guespin*. 1670
Doppet, F.-A., *Le Médecin de l'Amour*. Paris 1787
Drouet de Maupertuy, J.-B., *La Femme faible*. Amsterdam 1755 (1714?)
Duclos, C. P., *Considérations sur les mœurs de ce siècle*, ed. F. C. Green. Cambridge 1946
— *Histoire de Mme de Luz*, in *Œuvres complètes*, vol. viii. Paris 1806 (1714)
— *Les Confessions du Comte de ****, in *Romanciers du XVIIIe siècle*, vol. ii. Paris 1965
— *Mémoires pour servir à l'histoire des mœurs du XVIIIe siècle*, in *Œuvres complètes*, vol. vii (1751)

Elie de Beaumont, A.-L. Dumesnil-Molin, madame, *Lettres du Marquis de Rozelle*. Londres, Paris 1764
Etoile heureuse, L'. Berlin 1756
Eulalie ou les dernières volontés de l'amour. Londres 1777

Falconnet, A., *Le Début ou les premières aventures du Chevalier de ****. Paris 1770
Fenestre de Hotot, P.-A.-E., *Mémoires d'une provinciale*. Amsterdam, Paris 1764
Fielding, H., *Tom Jones*. New York 1964
Fontette de Somméry, mlle, *Lettres de Mlle de Tourville*. Paris 1788
Fougeret de Monbron, L.-C., *La Capitale des Gaules*. Londres 1760
— *Margot la Ravaudeuse*, postface by M. Saillet. Paris 1965
Furetière, A., *Le Roman bourgeois*, ed. A.

Adam. Paris 1958

Gacon-Dufour, M.-A.-J. d'Humières, madame, *L'Homme errant*. Paris 1787
— *Les Dangers de la coquetterie*. Paris 1788
Gaillard, P.-A., *dit* Gaillard de La Bataille, *Jeannette Seconde ou la nouvelle paysanne parvenue*. Amsterdam 1744
— *Mémoires et aventures de Monsieur le Comte de Kermalec*. La Haye 1749 (1740-1741)
Gillet de La Tessonerie, J.-B., *Le Campagnard*. 1657
Gimat de Bonneval, J-.B., *Fanfiche*, in *Bibliothèque choisie et amusante*, vol. iv. Amsterdam 1749 (1743?)
— *Le Voyage de Mantes*. Amsterdam 1753
Godard d'Aucour, C., *Histoire et aventures de *** par lettres*. n. p. 1744
— *Mémoires turcs*. Paris 1743
— *Thémidore*. Londres 1781 (1745)
Goldsmith, O., *The Deserted village*, in *Collected works*, ed. Friedman, vol. iv, Oxford 1966
Gorgy, J.-C., *Blançay*. Paris 1788
— *Victorine*. Paris 1789
Goudar, A., *L'Anti-Babylone*. Londres 1760
— *Les Intérêts de la France mal entendus*. Amsterdam 1756
Graffigny, F. d'Issembourg d'Happencourt, mme de, *Lettres d'une Péruvienne*, ed. Nicoletti. Bari 1967
Gresset, J.-B.-L., *Le Méchant*. 1745
Guer, J.-H., *Pinolet ou l'aveugle parvenu*. Amsterdam 1755

Hardy, S.-P., *Mes loisirs*, ed. Tourneux et Vitrac. Paris 1912
Haudart, *Vie et amours du pauvre diable provincial*. Genève 1788 (1784)
Hauteroche, N. Le Breton, sieur de, *Les Nobles de province*. 1682
Histoire de Gogo. La Haye 1739

Imbert, B., *Lecture du matin*. Paris 1782

Jèce, *Etat ou tableau de la ville de Paris*. Paris 1760
Jonval, *Les Erreurs instructives*. Londres, Paris 1765
Jullien, J.-A., *dit* Desboulmiers, *Honny soit qui mal y pense*. Londres 1761
— *Le Bon fils*. Amsterdam 1769

Karamzin, N. M., *Letters of a Russian travel-*

ler, 1789-90, trans. F. Jones. New York 1957

La Bruyère, J. de, *Les Caractères*, ed. R. Garapon. Paris 1962
Laclos, P.-A.-F. Choderlos de, *Les Liaisons dangereuses*, ed. Y. de Hir. Paris 1952
La Croix, J.-V. de, *Lettres d'un philosophe sensible*. La Haye 1769
— *Mémoires de Victoire*. Amsterdam, Paris 1769
Laffichard, T., *L'Amour chez les philosophes*. La Haye, 1748
Lambert, C. F., *Aventures de trois coquettes*. Paris 1779 (1740)
— *La Nouvelle Marianne*. La Haye 1740
— *Mémoires et aventures d'une dame de qualité qui s'est retirée du Monde*. La Haye 1741
La Morlière, C.-J.-L.-A. Rochette de, *Angola*, ed. O. Uzanne. Paris 1879 (1740)
La Peyre, *Les Mœurs de Paris*. Amsterdam 1747
La Salle d'Offement, A.-N. Piédefer, marquis de, *Le Maladroit*. Paris 1788
La Solle, H.-F, de, *Mémoires de Versorand*. Amsterdam 1750
Leblanc, J.-B., *Lettres d'un Français*. La Haye 1745
Lennox, C., *Henrietta*. London 1758
Le Prince de Beaumont, Marie, *Œuvres mêlées*. Maestricht 1775
Leroy de Lozembrune, F.-C., *Tableau des Mœurs*. Mannheim 1786
Lesage, A. R., *Histoire de Gil Blas de Santillane*, in *Romanciers du XVIIIe siècle*, vol. i. Paris 1960
— *La Valise trouvée*. n. p. 1740
— *Le Diable boiteux*. *ibid*.
— *Turcaret*. 1709
Lesbros de La Versane, L., *Caractères des femmes*. Londres 1773 (1769)
Lesuire, R. M., *Le Crime*. Bruxelles 1789
— *Le Repentir*. Bruxelles 1789
Lezay-Marnézia, C.-F.-A., marquis de, *L'Heureuse famille*. Genève 1766
Lintot, C. Cailleau, dame de, *Histoire de Mademoiselle Datilly*. La Haye 1745
Loaisel de Tréogate, J.-M., *Ainsi finissent les grandes passions; ou les dernières amours du Chevalier de ...*. Paris 1788 (1787)
— *Dolbreuse ou l'homme du siècle ramené à la vertu par le sentiment et la raison*. Amsterdam, Paris 1783
Longchamps, P. C. de, *Les Aventures d'un*

jeune homme. Londres 1765

Louvet de Couvray, J.-B., *Les Amours du Chevalier de Faublas,* in *Romanciers du XVIIIe siècle,* vol. ii

Luchet, J.-P.-L. de La Roche Du Maine, marquis de, *Le Vicomte de Barjac.* Dublin 1784

— *Une Seule faute ou les mémoires d'une demoiselle de qualité.* Bruxelles 1788

Mackenzie, H., *The Man of feeling,* ed. B. Vickers. London 1967

Magny, J.-B.-M., *Mémoires de Justine.* Londres 1754

Mailhol, G., *Le Cabriolet.* Amsterdam 1755

Marais, M., *Journal et mémoires,* ed. Lesuire. Paris 1864

Marchand, J.-H., *Les Avis d'un père à son fils.* Amsterdam 1751

— *Les Délassements champêtres, ou mélanges d'un philosophe séreux à Paris, et badin à la campagne.* La Haye 1767 (first part published 1759)

— *Le Véridique ou mémoires de M. de Fillerville.* Amsterdam 1769

Marchant, F., *Le Roman sans titre.* Paris 1788

Marivaux, P. Carlet de Chamblain de, *Journal et œuvres diverses,* ed. F. Deloffre and M. Gilot. Paris 1969

— *La Provinciale.* 1761

— *La Vie de Marianne,* ed. F. Deloffre. Paris 1963

— *Le Paysan parvenu,* ed. F. Deloffre. Paris 1959

— *Œuvres de jeunesse,* ed. F. Deloffre and C. Rigault. Paris 1972

Marmontel, J.-F., *Contes moraux.* Paris 1801-1805

— *Annette et Lubin.* (1759)

— *La Femme comme il y en a peu.* (1765)

— *La Mauvaise mère.* (1759)

— *Laurette.* (1765)

— *Le Connaisseur.* (1761)

— *Le Franc Breton.* (1791)

— *Le Misanthrope corrigé.* (1765)

— *Le Scrupule.* (1756)

Meheust, madame, *Les Mémoires du Chevalier de ***.* Paris 1734

Mérard de Saint-Just, A.-J.-F. d'Ormoy, mme, *Histoire de la Baronne d'Alvigny.* Londres, Paris 1788.

— *Mon journal d'un an.* Parme, Paris 1788

Mercier, L.-S., *L'An deux mille quatre cent quarante,* ed. R. Trousson. Bordeaux 1971

— *Le Campagnard ou le riche désabusé.* La Haye 1779

— *Le Tableau de Paris.* Amsterdam 1782-1788

— *Théâtre complet.* Amsterdam 1778-1784

Mirabeau, Victor Riqueti, marquis de, *L'Ami des hommes.* La Haye 1758

Moine galant, Le. n. p. 1756

Molière, J.-B. Poquelin, *dit, Les Précieuses ridicules.* 1659

— *George Dandin.* 1668

— *La Comtesse d'Escarbagnas.* 1671

— *Monsieur de Pourceaugnac.* 1669

Montesquieu, C.-L. de Secondat, baron de La Brède et de, *Les Lettres persanes,* ed. P. Vernière. Paris 1960

Montfleury, A.-J., *dit, Le Gentilhomme de Beauce.* 1670

Mouhy, C. de Fieux, chevalier de, *La Paysanne parvenue.* Amsterdam 1746 (1735-1737)

— *Le Danger des spectacles.* Paris 1780

— *Le Financier.* Amsterdam 1755

— *Paris ou le mentor à la mode.* Paris 1735-1736

Muralt, B. L. de, *Lettres sur les Anglais et les Français et sur les voyages,* ed. C. Gould. Paris 1933

Musset, L.-A.-M. de, marquis de Cogners, *Correspondance d'un jeune militaire.* Yverdun 1778

Nerciat, A.-R. Andréa de, *L'Œuvre,* ed. G. Apollinaire. Paris 1910

Nougaret, P.-J.-B., *La Paysanne pervertie.* Londres, Paris 1777

— *Le Danger des circonstances.* Bruxelles, Paris 1789

— *Les Astuces de Paris.* Londres 1775

— *Les Faiblesses d'une jolie femme.* Amsterdam 1779

— *Les Travers d'un homme de qualité.* Bruxelles 1788

— *Paris vu tel qu'il est.* Londres 1781

Pauvre diable provincial, Le. Avignon 1763

Perrin, J.-A.-R., *Henriette de Marconne.* Amsterdam, 1763

— *Les Egarements de Julie.* Paris 1806 (1755)

Prévost d'Exile, A.-F., *Le Monde moral.* in *Œuvres choisies.* Amsterdam, Paris 1783-1785, vol. xxix (1760)

— *Manon Lescaut,* ed. F. Deloffre and R. Picard. Paris 1965

— *Mémoires d'un honnête homme*, in *Œuvres choisies*, vol. xxxiii (1745)

Puineuf, baron de, *Mémoires et aventures du baron de Puineuf*. La Haye 1737

Pure, M. de, *La Prétieuse ou le mystère des ruelles*, ed. E. Magne. Paris 1938-1939

Puységur, F.-J. de Chastenet, marquis de, *Histoire de madame de Bellerive*. Londres 1780 (1768)

Quesnay, F., *Œuvres économiques et philosophiques*, ed. A. Oncken. Frankfurt, Paris 1888

Quinault, P., *L'Amant indiscret*. 1654

Restif de La Bretonne, N.-E., *Ingénue Saxancour*, preface by G. Lely. Paris 1965
— *La Malédiction paternelle*. Leipzig 1780
— *La Paysanne pervertie*. La Haye 1784
— *La Vie de mon père*, ed. G. Rouger. Paris 1970
— *Le Paysan perverti*. La Haye 1776
— *Le Paysan et la paysanne pervertis*. La Haye 1787
— *Le Pied de Fanchette*. La Haye 1769
— *Les Contemporains*. Paris 1962
— *Les Contemporaines*, ed. Assézat. Paris 1876
— *Les Nuits de Paris*. Londres 1788
— *Lucile ou les progrès de la vertu*. Paris 1768
— *Monsieur Nicolas*, ed. J.-J. Pauvert. Paris 1959

Riccoboni, M.-J. Laboras de Mézières, madame, *Lettres de Milord Rivers*. Paris 1777

Robert, M.-A. de Roumier, madame, *La Paysanne philosophe*. Amsterdam 1752
— *La Voix de la nature*. Amsterdam 1770 (1763)
— *Nicole de Beauvais*. La Haye, Paris 1767

Rousseau, J.-J., *Confessions*, ed. J. Voisine. Paris 1964
— *Emile*, ed. F. and P. Richard. Paris 1961
— *La Nouvelle Héloïse*, in *Œuvres complètes* vol. ii, ed. H. Coulet. Paris 1961
— *Lettre à m. d'Alembert sur les spectacles*, ed. M. Fuchs. Genève, Lille 1948

Rutlidge, J., *Alphonsine*. Londres 1789
— *Les Premiers et second voyages de Mylord de *** à Paris*. Yverdun 1777
— *Le Vice et la faiblesse ou mémoires de deux provinciales*. Lausanne, Paris 1785

Sade, D.-A.-F., marquis de, *Œuvres complètes*, ed. J.-J. Pauvert. Paris 1966-1967

Saint-Clair, de, *Les Egarements d'un philosophe*. Genève, Paris 1786

Sainte-Colombe, E.-G. Colombe, dit, *Les Plaisirs d'un jour ou la journée d'une provinciale à Paris*. Bruxelles 1764

Sainte-Croix, de, *La Comédienne, fille et femme de qualité*. Bruxelles 1756

Saint-Foix, G.-F. Poullain de, *Lettres turques*. Cologne 1744 (1730)

Saint-Lambert, J.-F., marquis de, *Les Saisons*. 1769

Scarron, P., *Le Roman comique*. Paris 1958

Sénac de Meilhan, G., *Considérations sur l'esprit et les mœurs*. Londres 1787

Sorel, C., *Histoire comique de Francion*. Paris 1958

Tencin, C.-A. Guérin, marquise de, *Mémoires du Comte de Comminges*. Paris 1885 (1735)

Tilly, J.-P.-A., comte de, *Mémoires pour servir à l'histoire des mœurs de la fin du XVIIIe siècle*, ed. Melchior-Bonnet. Paris 1965
— *Les Trois voluptés*. n. p. 1746

Uncy, mademoiselle, *Contes moraux*. Amsterdam, Paris 1763

Ussieux, L. d', *Nouvelles françaises*. Paris 1779

Vasse, C.-P.-B. Wouters, baronne de, *L'Art de corriger*. Londres 1783
— *Les Aveux d'une femme galante*. Londres 1782

Villaret, C., *Le Cocq*. Amsterdam 1742

Violaine, madame la comtesse de, *Mémoires de Saint-Gory*. Londres, Paris 1776

Voltaire, F.-M. Arouet de, *Epitres à Saint-Lambert, Œuvres complètes*, ed. L. Moland, vol. x. Paris 1877
— *Le Comte de Boursoufflé*, ed. Moland, vol. vii
— *Romans et contes*, ed. H. Bénac. Paris 1960

Yon, le chevalier, *Les Femmes de mérite*. n. p. 1759

Young, A., *Travels in France*, ed. M. Bethan-Edwards. London 1924

Secondary sources

Allem, A., *Le Marquis d'Argenson et l'économie politique au début du XVIIIe siècle.* Paris 1900

Babeau, A., *La Province sous l'ancien régime.* Paris 1894

Béclard, L., *Louis-Sébastien Mercier, sa vie, son œuvre, son temps, d'après des documents inédits.* Paris 1903

Behrens, B., *The Ancien régime.* London 1967

Bernard, L., *The Emerging city: Paris in the age of Louis XIV.* Durham, North Carolina 1970

Blanchard, J. M., 'Style pastoral, style des lumières', *Studies on Voltaire* 114 (1973), pp.331-46

Bourde, A. J., *Agronomie et agronomes en France au XVIIIe siècle.* Paris 1967

— *The Influence of England on the French agronomes 1750-1789.* Cambridge 1958

Bowling, T. W., *Life, works and literary career of Loaisel de Tréogate,* Studies on Voltaire 196 (Oxford 1981)

Brengues, J., *Duclos ou l'obsession de la vertu.* Saint-Brieuc 1971

Brocard, L., *Les Doctrines économiques et sociales du marquis de Mirabeau.* Paris 1902

Brooks, P., *The Novel of worldliness.* Princeton 1969

Buchanan, M., 'Les *Contes moraux* de Marmontel', *French review* 16 (1967), pp.201-12

Byrd, M., *London transformed: images of the city in the eighteenth century.* New Haven and London 1978

Cameron, M., *L'Influence des 'Saisons' de Thomson sur la poésie descriptive en France (1759-1810).* Paris 1927

Cherpack, C., *An essay on Crébillon fils.* North Carolina 1962

Chevalier, L., *Classes laborieuses et classes dangereuses à Paris pendant la première moitié du XIXe siècle.* Paris 1958

— *Les Parisiens.* Paris 1967

Citron, P., *La Poésie de Paris dans la littérature française de Rousseau à Baudelaire.* Paris 1961

— *City and society in the 18th century,* ed. P. Fritz and D. Williams. Toronto 1973

Clouzot, H. and R. H. Valensi, *Le Paris de la 'Comédie humaine'.* Paris 1926

— *Colloques, cahiers de civilisation. Paris, croissance d'une capitale.* Paris 1961. *Paris, fonctions d'une capitale.* Paris 1962

Coulet, H., *Le Roman jusqu'à la Révolution.* Paris 1967

— *Marivaux romancier: essai sur l'esprit et le cœur dans les romans de Marivaux.* Paris 1975

Crocker, L. G., *An age of crisis.* Baltimore 1959

— *Nature and culture: ethical thought in the Enlightenment.* Baltimore 1963

Crosby, E. A., *Une romancière oubliée, mme Riccoboni: sa vie, ses œuvres, sa place dans la littérature française et anglaise du XVIIIe siècle.* Paris 1924

Darnton, R., 'The high Enlightenment and the low-life of literature in pre-Revolutionary France', in *French society and the Revolution,* ed. D. Johnson, Cambridge 1976, pp.53-87

Davies, S. F., 'Diderot and the problem of the servant', *Quinquereme* 2 (1979), pp.180-90

— 'Louvet as social critic: *Les Amours du Chevalier de Faublas*', *Studies on Voltaire* 183 (1980), pp.223-37

Dawson, R., *Baculard d'Arnaud: life and prose fiction,* Studies on Voltaire 141-42 (Banbury 1976)

De l'Encyclopédie à la Contre-Révolution, Jean-François Marmontel (1723-1799), ed. J. Ehrard. Clermont-Ferrand. 1970

Delon, M., 'Vision du monde "préromantique" dans *Dolbreuse* de Loaisel', *Annales de Bretagne* 82 (1976), pp.829-38

Duncan, J. L., 'The rural ideal in eighteenth-century fiction', *Studies in English literature* 8 (1968), pp.517-35

Ducros, L., *La Société française au dix-huitième siècle.* Paris 1922

Etienne, S., *Le Genre romanesque en France, depuis l'apparition de la 'Nouvelle Héloïse' jusqu'aux approches de la Révolution.* Bruxelles 1922

Fage, A., 'Les doctrines de population des Encyclopédistes', *Population* 6 (1951)

Fahmy, J. M., *Voltaire et Paris,* Studies on Voltaire 195 (1981)

Fauchéry, P., *La Destinée féminine dans le*

roman européen du dix-huitième siècle, 1713-1807: essai de gynécomythie romanesque. Paris 1972

Fletcher, D. J., '*Candide* and the theme of the happy husbandman', *Studies on Voltaire* 161 (1976), pp.137-147

Forno, L., *Robert Chasles: intimations of the Enlightenment.* Rutherford 1972

Fosca, F., *Histoire des cafés de Paris.* Paris 1936

Foster, J., *History of the pre-romantic novel in England.* New York 1949

Fox-Genovese, E., *The Origins of physiocracy: economic revolution and social order in eighteenth-century France.* Ithaca 1976

Franklin, A., *La Vie privée d'autrefois*, vol. xxi: *La Vie de Paris sous la Régence.* Paris 1897

Gaiffe, F., *Le Drame en France au 18e siècle.* Paris 1910

Galliani, R., 'Le débat en France sur le luxe: Voltaire et Rousseau', *Studies on Voltaire* 161 (1976), pp.205-17

Gaxotte, P., *Paris au XVIIIe siècle.* Paris 1968

Gay, P., *The Enlightenment: an interpretation: the rise of modern paganism.* London 1967

George, M. D., *London life in the eighteenth century.* London 1965

Gilot, M., *Les Journaux de Marivaux: itinéraire moral et accomplissement esthétique.* Lille 1975

Godenne, R., *Histoire de la nouvelle française.* Genève 1970

Green, F. C., 'A forgotten novel of manners of the eighteenth century: *La Paysanne parvenue* by the chevalier de Mouhy', *Modern language review* 18 (1923), pp.309-16

— 'Further evidence of realism in the French novel of the eighteenth century', *Modern language notes* 40 (1925), pp.257-70

— *La Peinture des mœurs de la bonne société dans le roman français de 1715 à 1761.* Paris 1924

— 'Realism in the French novel in the first half of the eighteenth century', *Modern language notes* 38 (1923), pp.321-29

— 'The chevalier de Mouhy, an eighteenth-century novelist', *Modern philology* 22 (1925), pp.225-37

Grieder, J., 'The novel as a genre: formal French literary theory, 1760-1800',

French review 46 (1972), pp.278-90

Guitton, E., *Jacques Delille (1738-1813) et le poème de la nature en France de 1750 à 1820.* Paris 1974

Gusdorf, G., *Naissance de la conscience romantique au siècle des Lumières.* Paris 1976

Hinde, Stewart J., *The Novels of mme Riccoboni.* Chapell Hill 1976

Huet, M.-H., *Le Héros et son double: essai sur le roman d'ascension sociale au 18e siècle.* Paris 1975

Hufton, O., *The Poor of eighteenth-century France 1750-1789.* Oxford 1974

Jacoebée, W. B., *La Persuasion de la charité.* Amsterdam 1976

Johnston, E., *Le Marquis d'Argens: sa vie et ses œuvres.* Paris 1929

Joly, R., *Deux études sur la préhistoire du réalisme: Diderot et Rétif de La Bretonne.* Quebec 1969

Jones, J. F., *La Nouvelle Héloïse: Rousseau and Utopia.* Genève 1977

Jones, S. P., *A list of French prose fiction from 1700 to 1750.* New York 1939

Kaplow, J., *The Names of kings: the Parisian laboring poor in the eighteenth century.* New York 1972

Kranowski, N., *Paris dans les romans d'Emile Zola.* Paris 1968

Kunstler, C., *La Vie quotidienne sous Louis XV.* Paris 1953

Labriolle-Rutherford, M. R. de, 'L'Evolution de la notion du luxe depuis Mandeville jusqu'à la Révolution', *Studies on Voltaire* 26 (1963), pp.1025-36

Las Vergnas, R, *Le Chevalier Rutlidge, 'gentilhomme anglais' 1742-1794.* Paris 1932

Laufer, R., *Lesage ou le métier de romancier.* Paris 1971,

— *La Ville au XVIIIe siècle.* Aix-en-Provence 1975

— *Le Jeu au XVIIIe siècle.* Aix-en-Provence 1976

Loaisel de Saulnays, H., *Un méconnu, Loaisel de Tréogate.* Alger 1930

Mackrell, J. Q. C., *The Attack on 'feudalism' in eighteenth-century France.* London 1973

Mandrou, R., *La France au XVIIe et XVIIIe siècles.* Paris 1967

Martin A., 'Argent, commerce et autres thèmes bourgeois vers 1770: les romans et contes de Louis Charpentier', *Zeitschrift für französische Sprache und Literatur* 84 (1974), pp.307-24

Martin, A., V. Mylne, & R. Frautschi, *Bibliographie du genre romanesque français 1751-1800*. London 1977

Mauzi, R., *L'Idée de bonheur au dix-huitième siècle*. Paris 1960

— 'Ecrivains et moralistes du xviiie siècle devant les jeux de hasard', *Revue des sciences humaines* 90 (1958), pp.219-56

May, G., *Le Dilemme du roman au dix-huitième siècle*. New Haven 1963

Meister, P., *Charles Duclos 1704-72*. Genève 1956

Morineau, M., *Les Faux-semblants d'un démarrage économique en France au XVIIIe siècle*. Paris 1971

Morize, A., *L'Apologie du luxe au XVIIIe siècle et 'Le Mondain' de Voltaire*. Paris 1909

Mornet, D., *Le Sentiment de la nature en France de J.-J. Rousseau à B. de Saint-Pierre*. Paris 1907

Moser, W., 'De la signification d'une poésie insignifiante: examen de la poésie fugitive au xviiie siècle et de ses rapports avec la pensée sensualiste en France', *Studies on Voltaire* 94 (1972), pp.277-415

Mumford, L., *The Culture of cities*. London 1938

Mylne, V., *The Eighteenth-century French novel: techniques of illusion*. Manchester 1965

— *Paris in literature*, Yale French studies 32 (1964)

Paulson, R., *The Fictions of satire*. Baltimore 1967

Payne, H. C., *The Philosophes and the people*. New Haven and London 1976

Pitsch, M., *La Vie populaire à Paris au XVIIIe siècle*. Paris 1949

Pizzorusso, A., 'Situations and environment in *Margot la Ravaudeuse*', *Yale French Studies* 40 (1968), pp.142-55

Poirier, R., *La Bibliothèque universelle des romans*. Genève 1976

Porter, C. A., *Restif's novels, or an autobiography in search of an author*. New Haven 1967

Ranum, O., *Paris in the age of absolutism*. New York 1968

Raymond, A., 'Le problème de la population chez les encyclopédistes', *Studies on Voltaire* 26 (1963), pp.1379-88

Réau, L., *Le Rayonnement de Paris au XVIIIe siècle*. Paris 1946

Renwick, J., 'Jean-François Marmontel: the formative years 1753-1765', *Studies on Voltaire* 76 (1970), pp.139-232

Rieger, D., 'Rétif de La Bretonne und Jean-Pierre-Baptiste Nougaret', *Germanisch-romanische Monatsschrift* 17 (1976), pp.52-77

Rivers, J., *Louvet: revolutionist and romance writer*. London 1910

Rosbottom, R., *Marivaux's novels: theme and function in early eighteenth-century narrative*. Rutherford 1974

Rustin, J., *Le Vice à la mode: étude sur le roman français du XVIIIe siècle de 'Manon Lescaut' à l'apparition de 'La Nouvelle Héloïse' (1731-1761)*. Paris 1979

Sauvy, A. and S. Hecht, 'La population agricole française au xviiie siècle et l'expérience du marquis de Turbilly', *Population* 13 (1958)

Sée, H., *La France économique et sociale au XVIIIe siècle*. Paris 1967

Sekora, J., *Luxury: the concept in western thought, Eden to Smollett*. Baltimore 1977

Sgard, J., *Prévost romancier*. Paris 1968

Sheppard, T., *Lourmarin in the eighteenth century: a study of a French village*. Baltimore 1971

Showalter, jnr, E., *The Evolution of the French novel, 1641-1782*. Princeton 1972

Spengler, J. J., *French predecessors of Malthus*. New York 1965

Starobinski, J., *Jean-Jacques Rousseau, la transparence et l'obstacle*. Paris 1957

Stevenson, N., *Paris dans la 'Comédie humaine' de Balzac*. Paris 1938

— *Studies in eighteenth-century French literature presented to Robert Niklaus*, ed. J. H. Fox, J. H. Waddicor and D. A. Watts, Exeter 1975

Stewart, P., *Imitation and illusion in the French memoir novel, 1700-1750*. New Haven 1969

— *Studies in the French eighteenth century* presented to John Lough, ed. D. J. Mossop, G. E. Rodmell, D. B. Wilson, Durham 1978

Sturm, E., *Crébillon fils et le libertinage au dix-huitième siècle*. Paris 1970

Testud, P., *Rétif de La Bretonne et la création littéraire*. Genève, Paris 1977

Thompsett, E., 'The theme of seduction in the eighteenth-century French novel: Barthe's *La Jolie femme*', *Forum for modern language studies* 12 (1976), pp.206-16

Tompkins, J. M. S., *The Popular novel in England 1770-1800*. London 1932

Trahard, P., *Les Maîtres de la sensibilité française au XVIIIe siècle*. Paris 1931-1933

Vaissière, P. de, *Gentilshommes compagnards de l'ancienne France*. Paris 1903

Vance, C. M., *The Extravagant shepherd: a study of the pastoral vision in Rousseau's 'Nouvelle Héloïse'*, Studies on Voltaire 105 (1973)

Van de Louw, G., *Baculard d'Arnaud: romancier ou vulgarisateur: essai de sociologie littéraire*. Paris 1972

Van den Heuvel, J., *Voltaire dans ses contes*. Paris 1967

Van Tieghem, P., 'Le roman sentimental en Europe de Richardson à Rousseau', *Revue de littérature comparée* 20 (1940), pp.129-51

Varga, A. K., 'La désagrégation de l'idéal classique dans le roman français de la première moitié du XVIIIe siècle', *Studies on Voltaire* 26 (1963), pp.965-98

Versini, L., *Laclos et la tradition*. Paris 1968

Wagner, J., *Marmontel journaliste et le Mercure de France (1715-1761)*. Grenoble 1975

Watt, I., *The Rise of the novel*. London 1957

Wilcox, F. H, *Prévost's translations of Richardson's novels*. Berkeley 1927

Williams, I., *The Idea of the novel in Europe, 1600-1800*. London 1979

Williams, R., *The Country and the city*. London 1973

Wolper, R., 'The toppling of Jeannot', *Studies on Voltaire* 183 (1980), pp.69-82

Index